ILLINOIS CENTRAL COLLEGE
PN2189.W5
STACKS
The theater event :

A12900 726874

A12900 726874

W9-BSA-396

PN 2189 .W5   72582

Wiles, Timothy J.

The theater event :

WITHDRAWN

Illinois Central College
Learning Resources Center

THE
THEATER
EVENT

Timothy J. Wiles

THE THEATER EVENT
Modern Theories of Performance

T.C.C. LIBRARY

THE UNIVERSITY OF CHICAGO PRESS
Chicago & London

72582

TIMOTHY J. WILES is assistant professor of
English at Indiana University at
Bloomington. He spent two years in
Poland, studying and acting in the theater,
and has directed ten plays, including *The
Measures Taken*, *Endgame*, *Ubu roi*, and, for
television, Mayakovsky's *Mystery-Bouffe*.

THE UNIVERSITY OF CHICAGO PRESS, CHICAGO 60637
THE UNIVERSITY OF CHICAGO PRESS, LTD., LONDON
© 1980 by The University of Chicago
All rights reserved. Published 1980

Printed in the United States of America
84 83 82 81 80   1 2 3 4 5

Library of Congress Cataloging in Publication Data

Wiles, Timothy J
  The theater event.

  Includes bibliographical references and index.
  1. Theater—History—20th century.   2. Artaud,
Antonin, 1896–1948.   3. Brecht, Bertolt, 1898–1956.
4. Grotowski, Jerzy, 1933–   5. Stanislavskii,
Konstantin Sergeevich, 1863–1938.   I. Title.
PN2189.W5   792'.028'0922   80–12206
ISBN 0–226–89801–6

Contents

Acknowledgments

I wish to thank the many people who have helped me evolve the ideas about theatrical performance that I present in this study. The most important are too many and scattered to name: my students in courses on various dramatic canons, in seminars on critical thought and performance theory, and students in the casts and crews of plays that I have directed or with which I have assisted at a number of college theaters. Let one student stand for them all, since Scott Sala fits into most of the categories I mention; they all have made a contribution.

Several scholars working in the broad field of modernism, theater, and literature have kindly read my manuscript and offered extensive advice. I thank Herbert Blau of the University of Wisconsin-Milwaukee, my colleague Matei Calinescu at Indiana University, Ruby Cohn of the University of California-Davis, David Halliburton and Herbert Lindenberger of Stanford University, Leonard Pronko of Pomona College, and Andrzej Wirth of the Free University-Berlin for their generous readings and assistance. I also wish to remember the late Michel Benamou, former director of the Center for Twentieth Century Studies at the University of Wisconsin-Milwaukee, who read and encouraged my expansion of an early version of the Grotowski section, which I presented at the Center in 1978. And I have many teachers to thank, as well as colleagues, for their aid in stimulating my ideas and providing me nurturing communities within which to work.

There are also many people to whom I wish to make a personal acknowledgment for their support and friendship during the evolution of this book, too many to single out. But four individuals who were most important must be named: Teresa Kieniewicz of Warsaw University, who aided me greatly during my researches in Poland; my parents, Ruth and James Wiles; and my wife, Mary McGann.

Introduction

The belief that art reflects reality is as old as Aristotle, yet equally persistent is the hope that art might affect reality as well. Aristotle's *Poetics* proposes both a mimetic and a cathartic theory of dramatic literature, a means and an end. The implications of both these enterprises have occupied Aristotle's readers throughout the centuries in which his texts have been read, and in some of the centuries in which Aristotle's words were known only by hearsay. His premises have gained the status of myth in our culture, in part because textual corruption and philological cruxes prevent us from knowing exactly what he *said*. Determining what Aristotle *meant* has occupied writers and critics with sensibilities as diverse as those of Corneille, Nietzsche, and Northrop Frye. Philologists and translators have doggedly tried to inform us what Aristotle's theory *does* discuss; on the other hand, an equally important group of readers has dealt with the implications that his theory initiated, by virtue of both its excellence and its mythic stature, even the implications that Aristotle would have contradicted. "Aristotle has not defined pity and fear," says Stephen Dedalus, "I have."

Among the most recent thinkers to wrestle with the *Poetics* are the creators who bring drama to life through theatrical performance, the actors, directors, and dramaturgs. The phenomenon and the cult of the theater director are modern innovations, although they have a background ranging from Sophocles (who staged and acted in his tragedies) to the actor-managers of the eighteenth and nineteenth centuries. The paradox of acting occupied Diderot and the theater's first professional dramaturg, Lessing, but before the nineteenth century little cogent speculation existed on the relationship between the enactment of drama and its effect upon the participants in performance, the actor and audience. We possess considerable documentary information about the means of imitation, the acting and staging styles employed in the great periods of theater activity in our culture; what we lack are coherent philosophical speculations about the affectivity of these means, about the anticipated changes which these technical means were intended to bring about.

In this study, I shall examine the writings of four theater thinkers—Stanislavski, Brecht, Artaud, and Grotowski—whose work leads to a theory of theater affectivity. Such a theory can be formulated only by a theater worker who oversees all the elements of performance and believes that each of them is creative in its own right and is not simply an illustration of the creativity of the playwright. This kind of theory admits the actor into the creative process; we know that he changes the writer's words through inflection and accompanying gestures, but he also introduces a component of his own psychology, emotion, and existential particularity to the artwork provided by the playwright, that is, to a character outline which can be fleshed out by innumerable interpreters but which has no flesh except that which its interpreters lend it. The theory also admits the audience into a creative role. We know that performances of the same production differ from night to night according to the makeup of their audiences, but we usually discount "audience response" as being peripheral to the art experience itself; however, if art exists not only in objects by which we know it but also in the experience of those who perceive it, their existential presence is also a component of art. In other words, art is not art "in general" but is made up of the particular, unrepeatable interactions between the original creator's work and each of its new recipients, a transaction which leaves neither party unchanged. Of course, art possesses an aspect as a tangible and unalterable object, like a statue, just as it possesses an aspect as a changing and change-making interaction. Perhaps theater exists to illustrate this second aspect of art; for more than any other, theatrical art depends upon living and present mediators, actors and audience, for both its meaning and its existence. Dramatic literature is not complete until it is performed, and even if we know it only through reading, we experience it fully only if we conceive it "in the mind's eye" as staged. By this I do not simply mean that we imagine what a particular acting style, scenery, blocking, timing, and directorial concept can bring to the script (that actor's term which attests to the sense in which all dramatic literature is but outline and prologue to the complete art experience of performance). What is more obvious, and perhaps more difficult, is that we must read as if we were the performance's authentic audience. I do not mean that we must assume the beliefs and attitudes of the play's original audience, although this knowledge is also essential for the fullest understanding of any artwork. Beyond this historical "acquiescence" to the play, we must allow it to address us personally, particularly, and we must imagine the existential participation of our own being in the being of the artwork. Seen in these terms, theatrical performance is an enactment of more than just the play at hand: it is an activity in which we of the audience act, much as do the actors. The root of the Greek word for drama originally meant "to do," and all theater is essentially a deed.

In this study, I refer to the creative interaction of literary text, actor's art, and spectator's participation as "the theater event." I examine the theories of a few theater workers who believe that their conception of this event integrates the creative aspects of literature, actor, and audience into a totality, one which may change all the parties involved. In the contemporary theater, the artist who possesses the training and the responsibility for formulating this kind of theory is the director; the theoreticians whom I examine are all directors, and they have contributed more than any others to the contemporary cult of the director, which elevates him to the status of *auteur* of all the elements of production and performance, to borrow a useful term from cinema criticism. Constantin Stanislavski, Bertolt Brecht, Antonin Artaud, and Jerzy Grotowski all changed the style and the function of acting in significant ways; Stanislavski, Brecht, and Grotowski initiated the three dominant styles of acting in twentieth-century theater practice and provided the methods of training which further them. Artaud's influence on Grotowski and on the most recent developments in performance style has been more theoretical than technical, but along with Stanislavski, Brecht, and Grotowski, Artaud wrote a major theoretical work which extends the definition of acting beyond *praxis* toward speculations about philosophical issues: concepts of time and space, mimesis, myth, the didactic potentiality of art, and existential questions about being. Works like Brecht's *Short Organum for the Theater* and Artaud's *The Theater and Its Double* already belong to the canon of "intellectual background" for modernism; Stanislavski's *An Actor Prepares* and Grotowski's *Towards a Poor Theater*, although more technical, contain passages which well might join this canon. In this study, I examine the way that each of these directors connects his technical innovations in acting style to larger conceptions of the theater event itself, the way in which acting is oriented in one direction toward the text of dramatic literature, and in the other direction toward the audience which completes the transaction with art that I discussed above.

Each of these acting styles proposes a theory of affectivity as well, a notion of catharsis. And with Brecht in particular, this notion conflicts specifically with Aristotle's catharsis clause. Brecht's theory of an "anti-cathartic" epic theater has contributed significantly to the mythologizing of Aristotle which is still being practiced in this century. This myth consists in large part of what Aristotle is thought to have said, or ought to have said, and since the Renaissance creative reinterpretations or misinterpretations of the *Poetics* have contributed immensely to both literary and intellectual history. They attest to the importance of the original speculations themselves. In the next section of this introduction, I will examine the different interpretations of

Aristotle's catharsis clause which have led to the notions of catharsis and affectivity present in modern performance theory. These relate to acting theory in an essential way. For theories of acting are both descriptive and prescriptive—they tell us what an actor does and how he ought to do it. By extension, they address the actor's audience as well—they are models and recipes of both *being* and *behaving* in life as well as on the stage. We have long looked to dramatic characters and to the acting which portrays them as positive or negative models of behavior; I believe that the innovation of modern performance theory is to suggest that, in their place, we look to the *function* of the actor as a behavior model. Earlier styles of acting, such as the one proposed by Hamlet to the players, sprang from the mimetic tradition which sees art as a reflection of reality; these styles indicate what men *are* and hence how they might be faithfully copied in art. The innovation of modern acting theory, beginning with Stanislavski, is to move art from reflecting reality to being a kind of reality of its own, capable of affecting the "real world" of which it is a *part*, not a *copy*. Modern performance theory proposes models of what men *ought to be*, and hence how they might be enacted in life.

Aristotle's catharsis clause appears in section 6 of his *Poetics*, at the end of his definition of tragedy. After he defines tragedy as the imitation of a complete action which is presented in dramatic form, he concludes that it achieves, "through the representation of pitiable and fearful incidents, the catharsis of such pitiable and fearful incidents."[1] This is the translation of the catharsis clause suggested by Leon Golden, and I am convinced of its appropriateness *for Aristotle*. However, critics in the formative centuries for modern performance theory read Aristotle differently, and we shall see that this translation is inappropriate for many of their heirs today.

Golden's interpretation of *katharsis* as a "clarification" of the play's incidents reverses the more common notion that tragedy purges pity and fear from its hero or from its audience. Yet when we consider the catharsis clause in the context of the rest of the *Poetics*, "clarification" makes good sense. In his commentary to Golden's translation, O. B. Hardison argues that the *Poetics* is a *technē*—"a technical treatise concerned with the nature of tragedy, not with the response of the audience," as the notion of "purgative" catharsis forces it to be.[2] Nowhere in the *Poetics* does Aristotle specify the effect which dramatic literature ought to have on its audience; the word "catharsis" appears only twice in the *Poetics* itself. Since it occupies such a small position within the treatise, catharsis ought to be integrated into the general notion of tragedy which Aristotle develops throughout, and if a translation like "purgation" forces us to view catharsis as a new topic otherwise not dealt with in the *Poetics*, or as an afterthought or even a possible textual corruption, we can question that translation on philological grounds alone.

A clarificatory catharsis of incidents, on the other hand, connects the definition of tragedy found in section 6 with the theory of imitation proposed in sections 1–4 and Aristotle's concepts of probability and necessity in section 9.[3] Before making a definition of tragedy, Aristotle had speculated on the paradox of imitative art, the fact that it causes pleasure even when portraying painful or disgusting objects, such as corpses. The death of a virtuous man may provide us with a similar pleasure when we encounter it in literature, although it would appall us in everyday life. Aristotle associates learning with pleasure, and in art even the repellent has the capacity to instruct us. Learning is the kind of pleasure we ought to seek in tragedy, Aristotle argues in section 14: "We should not seek every pleasure from tragedy but only the one proper to it. Since the poet should provide pleasure from pity and fear through imitation, it is apparent that this function must be worked into the incidents." These incidents gain their ability to instruct us, and to be understood in general, Aristotle argues in section 9, when they are related to universal principles such as probability and necessity. The artist moves the incidents out of the realm of the contingent and acci-dental (the realm of history, or reality), and orders them into a dramatic action to show how and why they occur, particularly connecting them with the qualities of the men who perform them. Thus Aristotle can claim that the poet performs a task which is quite different from that of the historian, even though they both may deal with the same incidents. As Hardison explains tragic clarification,

> The tragic poet begins by selecting a series of incidents that are intrinsically pitiable or fearful. He may derive them from history or legend (the usual Greek practice); but he may also . . . make them up, as do most modern writers. He then presents them in such a way as to bring out the probable or necessary principles that unite them in a single action and determine their relation to this action as it proceeds from its beginning to its end. When the spectator has witnessed a tragedy of this type, he will have learned something—the incidents will be clarified in the sense that their relation in terms of universals will have become manifest—and the act of learning, says Aristotle, will be enjoyable.[4]

This reading of the *Poetics* makes the treatise more coherent and self-explanatory, and it also proposes a model for literature which empha-sizes coherence. The greatest tragedies, and by extension the greatest works of literature, will be those which present the most inclusive and unified pictures of experience, which tie together contingent, disparate elements; these elements confound us in life, but in art they may be reconciled and "made one" by being gathered together in a personification such as a symbol. This emphasis in the *Poetics* has led to modern notions of writing and criticism as divergent as Joyce's theory of "epiphany" and the structuralism and neo-Aristotelianism among contemporary literary critics. Seen in this light, the translation of "catharsis" as a clarification of incidents solves a minor yet persistent crux in Aristotle's larger argument.

But the history of criticism has not read Aristotle so fairly, and for centuries catharsis has been taken to mean either the purgation of emotions from an audience or the purification of its emotions. Neither meaning is well supported by a close reading of the *Poetics*, but ample evidence exists in Aristotle's other writings, and in Plato, to support either of them. A theory of purgation suggests that mimetic art in general, and drama in particular, arouses certain emotions within its audience, but through the principle of homeopathic medicine ("like drives out like") the intense excitation of particular emotions drives them out of the onlooker. The purgation theory would seem to be Aristotle's rebuttal to Book 10 of the *Republic*, where Plato cites the ability of tragedy to arouse pity and to make its spectators timid, and goes on to ban the tragic poet from his ideal republic. Aristotle accordingly replies that tragedy has the medicinal capacity of exciting dangerous emotions to rid us of them. Part of the evidence for this argument stems from his *Politics*, in which he does intend *katharsis* to mean purgation. He talks about the ability that music has to arouse pity, fear, and enthusiasm in certain persons, driving them to a "mystic frenzy"; but when they have gone through the experience, they appear to be "restored as though they have found healing and purgation. Those who are influenced by pity and fear, and every emotional nature, must have a like experience . . . and all are in a manner purged and their souls lightened and delighted." But if we transfer this notion to the *Poetics*, a problem arises. Such a reading forces Aristotle to accept Plato's arguments about the deterimental effects of the emotions. But Aristotle did not believe that the emotions were a threat to the intellect; for him, both intellect and emotions make up the complete human being. Nevertheless, the attractiveness of the Platonic intellectual bias, the evidence of the *Politics*, and belief in homeopathic medicine have led a number of Aristotle's readers to view catharsis as a purgation. In his preface to *Samson Agonistes*, Milton proclaimed that

> Tragedy [is] . . . said by Aristotle to be of power, by raising pity and fear, or terror, to purge the mind of those and such-like passions . . . . Nor is Nature wanting in her own effects to make good

his assertion; for so in physic things of melancholic hue and quality are used against melancholy, sour against sour, salt to remove
salt humours.

Psychoanalysis offers us a more modern example of homeopathic
medicine; Freud's early discovery that the recalling of painful childhood
experiences under hypnosis could alleviate neurotic symptoms nearly
led him to name his therapeutic treatment "the cathartic method." His
writings on dramatic literature support this purgative interpretation of
catharsis, and this is the interpretation which Stanislavski evolved at
virtually the same time as a means of helping the actor to portray emotions while playing a character—the technique of affective memory.
Brecht attacked the notion in both men as one that treated the symptom
of social imbalance, not the cause; his "anti-Aristotelian" and "anti-
cathartic" theater proposed to clarify the dialectics of social change.
Ironically, this clarification of historical incidents is remarkably similar
to Aristotle's own notion of catharsis.

A more moderate notion than purgation is the alternative translation
for *katharsis*, purification. This interpretation supports Aristotle's belief
that both the intellect and the emotions ought to be present in the
complete human being, but in balance and harmony. Tragedy might
purify our emotions, not by purging us specifically of pity and fear, but
by reconciling and inuring us to pity, fear, and other emotions. Tragedy
teaches us the proper use of pity, fear, and like emotions. This interpretation stems from Aristotle's own view of the emotions, rather than
from Plato's, as proposed in Aristotle's *Nichomachean Ethics*. Here he
develops a notion of mental hygiene as the balance between extremes:

> both fear and confidence and appetite and anger and pity and in
> general pleasure and pain may be felt both too much and too little,
> and in both cases not well; but to feel them at the right times, with
> reference to the right objects, toward the right people, and in the
> right way, is what is characteristic and best, and this is charac-
> teristic of virtue.

Although the *Ethics* does not refer us directly to tragedy or to art in
general, this notion of Aristotelian balance has attracted many interpreters of the *Poetics*. Such a reading makes theatrical affectivity more
anesthetic than purgative. For example, Castelvetro held that watching
deaths occur in tragedies resembled the experience of soldiers watching
men die on the battlefield: both spectator and soldier became inured to
death through watching its constant repetition. Milton argued that epic
verse served "to calm the perturbations of the mind and set the affections in right tune" (*The Reason of Church Government*); Lessing believed that tragedy purified the audience by increasing its sensitivity.

Recent exponents of purificatory catharsis include Stanislavski and Grotowski, who both have conceived of the theater as a surrogate church in which participants may become "priests of art" and achieve "secular sainthood."

The long history of interpretations of the catharsis clause suggests that Aristotle touched upon an aspect of art, particularly of dramatic art, which is of universal importance. Catharsis suggests a final cause for art which demonstrates how it affects us, and a *technē* of catharsis would explore the extent to which the creators of art can incorporate an intended affectivity into the art experience itself. In this study of the theories of catharsis in Stanislavski, Brecht, Artaud, Grotowski, and selected works of dramatic literature which are associated with their innovations, I do not propose a specific interpretation for catharsis which will choose between "clarification," "purgation," and "purification." Aspects of each of these interpretations can be found in modern performance theory, and they reinforce one another. In the chapters which follow, my definition of catharsis will not be imposed by Aristotle but will be determined by the particular directors and playwrights under discussion. What connects all these creators is their confidence that catharsis *is* the final cause of drama and theater. But for each of them, the theater event does not result simply in a literary art object which obeys Aristotle's technical treatise: it also results in an art experience which affects and is affected by all its participants. Stanislavski, Brecht, Artaud, and Grotowski expand the *Poetics* to include the director, actor, and audience; an examination of their theories suggests that we should interpret catharsis as a general metaphor for the affectivity of theater art.

My study undertakes to record the history of catharsis in what I take to be the dominant and most characteristic theater theories of our time. The theoretical works of Stanislavski, Brecht, Artaud, and Grotowski possess an importance for modern intellectual history which extends beyond stagecraft and dramatic literature into the realms of aesthetics and philosophical speculation. I have strayed into these areas upon occasion, and borrowed ideas from such disciplines as structural anthropology, existential phenomenology, linguistics, and communication theory. But the achievements of dramatic literature remain the most concrete examples of the dramaturgical theories at hand, and between my discussions of theory I have interspersed chapters which deal with exemplary plays. Each of the directors in this study is associated with a body of dramatic literature which contributed to his notion of the theater event. Brecht, of course, wrote the plays which defined his epic

theater, and Grotowski's most recent production can virtually be attributed to his authorship. Stanislavski developed his style of theater
through directing the plays of Chekhov, although the playwright dis-
agreed with the director about the appropriateness of this style for the
production of his plays.

Ironically, a similar "disagreement" exists between theory and practice in the work of Brecht and Grotowski, although in each case the
same individual created both the theory and the artwork that was supposed to embody it. I am not interested in proving the "theoretical
inadequacy" of the thought of the German playwright or the Polish
director, but the fact remains that vital aspects of each artist's theory of
theater can be learned only through imagining an engaged participation
in a performance of one of his plays. Through my readings of Brecht's
The Measures Taken and Grotowski's *Apocalypsis cum figuris* I seek to
augment the ideas of theater that the artists outline in their theoretical
essays. My argument is continuous throughout this study, from theory
to play and then back to theory. The chapters dealing with specific
illustrations in each part map the extremes to which a particular theater
style may go before it breaks out of the boundaries of that style and
merges with another; these chapters attempt to show the affinities between the discoveries of Stanislavski, Brecht, Artaud, and Grotowski,
the sense in which they all contribute to one theory of performance.

PART I

On Catharsis
of Character in
Naturalistic Acting
and Dramaturgy

1. Stanislavski's Theater of Affective Memory

A legion of "great reformers" has altered the shape of European theater profoundly over the last century—Wagner, Meiningen, Strindberg, Appia, Craig, Meyerhold, Piscator, Brecht, Artaud, and Grotowski all changed the nature of the theater event through their contributions to staging, design, treatment of the text, acting, and attitude toward the audience. Although they were not all principally "stage directors" in the contemporary sense of the word, each was an artist concerned with redefining the "total putting-on-stage" of theater (by which I mean the positioning of the theater event in a significant relation to its audience, as well as the more technical procedure implied by our limited English term "staging"): each was an artist of the mise-en-scène. But Constantin Stanislavski must come first in any history of theatrical innovation that unites acting practice with philosophical implications. For Stanislavski was the first to work out and transcribe a consistent acting methodology which also refers to larger concerns beyond theater practice. He did not invent his system all at once, of course—he is prominent among the "great reformers" as an artist-hero who devoted himself to the constant renewal of his system and to its continual refertilization of his own life. Nor was Stanislavski without antecedents. He owed much to Wagner's notion of the integrated work of theatrical art and to Meiningen's example of ensemble acting; and though he was not aware of Strindberg's comments on acting, he would have agreed with Strindberg's belief that actors convince us of their characterizations by living the parts.[1]

But Stanislavski was a practical theater worker, not a scholar, and he derived most of his system through lifelong observation of his own acting and decades of work with generations of student actors. Considering his scanty awareness of the main trends of modernism in the first decades of this century, it should startle us to note how much he anticipated unconsciously. Stanislavski was the first to identify a psychological basis for the actor's creation of a character, and the first to develop what he called a "psycho-technique" (his "affective memory" system) which would enable the actor to portray a character's unconcious. His psycho-technique links him with Freudian psychoanalysis, and its affective aspect contains his theory of catharsis. Stanislavski was the first to suggest that the actor was an integral part of the theatrical artwork, not just its transmitter, and that as the actor changes over time, the artwork changes as well. This suggestion links Stanislavski with the idea that art is more a process than an object, and to the notion common to the symbolist movement, phenomenology, and structural linguistics that art is a transaction between its creators and its audiences. Of all the philosophers and writers who constituted the naturalist school, Stanislavski was the first to sense (although not to specify) that what is essentially "real" about theatrical realism lies as much in the reality of the performance itself as in the true-to-life quality of a play's details. (For him the two levels of reality are mutually supportive, so that his ultra-naturalistic acting style is also a basis for later theories of theatricalism.) Finally, Stanislavski was the first to argue passionately for acting as an ennobling activity, a mission and a life-role that result in a "life in art" (as he titled his autobiography), which can change the actor as a person, and which has the potentiality to similarly affect the audience. This affectivity is the broadest extension of Stanislavski's theory of catharsis, and his heroic role for the theater artist links him with images of the artist already developed in the avant-garde poetry and fiction of his time.

Throughout his mature career, Constantin Stanislavski insisted upon two facts in regard to his system of acting. First, he had not really invented a "Stanislavski system"; what he had discovered about acting was already there, an organic and natural truth waiting to be released within the actor, "an innate capacity for creativeness."[2] Second, if he had been able to codify this process into a system of acting, his primary inspiration had come from directing and acting in the plays of Anton Chekhov. Stanislavski believed that his system "must be approached through Chekhov," but also that it "serves as a bridge to the approach of Chekhov."[3] Chekhov, however, felt that the director consistently misinterpreted his plays. His misgivings were not groundless: to this day, most readers, not to mention directors and actors, filter his plays through some understanding of the "Stanislavski system." To a lesser extent, Stanislavski's work is known through his interpretations of Chekhov's plays; some of his Chekhov productions played in the repertoire of the Moscow Art Theater for decades. In fact, as I want to show later, scattered insights and philosophical speculations in Stanislavski's acting treatises take on a new coherence when seen as the attempt to justify certain assumptions about staging gleaned from Chekhov (not always with the playwright's sanction). But if Stanislavski wrested the optimistic ideal of a "life in art" from a Chekhov who never intended to illustrate such an ideal, it was nevertheless a fine one, an ideal which stands behind all the major theories of theater which have been developed in this century.

Born in 1863 of a wealthy merchant family, Constantin Sergeievich Alexeiev (he used the stage name "Stanislavski" only in the theater) grew up on a country estate near Moscow similar to those described by Chekhov. His parents passed no theatrical talent or tradition on to their son, but they did provide him with the means which allowed him to devote all his energies to art. Throughout his life, even after the Revolution, he defended the values of the landholding class, and especially the civilizing effect of the urban intelligentsia when it was isolated, by choice or necessity, in the backward provinces. (These, of course, are the themes of *The Three Sisters*.) Stanislavski engaged in amateur theatricals in his youth, often acting with his brothers and sisters at the family estate.

Thus he began his apprenticeship in the theater. We should always remember that he attributed his later genius as a director to hard practice and self-education, not to "inspiration"; his system of acting denies that "truth in art" could ever spring from anything so immaterial. In his autobiography, Stanislavski gives every indication that he learned each aspect of his craft through conscious effort. He claims to have been guilty, at first, of all the faults of the melodramatic actor, and apparently he suffered from acute stage fright throughout his career. To overcome these shortcomings, he studied the realistic school of Russian acting which dated back to Mikhail Shtchepkin in the early part of the nineteenth century. The extreme naturalism of the Hessian director the duke of Meiningen was a more contemporary influence during his early years. (Meiningen's company played in Moscow in 1885 and in 1890.) Stanislavski admired Meiningen's surface realism, the settings designed to look like rooms in real houses, and the multitude of small objects and hand properties, and he was especially drawn to the duke's autocratic control of his ensemble. It was one of the first "director's theaters" in which the productions had no stars and all the details were planned by one mind.

Stanislavski had acted in few plays which we remember today, and had been directing plays for only six years, when he met the playwright and critic Vladimir Ivanovich Nemirovich-Danchenko in 1897. The next year they formed the Moscow Art Theater, with Nemirovich-Danchenko serving as dramaturg and Stanislavski acting and directing. The goal of the company was to escape from the melodramatic theatricalism then reigning in Russia, and to find a "truth in art" by embracing the then avant-garde concepts of naturalism which were being demonstrated on small coterie stages across Europe. The Moscow Art Theater achieved its first critical success in the year of its formation with Chekhov's *The Seagull*; this production also marked Chekhov's first triumph on the stage, for earlier productions of his plays had convinced most Russians that he should confine his talents to writing short stories. In the next few years, the Moscow Art Theater produced each of Chekhov's subsequent plays, *Uncle Vanya* in 1899, *The Three Sisters* in 1901, and *The Cherry Orchard* in 1904, the year of the playwright's death.

During this time, Stanislavski was not particularly aware that he was developing a new system of acting. He tells us in this autobiography that by 1907 he realized that actors could not depend upon inspiration alone but required what he called a "psycho-technique" which would prepare the ground for it.[4] The established actors in his company balked at the idea of relearning their skills from the point of view of psychoanalytic theory, so Stanislavski founded the First Studio of the Moscow Art Theater as a school for beginning actors and a laboratory in which to test his emerging theories. Subsequent studios followed, before and after the First World War and the Russian Revolution, and by the 1920s his earliest students were teaching "the Stanislavski system" abroad, especially in New York, where it has had its greatest influence in so-called "method acting." But Stanislavski did not describe his system in writing until the end of his life. He published a partial account in 1924 in his autobiography, *My Life in Art,* and in an article on "The Art of the Actor and the Art of the Director" written for the *Encyclopaedia Britannica* at the end of the decade.[5] This article contains his most specific definition of "affective memory," the cornerstone of his "psycho-technique." Stanislavski's fullest account of his system of acting is contained in the companion volumes *An Actor Prepares, Building the Character,* and *Creating a Role,* which are written in the form of fictionalized acting lessons given by the great director Tortsov (Stanislavski) and recorded by his most avid student, Kostya Nazvanov (who resembles Stanislavski in his untrained youth).

Stanislavskian acting begins as a reaction to what he calls the "moldy theatricality" inherited from the stages of Goethe and Hugo. He objected to the actor who donned his roles as he donned his costumes, playing the external details of a character and repeating them in frozen form at each performance. In place of this externalized acting, he asks the actor to live the part he is playing in his own self: "You must live [the role] by actually experiencing feelings that are analogous to it, each and every time you repeat the process of creating it."[6] The actor accomplishes this by seeking out the aspects of his personality which resemble characteristics of the role he is playing. His characterization grows out of his own self, and he can display "the reality of the inner life of a human spirit in a part and a belief in that reality"[7] which Stanislavski demands, because he believes in the reality of his own personality and feelings.

Stanislavski conceived of a number of devices which would aid the actor in his task of living the part. The actor should experience "solitude in public," forgetting that an audience is watching him, and concentrate all his attention on a small circle surrounding the character he plays; only occasionally does he expand his circle to include the other characters and the larger actions in the play. He should divide his role into units of action, and be able to express the character's objective in each unit by means of an active verb in the infinitive form. The actor composes and memorizes a "subtext" consisting of the unexpressed thoughts of his character which accompany the words the playwright writes for him. Stanislavski called this "the inwardly felt expression of a human being in a part, which flows uninterruptedly beneath the words of the text, giving them life and a basis for existing."[8] His statement indicates an assumption residing behind all these devices which appear to be mere technical aids. The subtext, he says, gives the text a life and a basis for existing. Hence the actor who creates the subtext has joined, if not replaced, the author as the creator of a work of art.

Stanislavski's system offers the first unified argument that the actor himself is an artist and a work of art, not merely a technician who illustrates the artwork of another. In Stanislavski's words,

> We know that Shakespeare re-created stories by others. That is what we do to the work of the dramatist, we bring to life what is hidden under the words; we put our own thoughts into the author's lines, and we establish our own relationships to other characters in the play . . . we filter through ourselves all the materials that we receive from the author and the director; we work over them, supplementing them from our own imagination. That material becomes part of us, spiritually, and even physically . . . that is creativeness and art.[9]

Ironically, this artist who creates by using his own self as material appears to the audience to be the most truthful recreation of the character written by the playwright. The logical extension of Stanislavski's thinking is that the actor creates an artwork out of his own self and for his own self, not for the audience, which may not even be aware that the actor has created anything. Although Stanislavski did not draw such a conclusion, many of the devices in his system serve this purpose of cutting the actor off from his audience. For example, the director provides his actor with a detailed and realistic mise-en-scène of setting, costumes, and properties; Stanislavski says that they are for the sake of the actor's belief in his character, not for the sake of the audience's belief. Another example: the actor devises a series of speech and body rhythms which correspond to the text and subtext of the play. During exercises, Stanislavski asked his actors to play their parts silently and to express the text by means of these rhythms alone; when they complained that no one could fathom the verbal content being expressed by others, Stanislavski replied that concentration on what he called the "tempo-rhythms" of a part aided the actor's belief in his character, and was not to be thought of as an aid to the audience.[10] Likewise, each actor was to draw the "through line of action" by which he discovered his character's continuous development throughout the play, but Stanislavski held that this "through line" must "remain on our side of the footlights, and not stray once into the auditorium."[11] The result of these practices is to limit the audience's role in performance to a passive "belief" in the reality of what is being presented, a role which later critics like Brecht would attack for being apolitical and for stifling participation.

Still, Stanislavski could never forget that the actor is the only artist who creates in public. He discusses the phenomenon of stage fright in each of his books and knows that the mature actor as well as the student suffers from it. During the first fictional acting lesson recounted in *An Actor Prepares*, the only students who demonstrate any truth to the inner lives of their characters do so through a creative grappling with a fear of the "black hole of the proscenium arch."[12] (In unashamedly acknowledging this fear, Stanislavski may be attempting to imply what he cannot admit into his conscious system: that the actual actor-audience dynamic and tensions become part of the psychological subtext of dramatic art.) Even Stanislavski's concern for the quality and quantity of life-like detail on the stage, not only in the objects but also in the minute variations of expression displayed by the characters, stems in part from a fear of boring his audience; to overcome this, he would fill up the time with a multitude of naturalistic details. But once this has been done for the spectator, it is his responsibility to be engrossed in the characters portrayed, and it is not the actor's function to be interested in the audience. The only way for the audience to become engrossed in the actions and relationships of the characters is for the actors to be engrossed in these actions and relationships themselves. Then the audience will experience empathy with both the author's characters (through intellectual understanding) and the actors' characterizations (through emotions). As Stanislavski puts it.

When a real artist is speaking the soliloquy "to be or not to be," is he merely putting before us the thoughts of the author and executing the business indicated by his director? No, he puts into the lines much of his own conception of life.

Such an artist is not speaking in the person of an imaginary Hamlet. He speaks in his own right as one placed in the circumstances created by the play. The thoughts, feelings, conceptions, reasoning of the author are transformed into his own. And it is not his sole purpose to render the lines so that they shall be *understood*. For him it is necessary that the spectators *feel* his own inner relationship to what he is saying. They must follow his own creative *will* and desires. Here the motive forces of his psychic life are united in action and interdependent.[13]

Now we can begin to see how Stanislavski admits the audience into creative partnership within the theater event. By his concept of "affective memory" Stanislavski unites that part of the artwork created by the playwright and expressed in words, the actor's contribution to the artwork created out of and expressed by feelings, and the audience's intellectual understanding of and emotional empathy with both of these. Affective memory begins as a device by which the actor can identify himself with the character he is playing. First he determines what emotions his character is experiencing at a given point in the play. Next he searches in his personal memories for an event which caused him to experience similar emotions at some time in the past. For example, while he is playing a character whose friend dies during the play, he may remember his feelings at the death of one of his own friends. To sharpen this remembering of emotions, or "emotion memory" as Stanislavski calls it throughout *An Actor Prepares,* he employs "sensation memory," recalling not only the circumstances surrounding this event from his own past but also the sensory impressions accompanying it, the visual aspect of the scene, the sounds it produced, even appropriate tactile and olfactory impressions.[14] This concentrated recalling of sensations causes the actor to experience again the emotions surrounding the incident from his life; in turn, the process causes the audience to empathize with the actor's displayed emotions as if they were those emotions which the literary character would be expected to experience, given the text by which the playwright makes his character express himself. "Affective memory" affects both the actor and the spectator. Stanislavski gives his fullest definition of the concept in the article he wrote for the *Encyclopaedia Britannica* on acting and directing:

> We cannot directly act on our emotions, but we can prod our creative fantasy in a necessary path, and fantasy, as scientific psychologists have discovered, stirs up our *affective memory,* calling up from its secret depths, beyond the reach of consciousness, elements of already experienced emotions, and regroups them to correspond with the images which arise in us.[15]

The actor who uses the process of affective memory to create a role out of his own history and feelings takes over from the author part of the responsibility for creating a work of art. According to Stanislavski's ideal understanding, the actor is not merely using affective memory as a technique by which to impress his audience. His more profound motivation arises from a belief that a character might logically be expected to be experiencing certain emotions if it were a living human being, and that the playwright has given these feelings the same degree of intentionality which he has given to the words he has written for the character to speak. In fact, Stanislavski's concern with the play's "subtext" suggests that unspoken feelings and pregnant pauses contain more of the content of dramatic art than does the text, which he treats as a subterfuge and pretext for emotions. Many dramatists writing in the tradition of Chekhov *do* interpolate significant pauses and even lacunae into their texts. It is a mark of Stanislavski's genius that he recognized this aspect of play writing not as the naturalistic imitation of inarticulateness to be made palatable to an audience by acting skills but as an aesthetic component for which an acting style should be created so that this component might be illuminated. Stanislavski resolved the problem of what he called "psychological pauses"[16] by filling them with psychological content from the actor's own psychology, *as if* it were shared by the character. He does not seem to have been able to consider the possibility that some "holes in the play" could be intended to be *holes*, empty pauses, and that their significance lies in their emptiness, not in the extraneous content invented by means of affective memory. When Chekhov objected to Stanislavski's additions of naturalistic details, both physical and psychological, and protested "Listen, I wrote it down, it is all there," Stanislavski merely smiled.[17]

Stanislavski's attitude stems only in part from egocentricity and a desire to leave a personal mark on the artwork. More important is his realization that, although the external skeleton of a play is fixed within the dialogue the playwright has written for it, the meaning imparted to the audience differs with each new production, and with each performance of a production: each dramatic image created on the stage "is unique and cannot be repeated, just as in nature."[18] Although he uncritically equates "meaning" with psychological "inner truth," the imprecise term he uses throughout his work, he is not frightened by the possibility that this will be created differently by different actors, who all use their own life memories to produce unique affective memories. And by extension, it does not bother him that a unique experience is imparted to each audience, and even to each member of that audience. Stanislavski's unquestioned acceptance of the recipient's participation in the creation of a work of art breaks new ground in the history of theater performance theory. Here is something remarkable: Stanislavski does not grapple with the idea and seek to justify it, indeed he does not seem to notice that it is something new; instead he openly accepts it as an "organic and natural" aspect of the art phenomenon, to use his own imprecise yet reverent language.

Though what the playwright intends within his work of art remains unchanged, what is taken by its recipients is always unique, re-created anew by each act of reception. A spectator is always a recipient, of course, and in most theater this is his only function. But notice that Stanislavski's logic requires us to see the actor in two ways, simultaneously: along with the playwright, he is a fellow creator (especially in rehearsals, where he builds his "score" of gestures and inflections), but he is also a recipient, along with the spectators (especially in successive performances). Recall that Stanislavski observes that the actor's unique contribution lies in the affective memories which he employs. He should change these with each performance, and find new memories that are appropriate not only to the unchanging play but to the mutable actor, the different person he is on each new day of performance. Like the recipient-spectator at any one performance, the recipient side of the actor receives something unique from the play at every performance, depending on "who he is" that day, and he should respond with different emotion-stimulating memories. Stanislavski does not make this recommendation because he fears that an actor will exhaust the technical effectiveness of a certain memory, although "method" actors do report that they use up the affective potentiality of a personal memory rather quickly. Stanislavski's justification reflects a philosophical awareness, not a technical practicality: "Bend your efforts to creating a new and fresh inspiration for today. There is no reason to suppose that it will be less good than yesterday's. It may not be as brilliant. But you have the advantage of possessing it today."[19] Here, in embryo form, is the origin of a notion which Grotowski will develop later into a central premise: the belief that an artwork such as a theatrical production is not a fixed object whose meaning and even existential makeup remain unchanged, but a series of transactions among all its co-creators and co-recipients. An overall *structure* for any category of transactions might be extracted from viewing (or imagining) all the performances—for example, the category of transactions between the unchanging text and the mutable recipient-actor (a spectrum bounded by the text's possible connotations, the director's dictates, and the actor's store of appropriate emotions). Indeed, it is essential to perceive these structures, for they convey the artwork's connotations as well as define what it existentially "is." But this artwork is the play's production, an ideal object perceived over time (the time of its "run"), and no one performance within the "run" contains *all* the transactions which potentially exist within a production. We are left with two conclusions, which need not be mutually exclusive: (1) the idea that an artwork has no exclusively corporeal existence but is a mental structure which is intellectually and emotionally perceived from successive acts of reception (for theater, "artwork" equals "production"); and (2) the thought that each unique act of reception is a new artwork itself (for theater, "artwork" equals "performance").

This idea that a work of art is continually re-created by its new reception does not originate with Stanislavski. The antecedents most immediately available to a late nineteenth-century Russian who considered himself to be "cultured" but not a scholar would have been the impressionist school of painting from France, and the symbolist movement in poetry, which Stanislavski knew indirectly through the plays of Maeterlinck and Hauptmann; Stanislavski also correctly interpreted the precursor Ibsen as a symbolist.

But Stanislavski's reaction to this literature is complex; he treats it both as a repository for useful naturalistic detail and as an indicator for a quality beyond what is commonly suggested by the term "naturalism." Whenever Stanislavski recommends that his students study the recent history of art and literature, he speaks of the "truth to life" and variety of natural details which they will observe in such work, and will want to incorporate into their store of memories to be drawn upon when affective memory is employed. He never observes the artificial quality of much of this art, how it plays with perspective and perception, and encourages the recipient to assist in the creation of an artifice rather than to observe a direct "slice of life." But these "true-to-life" details lead in turn to as much of an emphasis on the reality of a theatrical performance (as something that really exists) as on the realism of a given play (as something which very much resembles our daily activities). In one speech which he made to his actors in 1915, he referred to these literary researches as aids to displaying a "spiritual naturalism."[20] In turn, this constantly renewed arsenal of detail will allow the actor to experience and display the character's feelings *as if for the first time* during each performance, a capability that will help him to create the illusion that the characters are living their lives for the first time on the stage, not that they are being reenacted *again*. The actor has taken over some of the playwright's decisions (e.g., what the character's emotions are and whether the playwright intends that there are any, apart from emotions specified by the text) for the purpose of furthering the illusion that the play is real, that its events are taking place during each moment of performance. (He also takes responsibility for the assumption that the playwright intends that the illusion be taken as "real.") Not only does Stanislavski assume that the character's *present* existence be taken as real, he also indicates that the fact of the actor's presence, his own circumstances and emotions which vary his performance from day to day, be seen as an integral aspect of the work of art: "an actor cannot be merely someone, somewhere, at some time or other. He must be I, here, today."[21]

We can clarify Stanislavski's embryonic suggestions by looking at them from the perspective of phenomenology. One might even suggest that Stanislavski's proximity to the philosophical movement demonstrates his larger connection to the general trends of modernism.

From the point of view of contemporary theory of perception, any work of art from the past can be interpreted through a model of "inter-subjectivity" such as it is understood by phenomenologists like Marcel Merleau-Ponty. If we recapitulate his argument about the transmission of language between speakers, we discover that a model may be employed to describe the transmission of the artwork from creator to receiver that resembles his model for the transmission of *la parole*. He rejects the empiricist's belief that the word equals its verbal image, and the idealist's assumption that the word equals its concept. These equations share the tacit assumption that the word itself has no meaning; the empiricist believes it to be only a psychic phenomenon on the order of a nerve stimulation, while the idealist believes that it is an exterior sign which is unnecessary to the interior operation of recognition. From their opposing points of view, both the empiricist and the idealist believe that complete transmission of meaning can take place, and that the mechanism will operate in identical manner upon each listener. Saussure had already demonstrated the naiveté of this assumption and replaced it with the contrast between the "significative" (*significant*, the expression intended by the speaker) and the "signified" (*signifié*, the expression as achieved in the listener). Merleau-Ponty views communication as "the transcendence of the 'significative' by the 'signified' that it is the character of the 'significative' to make possible,"[22] or that transaction between what is intended and what is received which differs with each new listener and yet is governed by the same intention of the speaker. But since meaning lies within the transaction *between* the two (and not in ideal concepts shared by the two that are left unchanged by the transaction and merely triggered within their consciousnesses by the word acting as a stimulus), then the varying receptions within the listeners of unique *signifiés* reflect back onto the speaker and change and renew his own expressive intention. Philip E. Lewis explains this in his discussion of Merleau-Ponty's work *The Phenomenology of Perception:*

> Communication cannot be explained as a re-creation of mental representations by the listener; understanding of a speaker's message takes place in the same way that we understand his gestures,

i.e., there is a renewal of the speaker's expressive intention which is, for the listener as for the speaker, a "synchronic modulation of his own existence, a transformation of his being."[23]

Or, as Merleau-Ponty says in another work, "We who speak do not necessarily know what we express better than those who hear us."[24]

Translating this into the terms of the transmission of the work of art, particularly of the play transmitted by way of the actor, we can compare the "speaker" of Merleau-Ponty's model with the playwright, or more specifically, with the artwork's intentionality, and we can compare the "listener" with the recipient of the artwork, in this case the audience. The actor exists as a new third term between the two. Since, like the audience member, he first hears or reads a play text which has been given intentionality by its author, he shares in the function of the recipient of the artwork. But Stanislavski has insisted upon the actor's contribution to the creation of the artwork by the very fact of his presence. For the theater event, whether the play be staged or simply read with the assumption that its *being enacted* is an integral part of its existence, meaning resides in the transaction between the artwork and the recipient by means of the actor (who is considered as an aspect of both poles), and in the reciprocal "synchronic modulation" of both, to repeat Merleau-Ponty's phrase. No part of this conclusion is drawn by Stanislavski. It was not his genius to originate such a concept, which was already being hypothesized in poetic terms by Mallarmé and the impressionist painters. Stanislavski's contribution lies in the development of an acting style in which the assumption is inherent. And with the assumption embodied, as it is, in a staging technique, subsequent playwrights have given new significance to the process by which their works are transmitted to their recipients; a consciousness of the act of transmission and varying significations drawn from the existence of the transmission mechanism have been incorporated as part of the work's intentionality itself. From this, we should not conclude that contemporary playwrights feel obliged to create characters who are conscious of the fact that they are merely roles in a play, characters who announce their lack of "reality" to the audience. Stanislavski preferred plays which maintain the convention that play characters are actual persons whom the audience observes from behind an invisible "fourth wall." But today playwrights must be conscious of the fact that whatever degree of "reality" or "artificiality" their characters exhibit will be transmitted by actors who *are* really there, whose very presence becomes a part of the work of art. Although we can use the same model of transmission to discuss artworks created before there existed a philosophical or artistic consciousness on the order of Merleau-Ponty's or Stanislavski's, there is a qualitative difference between classical works created

by artists who possessed the idealist belief that the eternal and unchanging work and its meaning will be experienced the same way by
each recipient, and modern works created by artists who are conscious
of the role which perception plays not only in the meaning of their
works but in their very essence itself.

Perhaps the stage offers the archetypal paradigm of this phenomenon, for of all the verbal arts drama is the only one which needs to be
transmitted by means of a living and present mediator. Furthermore, it
offers the most concrete example of the variety of interpretations and
meanings which can be taken from the "one" work, for each new production and each authentically received performance is a different and
potentially valid interpretation. And because of the necessity of live
enactment for the work to come into existence (either on stage, or as
understood in reading), drama speaks most concretely of the *being* of a
work of art, for the work's *presence* is not only a factor of its transmission but of its meaning as well. Stanislavski initiates a direction of
thought within drama which is later reflected in such a statement as this
one by Alain Robbe-Grillet:

> The human condition, Heidegger says, is *to be there*. Probably it is
> the theatre, more than any other mode of representing reality,
> which reproduces this situation most naturally. The dramatic
> character *is on stage*, that is his most primary quality: he is *there*.[25]

Stanislvaski did not invent the concept of affective memory in a vacuum. He claimed not to have invented it at all. At the end of his second
volume of fictional acting lessons, after he has discussed the psychological preparation for acting (in *An Actor Prepares*) and the refinement
of the actor's physical apparatus so that it may effectively display the
psychological groundwork (in *Building a Character*), Stanislavski's *per-
sona* Tortsov refers to the "Stanislavski system" by name only to deny
that he has concocted it. For Stanislavski, no qualitative difference
exists between the human creation of an artwork and the birth of a
human being. We are born with the potentiality for producing either
one "inside us, . . . an innate capacity for creativeness," and hence any
method which fosters the emergence of an artwork from within the self
is no invention, but a "natural system."[26]

This failure to distinguish between artistic creation and creation in
nature indicates a confusion in Stanislavski's thinking, a confusion
arising from his failure to complete the line of thought initiated by his
genuine contribution to performance theory: the role of the mediating
actor and his creation of an artwork out of his self. The *fact* of this
mediation is true for any theater performance. Stanislavski acknowledges that he does not invent this fact, although he does not openly

state that he is among the first to incorporate its inevitability into a system of acting. But the *means* by which any system is effected, how it affects the actor and audience, differs according to the prevailing theory of psychology within a given society, and the social functions, overt and covert, of a given psychology. Earlier in the discussion, we observed how the playwright's awareness of the existence of a mediating process between his creation and its recipients reflects back upon the artwork, as well as reflecting forward onto its recipients. The playwright incorporates a critique of the process of mediation into the work itself. The varying significances given by authors to the fact of mediation reflect varying concepts of psychology and alternative social uses of them. These significances acknowledge, as Stanislavski does not, the artificial quality of the work of art, even though it is always transmitted to its receiver by means of human perception, which invariably alters it and adds an aspect of the receiver's self to it. When Stanislavski's thinking is carried beyond his own formulations, it results in notions of "truth to life" which he did not acknowledge in his own theater practice but which are rooted within it. For example, many dramatists writing after Stanislavski believe that the actor's closeness of feeling with the character he portrays does not represent the pinnacle of realism and "truth to life" upon the stage. Far more "true" is the fact that the actor *is* an actor and is performing in a theater, not living in the character's quarters which he has re-created so slavishly by means of affective memory. An examination of the intellectual traditions out of which Stanislavski's system of acting emerges will demonstrate more concretely the degree to which it is bound to particular social circumstances. I suspect that Stanislavski's unwillingness to acknowledge this fact to himself led him to write his books on acting through the voice of the fictitious Tortsov, who could claim that the system was "organic" and could show it as emerging from neophyte actors by means of subtle prodding. In this way Stanislavski did not have to speak in his own voice, that of the autocratic director who implanted the system into many generations of student actors.

The realistic school of acting begins on the Russian stage with Mikhail Shtchepkin. He acted and taught at the Imperial Little Theater in Moscow in the second quarter of the nineteenth century. Stanislavski knew Shtchepkin's work from the actor's correspondence and from his own apprenticeship at the Imperial Little Theater at a time when Shtchepkin's graying pupils were carrying on his tradition in a debased form. Stanislavski notes that Shtchepkin was the first to introduce simplicity and lifelikeness into Russian theater; more important, he encouraged his pupils to study the manner in which emotions are expressed in real life and to use this knowledge to "enter . . . into the skin of the role."[27] Stanislavski was fond of quoting Shtchepkin's maxim that "It is not important that you play well or ill; it is important that you play truthfully."[28] Shtchepkin regretted that the actor's art had not yet been codified into a system, but he left little more than occasional notes toward this end himself.

Stanislavski grounds his own technique for entering into the skin of a role by way of emotions, or affective memory, in the writing of the French psychologist Théodule Ribot, whose *Psychologie des sentiments* was published in F. Pavlenkov's Russian translation in 1896. But Stanislavski apparently took from Ribot little more than the anecdote with which he introduces his discussion of affective memory in *An Actor Prepares.* Two travelers marooned on some rocks by a high tide narrated their impressions after their rescue. One remembered all his actions, how, why, and where he had climbed to escape the tide. But the second man had no recollection of the place at all. Instead, he remembered the emotions he had felt, and used these to recount his tale in far more striking terms.[29] Stanislavski calls this technique "emotion memory," but at this point does not explicitly discuss how it affects the actor and audience.

Ribot's writings offer only a minor contribution to the psychoanalytic theory evolving at the turn of the century. Cultural distance and the lack of scholarly inquiry isolated Stanislavski from Freud's theories at the very time when Stanislavski was inventing the concept of affective memory. Nevertheless, it is a remarkable case of parallel evolution. Freud and Stanislavski hold the common assumption that beneath our superficial social transactions a subconscious life exists which is more real than the surface actions we perform, or the "text" we speak. Both assume that a manipulation at the subconscious level can produce a change at the level of consciousness. Both the psychoanalytic method and the acting technique ask the subject to search in his past for causative incidents and to reexperience the emotions surrounding them. Both methods encourage concentration upon the physical and sensory details surrounding these emotions; such awareness of detail enhances the felt quality of emotion. And both methods assume that the reliving of a past incident through emotions in the present will cause a result in this same present. For Freud, the result is cure, a consciousness of past trauma which rids the subject of the fear attendant upon it in the present. Ideally, the cure is a purgation, and, in fact, Freud considered naming his technique "the cathartic method" before he decided upon the term "psychoanalytic treatment," a phrase which emphasized the conscious understanding of the past more than it promised a cure for injuries in the present. Stanislavski's technique results more in a purification of our attitude toward traumatic events than an expulsion of the emotions attendant upon them; indeed, he believed that the actor should be able to reexperience the emotions accompanying an event in his life many times in performance. The actor's display of his own emotions awakens similar feelings within the audience; by the process of empathy with the actor's reexperienced emotions, the audience empathizes with the action being undertaken by the character he portrays. The result for the actor is an acceptance of his own past, and for the audience an acceptance of the character.

"Purgation" and "purification" were the common translations of Aristotle's term "catharsis" at the turn of the century. They were inherited from Renaissance and nineteenth-century interpretations of the *Poetics* which tended to ignore the technical aspects of Aristotle's handbook for writing poetry and to develop—or invent—a psychology of aesthetics from it. That is, these interpretations depart from Aristotle's view that poetry is a self-contained system of knowledge which obeys the laws of art, and they discuss instead the way poetry reflects and affects reality. In terms of the theater, they admit the actor and audience into the *Poetics.* I suspect that Stanislavski has in mind a late-nineteenth-century reading of Aristotle when, in *An Actor Prepares*, he makes his most conscious statement about catharsis. The passage follows immediately after the discussion of affective memory. In rather mawkish language, the student-narrator Kostya recounts a traffic accident he has seen, which has left a man mangled in the show beneath a streetcar. At the scene of the accident, Kostya feels nothing more than shock at the vividness of the physical details, the colors, the sobbing wife and indifferent crowd, and some children playing obliviously beside a stream of blood. But when he returns to the site after the wreckage has been cleared away and recalls the accident, using the newly learned technique of affective memory, he experiences an insight which inures him to the shock of sudden death. In the schoolboy-philosopher's language of Kostya:

> The stream of blood, that is the flow of man's transgressions. All around, in brilliant contrast, I see the sky, sun, nature. That's— eternity. The street cars rolling by, filled with passengers, represent the passing generations on their way into the unknown. The whole picture, which was so horrible, so terrifying, has now become majestic, stern . . . .[30]

Kostya does not leave his experience as an impassive observer. Later, when he tries to recall the emotions surrounding the event, he finds that the streetcar which mangled a victim who was unknown to him does not impress him nearly so much as the memory of a streetcar which he once had to help push back onto the tracks after it had been derailed. He now functions as an actor who uses his own past to create the character's history. When he tells this to Tortsov-Stanislavski, the director commends him, and observes that time "not only purifies, it also transmutes even painfully realistic memories into poetry."[31] The observation is trite, but the implications of the acting technique which emerge from it are large.

Freud's own analysis of catharsis in drama links the enjoyment of tragedy with the release of "the subject's [audience's] own affects"; this release corresponds to "the relief produced by their free discharge," and the sexual stimulation which, Freud assumes, accompanies every emotional excitation.[32] He believes, as does Stanislavski, that the audience should identify itself with the characters, but that it derives its pleasure through the knowledge that *another* is acting and suffering on the stage; the audience's emotional excitation is only *as if* it were in the place of the character.[33] (This parallels Stanislavski's oft-repeated formula of "the magic *if.*") Freud goes on to suggest that the audience derives pleasure only from witnessing mental anguish, not physical suffering, on the stage, for its empathy with the character is purely a mental relation.[34] Stanislavski's concern with subtext and hidden motivations suggests a similar constriction of attention; all his work with the physical apparatus of the actor in *Building a Character* is accompanied by the caveat that concern with this apparatus springs from and serves to display the "psycho-technique" elaborated in the first lessons described in *An Actor Prepares.*

Freud departs from Stanislavski when he assumes that the mental anguish of a character is a neurosis. The action of the play drives the hero to what Freud calls "a psychopathic state" because of a repressed desire which is similarly repressed in the audience; the hero's release is achieved in the audience by means of empathy, or, as Freud puts it, "it is thus the task of the dramatist to transport us into the same illness."[35] (In regard to repression, Stanislavski would concur, for he says that his actors are ashamed to display their most intimate and secret traits unless they may hide behind the mask of a characterization.) Freud goes on to make the equation between psychoanalysis and empathetic catharsis to which Brecht will so strongly react:

> it appears to be one of the prerequisites of this art form that the struggle of the repressed impulse to become conscious, recognizable though it is, is so little given a definite name that the process of reaching consciousness goes on in turn within the spectator while his attention is distracted and he is in the grip of his emotions, rather than capable of rational judgment. In this way resistance is definitely reduced, in the manner seen in psychoanalytic treatment, when the derivatives of the repressed ideas and emotions came to consciousness as a result of a lessening of resistance in a manner denied to the repressed material itself.[36]

In other words, Freud compares the process by which an audience's rational attention is distracted by emotional engagement in a play to the therapeutic distraction employed in psychoanalysis, that is, the analyst's dwelling upon peripheral events surrounding a traumatic past incident which the patient cannot consciously face. By this indirect means, the patient brings himself into a conscious engagement with the repressed incident itself, for the sake of a therapeutic end. In terms of an acting theory, Freud's statement would demand that the actors behave in such a way that the audience forgets the objective fact that it watches players on a stage, not persons in real life. To this end, Stanislavski forbade his actor to play to the audience, or even to acknowledge the audience's existence (the device which Brecht will later use to allow his audience to make conscious and rational judgments). But though his actor is oblivious of the audience, Stanislavski believed that the audience should be engrossed in the actor. He shares Freud's supposition that the release of repressed impulses takes place in the audience at the emotional rather than the rational level.

But Stanislavski's actor cannot afford to operate at this level: all the devices of Stanislavski's technique serve to focus the actor's conscious attention on the role he is playing. If catharsis is to be effected at the emotional level, whom does it affect? Not Stanislaviski's actor, who is consciously using his emotions and controlling them by rational means to achieve the end of resembling the character. The audience identifies with the character and experiences the character's release of repression by means of empathy. Since the audience does this at the emotional level, it achieves a catharsis, according to Freud, but Stanislavski does not inquire into the way performance affects the audience other than to link the effect to the experience of the character. In fact, the burden of catharsis in Stanislavski's theater falls upon the character, despite all the emphasis his technique places upon the actor. He believes that the actor's role in performance is a fluid and inventive one: the actor is constantly re-creating and renewing the artwork by means of fresh emotions in an endless series of "present moments" of performance. Even the audience appears to be somewhat dynamic; although in theory Stanislavski leaves it "beyond the footlights," he acknowledges that it changes from night to night and from moment to moment, and that these changes result in responses which the actors feel and incorporate into the performance, thus changing the artwork itself. Only character, in his system, seems passive and static. Character is tied to the "through lines of action" and "given circumstances" of the play; it is occasionally animated by the emotional outbursts of the actor inhabiting a role, and at the play's end it has achieved a rather conventionally optimistic inurement to the play's events, which now appear to be purified by the very process of the characters' having lived through them.

Stanislavski thought that he had found a perfect exponent for this kind of catharsis in Chekhov. As we noted earlier, he dutifully filled the playwright's ambiguous pauses with psychological content ("repressed impulses" in Freud's terms); then he released this content in emotional outbursts which were motivated by the actors' own emotions, and at the play's end he displayed the purified characters looking back with new understanding upon events which were now devoid of trauma. The thought that Chekhov's pauses might be empty, his tears motiveless, and his characters unchanged at the play's end never occurred to Stanislavski.

But before the question of Stanislavski's appropriateness to Chekhov is discussed, we should continue our examination of Stanislavski's contribution to psychoanalytic theory. In his comparison of Freud and Stanislavski, John J. Sullivan observes that while Freud's concern was with the relation between reality and the individual's intentions, and between these intentions and other mental processes, Stanislavski's concern was with the relation between mental processes and behavior.[37] Stanislavski moves psychoanalysis from a descriptive to an affective position; in fact, he always accompanies his descriptions of "psycho-technique" with the proviso that he does not study the subconscious but only the paths leading to and from it. In Sullivan's opinion, Stanislavski's contribution is essential for the development of "a psychology of aesthetics," for it serves to "explicate more clearly the relations of thoughts and feelings to expressive behavior."[38]

What is the nature of the "expressive behavior" prompted by affective memory? We have already observed that the actor draws upon his own life to create and constantly renew a work of art in the present. But like Wordsworth's formula of "emotion recollected in tranquility" or Proust's experience with the madeleine, which so resemble affective memory, the latter limits its effect to the past. To the extent that the character is created out of the actor's emotions (not out of the playwright's words), its enactment through affective memory allows it to achieve a catharsis for past trauma but in no way prepares it to anticipate or act in a future. Likewise, for the actor, affective memory has the effect of allowing him to portray characters who have no futures, only pasts, in plays the main action of which is to expose past suffering and expunge it from the characters, or inure them to it in the present. Specifically, the technique has proved particularly unsuited for chronicle plays such as Shakespeare's or Brecht's, which display characters in the process of making their futures.

In addition, the actor using affective memory encounters this technical drawback: he quickly exhausts the effectiveness of any particular personal incident for producing an emotion, and he has to search constantly in his own past for other incidents to put in its place. Paradoxically, the trauma associated with the incident for the actor has not only been purified by means of an artistic understanding, in the terms of Stanislavski, it has been purged away entirely, as in Freud's psychoanalytic catharsis. Stanislavski is ambivalent about this situation: he is convinced that although the actor's repertoire of memories is finite, like the finite elements of the color spectrum or sound scale, its elements can be infinitely rearranged to produce new emotions; on the other hand, he encourages the actor to replenish his stock of memories continually by making observations from life and the world of art. Neither suggestion helps the actor move toward a future; they only deepen his researches into a past. And when Stanislavski demands that the actor never portray anything externally which he has not experienced internally, he forces his actor either to limit his repertoire of characters severely—after all, Stanislavski's technique is most suitable to the portrayal of characters who do not *act* so much as they *remember*—or to substitute a trite or inappropriate experience as the analogue for a character's experience which the actor could never have had in his own life. Remembering all the sensations and emotions surrounding the slaying of a mosquito does little to illuminate the emotions of an Othello when he is about to murder Desdemona, but unfortunately such a situation is a commonplace of "method acting."

Richard Schechner contrasts Stanislavskian acting with child's play as a means of illuminating their temporal orientation.[39] Like the actor, the child in imaginative play often performs actions which he has never performed in life. Yet the child's lack of a set of experiences upon which to draw for models does not inhibit his "acting": rather than reliving his past he is "rehearsing" actions which he will later be called upon to perform in life. (Schechner's analogy is carried a step further in recent acting practice: troupes like Grotowski's Laboratory Theater improvise around a physical activity to find an action they wish to portray, rather than work backward through emotion to a remembered event.) Concerning child's play, Schechner observes:

> The child is testing and toying with his emotional apparatus. In a sense he is doing the opposite of affective memory which is a re-living; the child is pre-living, anticipating a set of emotions he may later, as an adult, find use for. The actor using affective memory is paying back old debts; the child is storing up resources.[40]

In terms of catharsis, the child and the actor who employ "pre-living" are *making* themselves, and for them catharsis involves change. Opposed to this position is Stanislavskian acting, which has the effect of instructing the character, actor, and audience to remain as they are: they are finding themselves, and catharsis involves confirmation.

The assertion that the result of his theater is an unspoken command to the participants in it to "remain as they are" would have surprised Stanislavski. It was Brecht's evaluation, and it led him to link Stanislavski's methods with Freud's and to criticize them both: "Stanislavski's methods of concentration have always reminded me of psychoanalysis. Both are concerned with fighting a social disease, but neither uses social means. Thus only the results of the sickness can be fought, not its bases."[41] Stanislavski's written statements do not support Brecht's later judgment. Throughout his career Stanislavski believed that he was espousing a "life in art" which would remake the man who engaged in it, the actor. For Stanislavski, the actor can never get away from *himself* on the stage,[42] and it is the *man* behind the characterization who is to be revealed on stage. In Tortsov's words to a student: "Now if it would ever occur to you to show us on the stage something we have never seen, if you would show us yourself as you are in real life, not the 'actor' Grisha Govorkov but the man—that would be splendid because the human being that you are is far more interesting and talented than the actor."[43]

At times, the language Stanislavski uses to describe the "rebirth" of this man, his actor, attains religious overtones. He virtually concludes *An Actor Prepares* with this statement, italicized in the original: "Our type of creativeness is the conception and birth of a new being—the person in the part. It is a natural act similar to the birth of a human being."[44] And the succeeding volume, *Building a Character*, describes a physical technique which parallels the infant's education in the most basic life-activities: he reinstructs the actor in walking, speaking, and the experiencing of body rhythms.

In his quest to give birth to "the man in the part," Stanislavski anticipates a line of thought which leads to such conceptions as Grotowski's "holy actor" and contemporary "communal" theater. He talks of the actor's "service" to art and his "mission," and compares him to the "true priest" who is "aware of the presence of the altar during every moment that he is conducting a service."[45] His system is no recipe book for concocting various roles:

> No, it is a whole way of life, you have to grow up in it, educate yourself in it for years. You cannot cram it into yourselves, you can assimilate it, take it into your blood and flesh, until it becomes second nature, becomes so organic a part of your being that you as an actor are transformed by it for the stage and for all time.[46]

He even proposed that his actors form a monastic community on a plot of land in the country, which they would till and build upon, combining the rhythms of subsistence farming with rehearsals of plays. Their audience was to travel from the city to the commune for the evening, and dine and sleep there as well as view a performance. Of this "spiritual order of actors," Stanislavski wrote: "Its members were to be men and women of broad and uplifted views, of wide horizons and ideas, who knew the soul of man and aimed at noble artistic ideals, who could worship in the theatre as in a temple."[47] Although he never carried out this plan, he did buy a plot of land on the Black Sea, and for several summers he sent his student actors there to farm the land and to continue their lessons.

The idea of art as a religion and a way of life was not uncommon among the avant-garde movements of the time. And at first, Stanislavski's work truly *was* avant-garde. Although it later became practically the state theater of the Soviet Union, the prerevolutionary Moscow Art Theater and especially Stanislavski's acting studios within it existed outside of and beyond the Russian popular theater for years, constituting "coteries," as discussed by Renato Poggioli in *The Theory of the Avant-Garde*. Such movements conceived of culture as "a center of activity and energy," a creation itself, not a thesaurus of attitudes taken from the society surrounding it; typically, their members gathered around "priests of the modern religion of poetry and art" like Mallarmé and Stefan George.[48] Although Stanislavski was less conscious of his priestly function than his European counterparts, he believed with them that his system could "save" the actor in some way and could remake the man behind him.

Toward the end of his career, Stanislavski revised his teaching methods considerably, and evolved what he called a "system of physical action" which closely resembles contemporary theater practice. He describes this system in his third book of fictional acting lessons, *Creating a Role*. Instead of depending upon remembered emotions with which the actor could display feeling in the present, the technique of affective memory, Stanislavski devised physical activities which would stimulate the desired feelings reflexively. The actor now worked from the exterior to the interior. Stanislavski called for a training the first two years of which would concentrate upon the actor himself, before he began work on particular roles; in *Creating a Role*, Tortsov-Stanislavski even claims that "One can act a play not yet written."[49] Stanislavski also stripped the actor of all realistic mise-en-scène as an aid to living the role, believing that he should be able to adapt his performance to the particular space in which he was playing. This appears to reverse the position taken in his first two books on acting, which demand that the actor work from his own interior to the character's surface. (In fact, toward the end of *Building a Character*, Stanislavski approaches the system of physical action through his discussion of "tempo-rhythms," internal but physically felt rhythms which must be sought in every characterization. Often they serve as "an almost mechanical stimulus to emotion memory," and "the correctly established tempo-rhythm of a play or a role can of itself, intuitively ... on occasion automati- cally ... take hold of the feelings of an actor and arouse in him a true sense of living his part."[50] Stanislavski wrote *Building a Character* and *Creating a Role* at the same time he was developing the system of physi- cal action.)

Such a system reflects a change in his affiliation with psychological theory. In effect, Stanislavski departed from Freud and turned to Pavlov and the stimulus-response mechanism of behaviorism. Vladimir Pro- kofyev, historian of the Moscow Art Theater, notes this reversal. Stanislavski was still working through a conscious approach to cause a reaction in the subconscious, as he insists throughout his books dealing with affective memory; however, late in life he realized that the feelings associated with this subconscious can best be stimulated by tangible and visible actions. But the new system of physical actions has the same goal as the old method of affective memory: "Because living the part means believing it and because it is easiest to believe in actions, the method of physical action became the simplest and surest means to truth on the stage."[51] Prokofyev does not question the goal, nor does he observe, that, in effect, affective memory operates as a comparable stimulus-response mechanism, although it lacks a physical and visible stimulus, or in Schechner's words, is "an effect without a cause."[52]

Contemporaries of Stanislavski and later practitioners whose work departs radically from his have sought to ground their practice in the system of physical action. His brilliant and rebellious student Vsevolod Meyerhold rejected any psychological technique for "a whole army of actors, psychologically 'experiencing' the parts of all those characters who do nothing but walk, eat, drink, make love and wear jackets."[53] Instead, Meyerhold proposed a method known as "Biomechanics" which he said Stanislavski himself was approaching in his later years. This description dates from 1922, from a lecture on "Biomechanics":

> There is a whole range of questions to which psychology is incap- able of supplying the answers. A theatre built on psychological foundations is as certain to collapse as a house built on sand. On the other hand, a theatre which relies on *physical elements* is at very least assured of clarity. All psychological states are determined by specific physiological processes. By correctly re- solving the nature of his state physically, the actor reaches the

point where he experiences the *excitation* which communicates itself to the spectator and induces him to share in the actor's performance.[54]

More recently, Grotowski has cited both the system of physical actions and Meyerhold's biomechanics as influences on his own work.[55] In 1952, at a time when his own theories were being contrasted unfavorably with those of the socialist realist whom Stanislavski had become in the eyes of Soviet Russia, Brecht called the system of physical action Stanislavski's greatest contribution to a new theater; Brecht added that the actors of the Berliner Ensemble had mastered the system of physical action without difficulty![56]

Whatever the reasons for citing Stanislavski as a source, it has not been realized that the system of physical action serves the same end as affective memory, the experiencing of the part by the actor which Meyerhold found so objectionable in the passage cited earlier. (In fact, Meyerhold's equivalent of catharsis is the "excitation" shared by actor and audience which he mentions in the passage dating from 1922; Stanislavski's catharsis is effected primarily in the character.) All the messianic programs which Stanislavski proposed as a means of renewing the man behind the actor—his theory of a "temple of art," theater communes in the countryside, and the system of physical actions which would remold the body—result in a philosophical failure. They contradict the primary goal of acting in his theater, which is living *the part*, not living itself, on the stage. Stanislavski proposes no new life in art but enables the actor to bring his old life from reality into the theater, and to continue to live it on the stage. When his students protest that they already know how to walk, move, and speak *in life*, Stanislavski convinces them of the difficulty of performing these most basic of physical activities *as if in life* upon the stage. He is unable to recognize that the fact that an actor *is* an actor upon the stage is a more primary reality than his attempt to live the part he plays. Neither can he imagine the possibility that living *as an actor* on stage may involve a technique, and thus a philosophical attitude, which differ from the actor's mode of being in his private person, the history of which Stanislavski introduces into the play by means of affective memory, but the future of which Stanislavski's thinking is incapable of affecting. Yet in spite of this failure, Stanislavski's practice and thought posed the problem, and his example of a life in art stands behind the attempts of more contemporary practitioners and philosophers to resolve it.

2. *The Three Sisters:* Stanislavski's Tragedy, Chekhov's Vaudeville

Anton Chekhov added the subtitle "A Drama in Four Acts" to his manuscript of *The Three Sisters* (*Tri Sestry*). It was the only play which he designated as a drama. His subtitle to *Uncle Vanya* is "Scenes from Country Life"; *The Cherry Orchard* he called simply "A Comedy." Stanislavski could not be convinced that Chekhov had comic intentions: he insisted that *The Three Sisters* was "a serious drama of Russian life,"[1] as was *The Cherry Orchard*, and of the latter play he wrote to Chekhov in 1903 that he had written neither a comedy nor a farce, as the playwright insisted, but a tragedy.[2] Chekhov was enraged at the maudlin and sentimentalized reading of *The Three Sisters* given by the Moscow Art company at the play's first rehearsal. He sat through it in silence, and then stalked out of the theater; Stanislavski reports that he never saw the playwright so angry as during this reading, and never had he defended his opinion so hotly as when he insisted that he had written "a gay comedy, almost a farce."[3] Although Stanislavski later admitted that during the first productions of Chekhov's plays the Moscow Art actors bathed in a sorrow inappropriate to Chekhov's characters, he never could admit that Chekhov was not an optimist. In *My Life in Art* he says of Chekhov's characters that they, like the playwright,

> seek life, joy, laughter, courage. The men and women of Chekhov want to live and not to die. They are active and surge to overcome the hard and unbearable impasses into which life has plunged them. It is not their fault that Russian life kills initiative and the best of beginnings and interferes with the free action and life of men and women.[4]

Chekhov's opinion of his plays was rather different. When he walked out of the first rehearsal of *The Three Sisters,* he exclaimed, "But what I wrote was a vaudeville!"[5] An examination of this play, which was both drama and vaudeville to Chekhov, will help to clarify Stanislavski's opinion that he had derived his acting system from Chekhov, and that his system was a key to understanding the playwright himself. I will pay particular attention to aspects of the play which manipulate audience reactions—unresolved dichotomies, pauses and lacunae, comic devices, and direct address to the audience—for these aspects reveal

Chekhov's own theory of affectivity (often in conflict with Stanislavski's).

The story which Chekhov relates in *The Three Sisters* might convince us to agree with Stanislavski and most subsequent interpreters that the play is practically a tragedy. Three young and well-educated women from the capital have become stranded in a provincial city along with their dull brother Andrei. They dream of returning to Moscow, where they will find love and intellectual stimulation. The only tolerable companions they find in their dreary surroundings are the officers in their dead father's regiment. The sisters entertain them at interminable social events on the country estate, and two of them find lovers among the officers. But even these pathetic remnants of the longed-for Moscow are lost when the regiment is transferred to Poland. Resigned to being a spinster, the oldest sister, Olga, takes a job which she despises as headmistress in a boarding school; Masha, married to a pedantic schoolmaster, loses her lover Vershinin when the regiment departs; the youngest, Irina, is to marry Baron Tuzenbach, an officer who has resigned his commission, but Tuzenbach dies in a duel as the final curtain falls. And Andrei's provincial wife, Natasha, successfully ousts the sisters from the estate.

Although Chekhov informs the audience of all these dismal events by the end of the play, he shows none of them happening directly upon the stage. The distance he imposes between his play's plot and his audience's apprehension of it in its unfolding cushions the immediate shock of the story's events. What Chekhov shows happening on the stage confirms the principle of literary criticism that the plot is not the same as the action. The plot events in *The Three Sisters* take place offstage or during the intermissions; the action portrayed emerges out of minor incidents from daily life which indirectly reflect the plot's events but are not caused by them. Chekhov organizes each act around a social gathering—a name-day luncheon, an evening party during carnival week, relief preparations when the town is struck by fire, and, finally, the departure of the regiment. Except for Tuzenbach's death, the play's final incident, none of these gatherings progresses to a climax, and Tuzenbach's duel is not causally related to the regiment's departure but simply takes place simultaneously with it. Instead, Chekhov shows the guests arriving, performing their social roles (and occasionally breaking out of them), and departing. While on stage, the characters speak banalities, interrupt one another, suffer silences, recount memories, and make confessions; if they live their lives in any more active sense, they do this offstage.

Stanislavski thought that Chekhov's seemingly random arrangement of trivial events revealed an extremely lifelike play which needed to be illustrated by an equally lifelike mise-en-scène. He believed that Chekhov had "painted pictures from life, not plays for the stage,"[6] and called for his actors to complement these pictures by means of much improvised detail; he also held that "Chekhov's characters cannot be 'shown,' they can only be *lived*."[7] Stanislavski thought that he had found a literary justification for many of the facets of his system in the writings of Chekhov. Like the playwright, he did not judge the characters but merely observed them, and asked his actors to identify with them. He took his theory of contradictory internal "tempo-rhythms" from Chekhov's dramaturgy, assuming that the character's verbal evasions and superficial statements must be animated by unstated conscious desires and unacknowledged subconscious drives, which should be reflected in the timing of speeches and hesitations, gestures and moments of stasis, all of which are ignored by the actor who merely reads the part and does not live it; the director claimed that whole plays of Chekhov were predicated on the combinations of contrasting tempo-rhythms, and cited *The Three Sisters* as an example.[8] He filled the "psychological pauses" with motivations and affective memories; the fact that the large crisis-incidents of the plot took place offstage allowed him to devise small characterizing incidents onstage, derived from improvisations and detailed observation of daily life.

Most important, Stanislavski found in the process by which Chekhov's characters discover themselves an analogue for his technique by which the actor discovers his characterization. For Chekhov's characters, life is a process of self-realization. They do not enter the scene with a fixed stereotype or "humour" out of classical comedy, and they do not change abruptly or suddenly come to know themselves at a turning point in the action, as does the hero of classical tragedy. Maurice Valency traces this means of characterization to Turgenev, whose heroes discover themselves little by little and appear to be surprised at their feelings and deeds. The audience gains insight into the character in the same gradual way that the character gains self-insight, and the audience is equally unprepared for the character's contradictory behavior.[9] When Stanislavski's actor builds a characterization, he repeats this process: instead of applying the surface characteristics of a "type" or "humour" to himself, he seeks the character within his self, gradually discovering and exposing the aspects of his personality and emotions which he shares with the character. Ideally, he renews the sources of his "affective memory" technique constantly, and thus renews the discovery of his own emotions, a process which will appear to the audience to portray the character's emergent self-realization.

But the actor who lives a part and re-creates within himself the process by which the playwright created his character does not necessarily understand what the character or his actions mean within the context of the play. Robert Corrigan has observed that Stanislavski's "ensemble" technique actually tends to isolate each character in a vacuum,[10] but the effect of this is not only that the character is cut off from interaction with the other characters, as Corrigan supposes, but also that the character is cut off from the play's structure itself, which controls and "motivates" the seeming incongruities and failures to make sequential or logical responses that are so typical of Chekhov's people. The actor in a Chekhov play must deny his character a conscious knowledge of the artifice of the playwright's structuring, but he cannot deny him a *response* to it. And the audience viewing the play must not be so engrossed in the isolated characterizations that it fails to see the structure which animates them. This premise approaches the position of Brecht. It was first suggested in regard to Stanislavski's interpretation of Chekhov by the director's protégé, Eugene Vakhtangov, who developed an acting style which allowed the actor to perform, according to John Gassner, "both the role in the play and his critical or detached view of that role."[11] Commenting upon his mentor's opinion that the audience attending *The Three Sisters* came as if invited to the Prosorov sisters' house, not to a theater, Vakhtangov observed that this led Stanislavski to "a dead end."[12]

A close analysis of *The Three Sisters* indicates that two large actions control the play's plot; the events of both of these take place offstage or during the intermissions, and only their results are actually portrayed in the characters' activities. The actions correspond to the contrasting poles of change and stasis. If we try to follow Stanislavski's system of tracing the "through line of action" for this play, we find that there are at least *two* lines involved—and they are contradictory. As we shall see, this initial opposition is a paradigm for several others in the play. The effect that all of them should have on an audience is to complicate and confuse its response by suggesting a world which is philosophically absurd. So from the onset, Chekhov challenged Stanislavski's belief in the consistency and "naturalism" of reality.

On the one hand, in the first large action everything changes, and most of these changes occur because of the schemes of Andrei's provincial wife, Natasha. She is the least likable character in Chekhov's major plays, the closest he came to portraying a villainess. Natasha's selfish concern for her children, who may not even be Andrei's, disrupts and finally dissolves the Prosorov household. First she moves Irina into Olga's room so that she may give Irina's room to Bobik, the baby; then she so harasses Olga's old servant, Anfisa, that Olga is forced to take lodgings in an apartment provided by her boarding school. At the end of the play, when the heartbroken sisters realize that life can deal them no further blows and that they can finally "go home," it is not their family home to which they will return. Masha and Irina both refuse to enter it again. Natasha even schemes to rearrange the exterior, announcing that she will cut down the venerable oaks and maples on the grounds, the trees with which Tuzenbach had identified himself in his last speeches before going to his death. The playwright maneuvers his characters through settings which reflect Natasha's house-wrecking: he sets the first two acts in the "public" living room where Natasha is only a visitor at first and where in the second act she becomes the force which disrupts all the other guests at a carnival gathering and cancels the evening party; in the third act Olga and Irina have retreated to their bedroom, the last stronghold against Natasha and, significantly, the only room in the house from which they cannot see the provincial town she symbolizes; the last act finds the sisters outdoors beneath the stately trees which Natasha threatens, while she herself is seen through an open window *within* the house.

Chekhov conceals the impact of Natasha's rearrangements by revealing them only as intentions or accomplished actions during the course of the four acts. He also keeps her part small and her person offstage during much of the play, and correspondingly underscores the weakness and inefficiency of the sisters in failing to resist her, a failure that makes them the perfect victims for her schemes. Robert Brustein has noticed that Chekhov's plots are actually reworkings of stock melodrama plots, usually the tale of the precious mortgage controlled by an arch-villain who will rob the family of its ancestral homestead; this is the skeletal plot that especially underlies *The Cherry Orchard*, in which Lopakin assumes the "villain's" part.[13] Chekhov disguises his sources by denying the "innocent sufferers" their innocence and by omitting the sudden reversal and happy ending expected at the denouement of melodrama; in fact, his plots lack a peripeteia altogether. Characters who neither learn from their experiences nor experience personal change cannot be expected to undergo Aristotelian "discovery" or "reversal." In fact, Chekhov counters the suggestion that everything changes because of Natasha's machinations with the suggestion that, on the other hand, everything stays the same.

Everything stays the same through the workings of the other large action of the play, the garrison's departure from the provincial town; this action is typical of Chekhov's dramaturgy in that it is unconnected with Natasha's house-wrecking. The garrison had not always been stationed in this neighborhood, just as Masha's lover, Vershinin, had not always been stationed with this particular garrison. Richard Schechner observes that both do not so much *depart* from the sisters' lives as they *pass through* them, and leave them effectively unchanged.[14] At the beginning, Olga is an unhappy schoolmistress; at the end, in spite of her desire to marry and stop teaching, she is a spinster head-mistress. Masha is married to Kulygin in the beginning, conducts a furtive affair with Vershinin during the play, and returns to the forgiving Kulygin at the end. Irina gains and loses a fiancé during the play; she changes her status only in that she stops suffering the drudgery of idleness and learns to suffer the drudgery of employment. None of them is any closer to or farther from Moscow at the end than at the beginning. Each is still hovering on the brink of a fuller life which she thinks she can somehow still experience.

Chekhov does not ask his viewers to choose between change and stasis in his play. He simply presents the pair as a contradictory polarity which animates the same events. The play is full of such dichotomies—work vs. idleness, faith in future happiness (Vershinin) vs. confidence in present happiness (Tuzenbach), remembering vs. forgetting, and, symbolic of all of them, being "there" in Moscow vs. being "here" in the provincial town. A close examination of each pair of dichotomies reveals Chekhov's belief in the absurdity of making an optimistic choice or of taking a positive action from any of them.

For example, if we examine work vs. idleness in *The Three Sisters*, we find that the characters who derive the most philosophical meaning from the concept of work are the characters who have not yet worked themselves. At the beginning of the play Irina expresses a faith in labor which reminds us of Tolstoy:

> Man should work and toil by the sweat of his brow, whoever he is—that's the whole purpose and meaning of his life, his happiness and joy. How wonderful to be a workman who gets up at dawn and breaks stones in the road, or a shepherd, or a schoolmaster who teaches children or an engine-driver. Heavens, better not be a human being at all—better be an ox or just a horse, so long as you can work . . . .[15]

Two of the jobs she mentions, those of the schoolmaster and the work-man breaking stones, become the occupations which she and her suitor Tuzenbach decide to pursue for their lifework. But here in act 1 when they make their declarations about the sanctity of labor, neither of them speaks from experience: Olga describes Irina as lying in bed until nine, and the Baron admits that his family had never worked and had pre-vented him from working, as well. His faith lies in a revolutionary return to labor which will "blast out of our society all the laziness, complacency, contempt for work, rottenness and boredom."[16] But Tuzenbach himself suggests no political or social program which would bring this about, though his statement does describe the play's milieu rather well. In act 2 he resigns his commission and announces that he will seek a job in the local brickyard as a common laborer, his idea of an exhausting job which would allow him to sleep undisturbed rather than suffer the guilty insomnia of the play's idle characters. But he dies before he can test his zeal for work by actually doing any. Irina finds employment in the post office, but despises it, and complains that it robs her of all genuine contact with life. She has not lost her illusions about salvation through work at the end of the play, when she cries for joy at her plans to become a teacher. Even after Tuzenbach's death, she perseveres in this plan, but she no longer views it with joy; now she resigns herself to serving those who may need her, and in her final speech associates her burial in work with the decline of the seasons: "It's autumn now and it will soon be winter, with everything buried in snow, and I shall work, work, work."[17]

The characters who actually work are far less optimistic about it. Regarding Irina's idolizing of the profession of teaching, Masha's schoolmaster-husband, Kulygin, says that her plan "lacks sense," "amounts to nothing," and "smacks of hot air"; he places his own faith in the mindlessness of repetition, stating that "That which loses its routine loses its very existence."[18] Olga has also devoted her life to teaching, yet she longs to leave the profession; it has brought her the same kind of gloom which the idle Irina says is caused by their family's hatred of labor. Ironically, Olga the spinster is the only character to express belief in marriage as an alternative to a profession, while Masha experiences only unhappiness in her marriage, and Irina, who has three suitors, loves none of them, and approaches marriage as a duty, not a salvation.

This questioning of the results of one's lifework in the future is linked in the play to the theme of time. Just before he departs, Vershinin announces his own formula for happiness, to be achieved in some distant future: "If we could only combine education with hard work, you know, and hard work with education."[19] Characteristically, Vershinin then looks at his watch and excuses himself from the scene rather abruptly. He never makes a confession of his true feelings toward Masha or to the world around him; instead, throughout the play, he hides behind long monologues and then summarizes his attitude toward the sisters with this cruel formulation. Unwittingly, proposing work and education, he exposes the futility of the sisters' work of educating the provincial town, and the futility of their own useless educations. All of Vershinin's monologues reiterate his faith in a happiness that will be achieved two or three hundred years in the future but that will be denied to everyone in his own generation. He proposes no plan or project by which this improvement will occur; somehow, the "civilizing" effect of three intelligent women stranded in this provincial town will be felt by a few others in the next generation, perhaps six, then twenty, and ages later everyone will think and feel with the same acuteness as the sisters, who nevertheless will have been forgotten long before. Vershinin places such faith in the inevitability of this gradual improvement that he takes no steps to initiate it in the present. He never responds to Tuzenbach's praise of labor with more than a cursory "Yes" before he changes the subject altogether, and he proves unable even to sort out his own personal affairs, failing to choose between his lover, Masha, and his suicidal wife. Chekhov arranges the monologues of Vershinin and Tuzenbach so that they form a philosophical debate. While Vershinin's faith lies in an unobtainable future happiness, Tuzenbach suggests that the future will be no better than the present and that he is happy in the present. Opposing Vershinin's theory of change through conscious education, which gradually creates a meaning for existence, Tuzenbach admires an unconscious immersion in existence that requires no meaning.

> Forget your two or three hundred years, because even in a million years life will still be just the same as ever. It doesn't change, it always goes on the same and follows its own laws. And those laws are none of our business. Or at least you'll never understand them. Think of the birds flying south for the winter, cranes for instance. They fly on and on and on, and it doesn't matter what ideas, big or small, they may have buzzing about inside their heads, they'll still keep on flying without ever knowing why they do it or where they're going.[20]

Masha, not Vershinin, responds to Tuzenbach. When she asks the point of such an existence in which meaning is unnecessary, he asks her to tell him the point of the snow which is falling outside. His quiescence does not satisfy her at this point (in act 2):

> I feel that man should have a faith or be trying to find one, otherwise his life just doesn't make sense. Think of living without knowing why cranes fly, why children are born or why there are stars in the sky. Either you know what you're living for, or else the whole thing's a waste of time and means less than nothing.[21]

But by the end of the play, when Vershinin leaves her, Masha has accepted Tuzenbach's position. She exclaims that the migrating birds are indeed happy, and in her final speech she resigns herself to a life in the present. The three final speeches of the sisters in which they reflect upon Tuzenbach's death and their broken dreams summarize the sisters' attitudes; Chekhov constructs the speeches so that they parallel and contrast each other. Irina's final words are a repetition of her faith in work, but Masha notes that their state is essentially unchanged from what it was in the play's beginning: "They're all leaving us, and one has gone right away and will never, never come back, and we shall be left alone to begin our lives again. We must go on living, we must."[22] In her last words, she indicates that she has embraced Tuzenbach's doctrine of living without striving for meaning. Chekhov's translator Ronald Hingley notes that Masha's speech was considerably longer in the original manuscript, and contained references to the flocks of birds which pass by their estate each year but do not know why they are traveling. The image provides a further link with Tuzenbach, but the actress who originally played Masha, Chekhov's future wife, found the speech unplayable and convinced the playwright to shorten it.

Although he converts Masha, Tuzenbach fails to convince the others of the rightness of his attitude toward a useful existence and happiness in the present. Although Chekhov arranges their long speeches to look like a debate, as I have said, and thereby leads the audience into expecting a resolution of the issue, Tuzenbach never manages to engage Vershinin in a discussion of his position; Vershinin ignores Tuzenbach, or tries to convince him that he is not really happy at all. These debates which fail to be enacted within the play's action parallel Chekhov's deliberate failure to resolve contradictions in the play's intellectual structure; in both cases, the result is to arouse and then thwart audience expectations.

One aspect of his belief in happiness in the future which Vershinin cherishes is the assumption that all those who are so unhappy in the present will be forgotten by that future. His desire for oblivion is shared by most of the play's characters. Chekhov begins the play by introducing the contrasting themes of forgetting and remembering: Olga reminisces about their father's funeral, which occurred one year ago to the day, and Irina responds, "Why bring up old memories?"[23] During the course of the play, the characters forget as much as they remember—Masha forgets her music and her mother's face; Irina forgets her Italian; the old family doctor and former admirer of the sisters' dead mother cannot remember his medical skills, or even whether their mother had loved him. When Chekhov brings Vershinin into the household for the first time, he creates a little palindromic structure of remembering and forgetting which shows in microcosm the pattern of failing to remember and failing to respond authentically to the other characters which is so typical of all the persons in the play. Vershinin had met the two older sisters years before in Moscow, but now all their memories are growing dim. Olga forgets that she had known Vershinin, and Vershinin forgets who Masha was. But he remembers having known Olga—while his future lover Masha remembers having known him. And when Olga suddenly remembers who Vershinin was, he fails to follow her response and, in a non sequitur typical of Chekhov, comments that he knew her mother.

Olga's last long speech at the end of the play concludes the discussion of remembering and forgetting which has been carried on throughout the play. She agrees with Vershinin that the future will soon forget them all, but that their suffering will bring about some measure of happiness in the future. If their existence is to be equated with suffering, as Vershinin suggests, then change is possible. But the context within which Olga speaks indicates that no one has changed throughout the play. Of her sisters, she says that "we still have our lives ahead of us,"[24] and this is not to be taken as simply a commonplace signifying that happiness is just around the corner, or some other cliché of consolation. The characters still understand nothing of the purpose of their lives and sufferings, as Olga says, and she ends by exclaiming "If only we knew, if only we knew!"[25] Olga indicates that the sisters have not yet lived their lives or gained an insight into them, which is the conclusion of Tuzenbach, the believer in changelessness. "If only we knew" at the end refers ultimately to the two positions stated, yet not successfully argued, by Vershinin and Tuzenbach; the sisters are no closer to knowing how to choose between them now than they were before. Structurally, Olga's last speech has returned us to the beginning of the play, which she opened with a long speech about her father's funeral. A military band was playing as he was carried to his grave, she had commented; another military band is playing now as she speaks (in the first version of the manuscript, Tuzenbach's body is carried across the stage at this point). The sisters' position during Olga's opening speech can be expressed in terms of potentiality: they have just finished the customary period of mourning for their parents, and now they may begin their independent lives. They are still standing before their lives at the end of the play. After Olga's first speech, which is filled with memories of the past and the purpose of reminiscence, Irina counters Olga with the curt question, "Why bring up old memories?"[26] Now, after her last speech, in which she projects a future and takes comfort in forgetting, not reminiscing, the old doctor and pessimist, Chebutykin, counters with another curt reply: "What's the difference anyway! What's the difference!"[27] Memory and forgetting, happiness and suffering, past and future, meaning and meaninglessness are all equated in Chebutykin's formula, and Olga can only reply to it that she has not yet learned to distinguish between any of these poles, and repeats her formula of "If only we knew, if only we knew!"

The play's most striking embodiment of all these contrasting pairs which come to resemble one another is found in the contrast the characters draw between life in faraway Moscow and life in the provincial city to which they have been exiled. For them, the two cities are worlds apart. Moscow contains the past for Masha, her freedom in an unmarried state. It contains a home for Olga, memories of stability within the family circle as opposed to the threat of being dispossessed in the province. Irina thinks that she would have found love in Moscow, instead of the duty match to Tuzenbach. Even Andrei believes he would have completed his education in Moscow and become a professor, instead of settling for the bureaucratic job he takes on the city council. In contrast to Moscow stands their city, in which only three educated people live out of a population of a hundred thousand, according to Vershinin (who cuttingly excludes Andrei from his census). Chekhov represents the local population in his play through Masha's kindly but dull husband Kulygin, who worships routine and prides himself on his having mastered the Latin form *ut consecutivum* and having received the Order of Stanislaus Second Class; Natasha, the scheming house-wrecker; and her lover Protopopov, not seen on stage, whose absurd name no one can pronounce but who patronizingly gives Andrei a job on the city council in exchange for cuckolding him. They seem to be the brightest people in town, not the dullest, and still the Moscow culture which the sisters attempt to introduce into the province is wasted on them. The sisters have found no one with whom they can speak the several foreign languages they have learned; when they propose a charity concert following a disastrous fire, Tuzenbach comments that no one in the city would be able to understand their music, and pompous Kulygin chides Masha about the propriety of a married woman playing in public.

It would be a mistake to think that Chekhov's characters would be much happier if they moved to Moscow. The playwright makes many small but cumulative suggestions that his characters' dreams of Moscow are delusions, that little difference exists between Moscow and the province. For example, the refined educations which the sisters received in Moscow serve them poorly in their daily lives; they lack the ability to make intelligent decisions or the resolve to act upon them and, for all their desire to pursue intellectual conversation, at their interminable social evenings they quickly lapse into gossip or melancholy. And the garrison of soldiers from Moscow gives us little reason to believe in the superiority of the citizenry in the capital. The facile optimist Tuzenbach believes in the sanctity of work but never works; his rival for Irina, Solyony, who kills him in a duel, adopts an equally superficial pessimism largely because he thinks that he resembles Lermontov. Vershinin grounds his faith in the future, a belief that conveniently prevents him from doing anything in the present. The old doctor Chebutykin forgets his medicine and takes to drink, and the minor characters Fedotik and Rode amuse themselves with guitars, cameras, gymnastics, and even coloring crayons! Vershinin admits that he sees little difference between the inhabitants of the provincial city and the soldiers from Moscow who are stationed in it—this from the character who has been in Moscow most recently, and whose attraction to the sisters stems largely from his association with the city. When Masha states that she wouldn't notice how bad the weather was if she lived in Moscow, Vershinin replies that she wouldn't even notice Moscow if she lived there. For the sisters, Moscow exists as an analogue to Vershinin's dream of a world two hundred or three hundred years hence: as their dreamworld recedes into the distance their scorn for their present surroundings increases, in direct proportion to their inability to change their present situation.

Chekhov deflates Moscow further through Andrei's old servant Ferapont, who has never been there but possesses his peasant's daydream of visiting the city. While Andrei dreams of the sense of belonging he would feel in the society gathered in a fine Moscow restaurant, Ferapont is more impressed with a tale he has heard of a man who ate either forty or fifty pancakes in Moscow and died of it. He also inquires whether there is an enormous rope stretching right across the city, as he has heard. Ferapont further equates Moscow with the provincial city by noting, during the fire which strikes in the third act, that Moscow had its fire too, in 1812—a comment which debunks Moscow's heroic effort when it burned during the successful resistance to Napoleon's invasion, a remembered heroism which stands in contrast to the characters' lack of that quality.

If Chekhov shows that his characters cannot change their lives in their present location, he suggests that they could not change in Moscow, either. He makes his most daring equation between the province and the capital, and his most scathing attack on both of them, in Andrei's diatribe in act 4:

> Where is my past life, oh what has become of it—when I was young, happy and intelligent, when I had such glorious thoughts and visions, and my present and future seemed so bright and promising? Why is it we've hardly started living before we all become dull, drab, boring, lazy, complacent, useless and miserable? This town's two hundred years old and we've a hundred thousand people living here, but the trouble is, every man jack of them's exactly like every other one, and no one here does anything really worth while. Or ever has. We've never produced a single scholar or artist or anyone else with a touch of originality to make us envy him, or decide we were damn well going to go one better

ourselves. All these people do is eat, drink and sleep till they drop down dead. Then new ones are born to carry on the eating, drinking and sleeping.[28]

By this point, Andrei has associated himself with the province so thoroughly that he speaks of it in the first person plural. But Chekhov does not direct his diatribe against the characters in the play who represent the province, none of whom are present at the time Andrei speaks. He instructed the actor who first played the part of Andrei to address his denunciation directly to the audience, and that audience was located *in Moscow* on the occasion of the first production. Chekhov told his actor that "He must be just about ready to threaten the audience with his fists!"[29] Chekhov's use of direct address here is the most consciously theatricalist device in all his later plays. Since it is such a rarity, I assume that Chekhov employs it here especially to impress the spectators of their complicity in the problem. This is Chekhov's closest approach to introducing direct actor-audience transactions into his plays.

Chekhov's equation of Moscow and the provincial city inhabited by the sisters serves to make their idealization of the capital even more remote and absurd. When his actor shakes a fist at the audience and denounces it as the "here" of one's present unhappiness as opposed to the "there" of an ideal Moscow, Chekhov is saying that that ideal exists nowhere, neither in the historical Moscow in which his play is being performed, nor in any other "there" in which it might be acted. The provincial city is everywhere; the town's namelessness and Andrei's habit of speaking of it as "here" add to its universal quality. Such a reading questions the attempt of Stanislavski to localize the source of the sisters' unhappiness in an unusually dull country town during the particularly discouraging time of the action (in terms of politics)—the eighties and nineties, to which the director refers in his postrevolution autobiography when he speaks of "the terrible realities of the Russia of Chekhov's time."[30] A Soviet critic like M. N. Stroyeva also limits the "here" of the play which Chekhov indicts when Stroyeva suggests that "although the forces of bourgeois triviality triumph, the moral victory goes to the anti-bourgeois characters, . . . the three sisters who inwardly free themselves from the power of the narrow confines of their existence."[31] Chekhov does not confine his critique to one particular class any more than he confines it to a particular province, and the Moscow-culture of the sisters is what any actor playing Andrei denounces when he addresses the audience. Maurice Valency's optimistic assertion that the sisters "will bring a little of Moscow with them into the wilderness"[32] can only be accepted ironically, from the point of view that this little bit of Moscow is exactly what Andrei refers to in his speech.

Chekhov's stage direction for Andrei's speech contradicts more than one of Stanislavski's assumptions. It denies that the play's meaning is limited to a particular historical setting which can be reproduced following the tenets of naturalistic mise-en-scène. It also works against the actor's technique of seeking a specific incident in his own life which will incite a particular emotion in him that corresponds to the character's feeling and gives the impression that the character is reacting to a similarly localized and specific motivation: Chekhov's character reacts to the general malaise of the playwright and his desire to express it in public, not some specific yet unspoken incident out of the fictional Andrei's past. This direct address to the audience suggests that Chekhov was not so bound to the "fourth wall" tradition as was Stanislavski, who insisted that a Chekhov production be completely lifelike and not acknowledge the presence of the audience at all.

When the actor addresses the audience directly and reveals the real nature of "Moscow," the actor playing Andrei shares a knowledge with the audience which is denied to the character Andrei. The actor who follows Chekhov's stage direction stands in a superior position to his character, and shares this superiority with the audience, even in the act of chastening the audience. Such a position gives us an indication that Chekhov wanted his play to be interpreted as a comedy, even a vaudeville. Comedy assumes that its characters are incapable of change; according to Henri Bergson, the actions of comic characters are funny when they fall into repeated patterns of mechanistic behavior. The limited perspective through which each character obsessively filters the world is often symbolized by the one overriding passion or "humour" which typifies each character—but the very fact that the actor can "put on" all of these "humours" in succession, and that the playwright can present them all to an audience, implies that actor, playwright, and audience stand in a superior position to comic characters.

Chekhov's characters, however, lack a governing "humour." Rather than being overdefined to the point of being "types," they are underdefined, more noted for their pauses, evasions, and failures to act than for speech or deeds which could limit them to one narrow perspective. Their constant *attempt* to define and discover themselves has led most interpreters, beginning with Stanislavski, to assume that they possess tragic proportions. The tragic hero is superior to the actor who portrays him and to the spectator who views him. Each tries to see a part of his self in the expansive tragic personality, and each feels awe when he realizes how much larger and unknowable the tragic hero is. The difference between the tragic hero and the Chekhov hero is that the tragic hero succeeds in knowing and defining himself *for himself*, even though this knowledge is much greater than that achieved by actor and audience, whose awe reflects the gap between what they have achieved and what the hero has accomplished (in terms of discovery); the Chekhov hero, however, attempts but fails to know and define himself for himself, but Chekhov succeeds in defining his limitations *for us,* the play's recipients, actor and audience. If all the Chekhov characters have a "humour," it is defined more by a lack than by a presence: this gap between what the actor and audience have accomplished (in terms of discovery) and what the character has achieved elicits exasperation from us, more than awe, and the possibility of laughter. Contrasting the "gaps" between character and recipients in tragedy and Chekhov, we can say that the tragic gap is infinite yet filled with mystery, while the Chekhovian pause (his concretization of the gap) is finite yet empty.

Such a reading contradicts Stanislavski's staging of Chekhov, which assumes an equality between the life Chekhov represents and daily life, between his character and the actor who "lives" the role (and by extension, the audience which lives it by means of empathy). Stanislavski's actor seeks to know the character in the same way that Chekhov's character acquires self-knowledge. The actor tries to motivate the play's incongruities—gaps, pauses, non sequiturs, and the like—through factors outside the play, what he imagines to be the unspecified life of the character when the character is offstage, and through his own life as well.

An alternative to this is the assumption that motivation lies in the play's structure, not in its characters' histories—in other words, that Chekhov knew what he was saying when he claimed that it was "all there" and that he had "written it all down." The contrasting themes we have already examined—the unresolved dichotomies between change and stasis, future improvement and present happiness, remembering and forgetting—attest to the characters' failure to achieve self-knowledge and their entrapment, not in the limited or obsessive perspective of comic "humour," but in the *non*perspective of unresolved arguments and contradictory attitudes, the obsessive *failure* to define themselves which is Chekhov's contribution to the psychology of humours. If this can be said to be comic in terms of structure, still none of it is particularly "funny." But Chekhov's plays do draw laughter, and a proper staging can bring out their "vaudeville." A reading (or performance) governed by the play's structure, rather than by the characters' psychologies, demonstrates the mechanisms into which the characters fall that bespeak the comic. Such a reading refutes the position of a critic like Francis Fergusson (who nevertheless has provided us with the instrumental terms). According to Fergusson,

It is certainly true that Chekhov reveals comic aspects of his action and expects the laughter of the audience; but his convention does not admit that relationship between stage and house, and the pretense of unarranged and untheatrical actuality is never broken. Comic genres, on the other hand, accept some sort of limited perspective, shared with the audience, as the basis of the fun; they show human life *as* comic just because they show it as consistent according to some narrowly defined, and hence unreal, basis. They fit Mr. Eliot's definition of a convention: they are agreed-upon distortions, forms or rhythms frankly imposed upon the world of action.[33]

The discrepancy between the character's and the actor's understanding of the symbol "Moscow" proved to be an instance of the character's limited perspective, one that the actor does not share and does not allow the audience to share. And Ferapont's absurd understanding of what might be found in "Moscow"—pancakes and a rope stretching across the city—introduced laughter into the symbolism. Beyond this exists a series of "distortions, forms and rhythms," which, when "agreed-upon" by actor and audience, imposes a comic perspective on the world of action: a grim comedy, not the "gay comedy" Stanislavski feared Chekhov had intended, but a comedy nevertheless. These distortions include juxtapositions, interjections, repetitions, and the non sequitur; being comic devices, they elicit tangible audience reactions, and must be included in any overview of the play which emphasizes audience affectivity (along with the tearful aspects stressed by Stanislavski).

The device by which the playwright's structure is seen to be completely outside the control of the characters' psychological motivations is juxtaposition. In Chekhov's plays, the device usually works this way: the author brings a new character into a scene to interrupt an ongoing conversation which the character has not overheard; he then gives the character an opening line which, through no conscious malice on the speaker's part, comments ironically on what has just been said. Since the character is clearly ignorant of this faux pas, no amount of imagined psychology or offstage biography can supply the motivation for, and thus defuse, the comic effect. Such a juxtaposition occurs at the beginning of *The Three Sisters*. Olga remembers the Moscow she left eleven years ago, but now imagines that they had departed "only yesterday," another instance of Chekhov condensing our consciousness of the long time elapsed in the play so that the action appears not to have moved forward or change to have occurred. Then Olga says that she feels she must return home to Moscow. Chebutykin and Tuzenbach appear at the door, in the midst of a previous conversation:

OLGA: . . . I felt so happy and excited, I felt I just had to go back home to Moscow.

CHEBUTYKIN: Not a chance in hell.
TUZENBACH: Absolute nonsense of course.[34]

By juxtaposition, Chekhov deflates the Moscow dream before he develops it as a symbol! The device has a grimmer aspect at the end of act 3, when Andrei is defending his behavior in mortgaging the house and marrying Natasha (while his sisters refuse to listen). Whenever Andrei pauses for a sympathetic response, which he does not get, Chekhov brings Kulygin into the doorway to ask where Masha is. In fact, Masha is cuckolding him with Vershinin, just as Natasha is cuckolding Andrei with Protopopov and thus causing his ruinous gambling with the family estate. Kulygin's inquiries about Masha have no causal connection to Andrei's confession, and the logical gap which the audience perceives between the two juxtaposed themes can bring forth a grim laughter if the juxtaposition is seen as a mechanical device in control of the characters; when the audience perceives that the non sequitur does in fact "follow" and that thematically Kulygin's cuckoldry "motivates" Andrei's outburst that Natasha is a "fine, decent woman,"[35] the gap between the audience's understanding of the character's statement and the character's understanding of it increases the comic dimension, even though it probably stifles the laughter.

Related to the device of juxtaposition is the unexpected and aggressive interjection by which characters habitually announce themselves. Such interjections seem comic and mechanical precisely because they mesh in no way with the conversation they interrupt, not even at an ironic level, as the juxtapositions do. Chebutykin likes to announce little snippets of information gathered from newspapers, such as his opening words at the name-day party about using naphthalene to cure baldness, or his interjection at the carnival party that Balzac got married in Berdichev. (This is a particularly inadequate response to the foregoing conversation, Vershinin's and Tuzenbach's philosophical debate about work and future happiness, which to the characters' perceptions has been the intellectual high-point of the evening. The fact that Chebutykin's comments deflates this philosophical interlude is another example of the play's structural mechanism controlling its characters—as is Irina's response to Chebutykin's news of Balzac: in Chekhov's stage direction, she repeats his statement "thoughtfully,"[36] as if it were a significant contribution to the conversation.) Chekhov builds entire characterizations around such interjections. Randall Jarrell notes that although the speeches of the other characters have an inner consistency and the quality of an aria when the roles are read separately, Captain Solyony's speeches lack these leitfmotifs.[37] Each is a violent interjection of failed wit, misquoted poetry, or brutal self-assertion, like his first words:

> With one hand I can only lift half a hundredweight, but if I use both hands I can lift two or even two-and-a-half hundredweight. From which I conclude that two men aren't just twice as strong as one, but three times as strong, if not more.[38]

But the interjection which most emphasizes the mechanical pattern in which the device traps the characters is found within a speech of Kulygin's, the only character who is concerned with numbers and exact time:

> And after that we're to spend the evening at the headmaster's. In spite of poor health our head does do his best to be sociable. What a wonderful inspiration to us all—a thoroughly first-rate chap. After the staff meeting yesterday he said to me, "I'm tired, Kulygin. Tired." (*Looks at the clock, then at his watch.*) Your clock's seven minutes fast. "Yes," he said. "I'm tired!"[39]

Kulygin interrupts himself to comment upon time. He cannot be aware of the mechanism governing him, or the irony of his apparently non-sensical interjection.

Repetition of single words and short phrases also adds to the pattern which controls the characters. When Vershinin appears at the name-day party in act 1, the fact that he comes from Moscow is repeated five times within twelve short lines, and the word "Moscow" appears nine times. An ironic staging of the scene would place a pause before each repetition, which lengthens after each instance of repetition, to reflect the playwright's taunt to the audience: "So you think that I don't dare repeat the word 'Moscow' yet another time, do you?" The repetition of instrumental symbols like the word "Moscow" also serves to inform the audience of their importance, but when trivial words are repeated by means of the same mechanism, they underline the absurdity of the repetition of the instrumental words, thus deflating their significance. This happens during the second act, when Solyony and Chebutykin argue over like-sounding words for Russian foods, *chekhartmá* and *cheremchá*, both of which they repeat four times within eight lines. Chekhov draws the connection between this absurd repetition and the Moscow repetition by engaging Solyony in another argument immediately following his fight with Chebutykin over *chekhartmá* and *cheremchá*. This time he argues with Andrei about whether Moscow has one or two universities, and the phrase "Moscow University" is repeated five times. These instances are obviously comic. Repetition gains a pathetic overtone toward the end of the play, when characters begin to repeat as assertions the phrases which they most want to convince themselves are true. Kulygin repeats that Masha loves him, and repeats the phrase "I am satisfied, I am satisfied" three times, to which Masha can only respond angrily: *"Amo, amas, amat, amamus, amatis, amant."*[40] Even Kulygin laughs at this. We do not laugh when the three sisters repeat instrumental phrases to conclude their last long speeches which form a coda to the play, but we must be aware of the comic framework in which the declarations "We must live" (Masha), "We must work" (Irina), and "If only we knew" (Olga) exist—not to mention Chebutykin's mordant reply, "What's the difference!"

The comic device which Chekhov employs most frequently is the non sequitur response to a sincerely meant question, request, or plea for sympathy, which demonstrates the second party's inability to understand or respond to the supplicant's need. Chekhov uses this structuring device to show characters trapped in the vacuum of self and severely limited in their knowledge of themselves and others. Examples occur on practically every page of the text. The play begins with such a failure of response: Irina's curt reply to Olga's lengthy musing about their former lives, "Why bring up old memories?" In act 2, after Vershinin has brought joy into gloomy Masha's life and she expounds upon the civilizing and cultivating effect of the military upon the provinces, all he can say is "I'm a bit thirsty, I could do with some tea."[41] When Tuzenbach declares that he would give his life for Irina, Masha simply tells him to go away. Even Andrei's long diatribe against the provincial town (discussed earlier) goes unheard by the one character on stage with him, deaf old Ferapont, whose only reply is "Eh? Papers for you to sign."[42] But the most pathetic instance in the play occurs when Tuzenbach takes leave of Irina for the last time. She does not know of his duel with Solyony, and has just told him that she will marry him even though she cannot love him. Tuzenbach is tempted to tell her of the duel, a confession which would certainly have prevented his death. He says goodbye once, starts to go, and then turns back and calls her name. Her reply is a blunt and uncomprehending single word: "What?"[43] After such a response, all he can do is to fumble some excuse about wanting a cup of coffee, and leave.

All these little scenes make their theatrical effect upon an audience only when the director inserts a carefully timed pause between the plea and the inadequate response. Stanislavski thought that Chekhov filled his texts with the stage direction "pause" because his characters know much more than they can say in speech—so Stanislavski filled these pauses with unspoken memories created by his actors, motivations derived from a logical extension of the characters' lives beyond the events which take place in the play, and with "subtext," the unspoken verbal and sensory content logically assumed to be existing within the characters' minds. But Chekhov claimed that he had written everything which he wanted to be known about his play into the play already. If we take his word, we are left with characters who pause not because they know more than they can say, but because they can barely say what they know. Their pauses are genuine gaps, and when they are played as such not only is the play funny but the basis for its comedy is brought out: the mechanism imposed by the playwright which governs and manipulates his characters.

With regard to the comic ignorance of Chekhov's characters, we should note that they are not only born outside of knowledge (of self or others), they pursue this ignorance actively. Whenever a character tries to make a confession about his inner self, or attempts to engage in a philosophical discussion which might further the knowledge of the lives of those around him, some other character stifles or ridicules the confession or discussion. When Tuzenbach begins to expound about the sanctity of labor, Solyony cuts him off by making a chicken's clucking sound, and when Tuzenbach tries to convince Vershinin that the key to future happiness lies in work in the present, Vershinin only mutters "Yes" and goes off to look at the flowers. No one listens to the major debate they conduct during act 2 about happiness in the future and in the present except Masha; the others are engrossed in a card game, and Masha's response is to laugh at both arguments. In act 3, when all the characters are exhausted by the fire and begin to confess their secret desires, Olga's main activity consists of stifling these confessions. She tries to prevent Irina from despairing about the lack of love in her life; she tries to prevent Masha from confessing her love for Vershinin and Andrei from confessing his gambling problem (during these last two incidents she hides behind a screen). As Randall Jarrell notes, all the characters make some intimate confession during the fire crisis of act 3 except the "incomplete character" Vershinin.[44] Jarrell does not notice that Vershinin tries to make just such a confession to Olga in the fourth act, when he attempts to tell her that he is aware he talks too much as a defense against making an intimate statement about himself. But Olga interrupts him to ask why Masha has not yet arrived.

If one aspect of Chekhov's "humour psychology" is the obsessive lack of governing perspective through which characters define themselves, then the complement of this lack is the characters' obsessive persistence in actively preventing themselves from gaining self-knowledge and knowledge of others which might allow them at least to have such a perspective. Such an "anti-humour" reflects not only upon the absurdity of the unspoken or stifled confessions, the real "subtext" within Chekhov's pauses, it casts doubts upon the significance of what is said in the speeches as well. Given such a situation, perhaps the most authentic communication in the play occurs in a scene which would appear at first to be the archetypal non sequitur. Early in act 2, Natasha carries on about baby Bobik in an attempt to elicit some response from her husband:

> NATASHA: Andrew, sweetie-pie, why don't you say something?
> ANDREW: I was thinking. There's nothing to say anyway.[45]

Chekhov does not impose a controlling mechanism upon his limited characters in order to write a comedy. Instead, he inserts "vaudeville" devices into his drama in order to expose the structural mechanism at its core and the significance to be taken from it. The pattern appears to be circular, for at the play's end the central characters seem to have arrived back at the same position which they occupied at the beginning. As the acts pass, a year's seasons pass, from the early spring of act 1 through winter in acts 2 and 3 to late autumn in act 4; however, four years pass in time. The four acts also follow a diurnal cycle, passing from morning to evening to late night to morning again. But the major characters do not so much move through this cycle as it moves through them; in fact, they do not move at all. The teasing hint of cyclic change makes the static reality more painful. Significant relationships and knowledge of the self or others do not progress.

Several symbolic repetitions allude to this pattern. Olga's first speech in act 1 recalls the band playing at her father's funeral; her last speech in act 4 comments upon the band playing as Tuzenbach is carried away. The music seems so happy and cheerful to her this second time that she believes that the sisters are on the verge of discovering the meaning of their lives and suffering. But they were equally on the verge at the beginning of the play, when their father's death freed them to begin their lives.

Another repetition which displays a character perpetually before life and filled with unrealized potentiality can be seen in Chebutykin's transference of his affections from the sisters' dead mother to the youngest sister, Irina. A generation passes, but Chebutykin is still the unrequited lover of a Prosorov woman. This illuminates the meaning of his gift to Irina of a silver samovar on her name-day, and all the sisters' dismay at such a gift, for Chebutykin has presented her with the gift two decades after he fell in love with her mother in Moscow, and a silver samovar is the traditional gift a Russian gives his wife on their twentieth wedding anniversary. When the drunken Chebutykin smashes an antique clock which had belonged to her mother, following Irina's announcement that she will be going to Moscow soon, he is doing more than striking back at Irina's desertion of his affections or acknowledging his own broken life: he kills time concretely, just as Chekhov slays it symbolically through his theme of inevitable stasis.

Chekhov extends the stasis into the following generation as well. Vershinin leaves for the even more remote province of Poland with his own two daughters, and admits that their lot will be no better than that of the Prosorov women, thus transforming them into the titular "sisters" of the next generation.

Chekhov's flattening out of time and his creation of a dual timescheme which seems to be both dizzyingly rapid and excruciatingly slow do not deny the reality of the sisters' decaying position (loss of home, departure of companions, failure of dreams) in the course of what Robert Brustein calls aptly their "tedious-rapid progress toward death."[46] But it does suggest that even their decay brings no change in their essential situation or knowledge. They stay as they are, while espousing great faith in change in the future, a future which has become their present and which will quickly recede into the past. Tuzenbach is the only character who believes in the impossibility of essential change, and, ironically, he is the only character whose situation changes essentially. He dies.

Several critics have observed the mechanism which has been described in this study as an unresolved contradiction between change and stasis; they have given it many names and almost as many interpretations. In his structural study "Approaches," Richard Schechner is content to describe it in terms of decay (Natasha's house-wrecking) superimposed upon stasis (the garrison passes through, passes in and out of the play).[47] Schechner's neutral approach stands in contrast to a thematic study like Robert Brustein's *The Theatre of Revolt*. This study wrests a significance from the play which accommodates it to Brustein's theme of revolt, which he finds in all important dramatic writing. For Brustein, Chekhov revolts neither by active deed nor by positive proposal; the simple *portrayal* of an intolerable circumstance cries out as an (unstated) protest against it. Not surprisingly, he makes Chekhov out to be an optimist who espouses all the values which he somehow neglects to portray in his plays.

Randall Jarrell makes a similar but less naive choice in his notes to his translation of the play. He divides the play's themes into categories of "meaning" and "meaninglessness" and demonstrates that Chekhov balances each theme from the optimistic category with its opposite in the pessimistic category.[48] Jarrell chooses to side with meaning; he cites with enthusiasm Olga's supposition that meaninglessness is merely divine meaning which mortals cannot understand, and her stubborn optimism concerning the necessity of "making an enclave of meaning in the middle of comparative meaninglessness."[49] For Jarrell, even Chebutykin's nihilistic "What's the difference?" reveals the difference, and the preference: "Here he acknowledges that there *is* so much difference between what is good and what is bad in human existence that he is unable to pretend that there is none, and wishes for the nonexistence in which there is no difference between nothing and nothing."[50] In his compulsion to choose between meaning and meaninglessness, Jarrell falls into the same trap that Chekhov prepares for his characters in the play. The playwright sets up untenable dichotomies which offer his characters no correct choice, and stages set-piece arguments (especially between Vershinin and Tuzenbach) from which neither position emerges as preferable. When Jarrell opts with Olga for meaning, he is forced to ignore that side of her personality in which she stifles the attempts of her sisters, brother, and even Vershinin to reveal meaning to her. (No wonder she needs to equate meaninglessness with divine meaning.) And Jarrell's clever transformation of Chebutykin into a tortured "unconfessed optimist" skirts the issue of "nonexistence" in Chekhov's play, to use Jarrell's own term. "Nonexistence" is simply a negative appellation for the "pre-existence" of Chekhov's characters, their habitually unfulfilled potentiality in their state of existing on the threshold of life; and the lack of "difference between nothing and nothing" which Jarrell detects but does not wish to acknowledge serves as a good description of Chekhov's flattening out of the distinction between, and equation of the values in, Jarrell's categories of "meaning" and "meaninglessness."

The playwright's own specific comments on Stanislavski's production of *The Three Sisters* all point to his dissatisfaction with Stanislavski's tragic yet optimistic reading of the play. Chekhov did not wish to choose between limiting categories like optimism and pessimism or "meaning" and "meaninglessness." But he does show characters trapped in the limiting mechanism of having to make a choice. He employs comic devices within the genre "drama" (or dramatic overtones within the comic genre—the label is not important) to point out the absurdity of such choices: this is his "vaudeville."

During rehearsals, Chekhov made small changes which underlined the comic and absurd aspects of *The Three Sisters*. After the disastrous first reading in which Stanislavski's actors interpreted the play as if it were a sentimental tragedy, he added several speeches, most of which reinforce the limiting mechanisms within which his characters' visions are trapped. Chebutykin's absentminded comment that the clock he smashed had belonged to their mother "if you say so," his callous comment in regard to Tuzenbach's duel that one baron "more or less" won't make much difference, and Solyony's comparison of himself with Lermontov all stem from this revision; Ronald Hingley notes that the changes Chekhov made in Vershinin's part emphasize the character's lack of interest in what anyone else has to say.[51]

In regard to Stanislavski's mise-en-scène itself, Chekhov made no major suggestions. Apparently he was unable to impress his interpretation of his own work on the Moscow Art company; instead, he let drop mysterious little hints concerning character interpretation which Stanislavski reports the company puzzled over for years. For example, his only comment on Stanislavski's performance as Astrov in *Uncle Vanya* was that Astrov ought to whistle as he leaves at the end.

Chekhov became especially dismayed when Stanislavski insisted upon filling the background with naturalistic country sounds, and even announced that he would write a play in which a character comments upon the loveliness of the silence around him: "How wonderful! We hear no birds, no dogs, no cuckoos, no owls, no clocks, no sleigh bells, no crickets."[52] Stanislavski dutifully quotes Chekhov's sarcasm and then adds that Chekhov loved sound effects on the stage himself. His filling of background emptiness with naturalistic sound corresponds to his filling of foreground gaps and pauses with naturalistic psychology. Both reveal Stanislavski's misunderstanding of the playwright. The gaps in Chekhov's plays should reflect an ideal void, and his words should fall into the emptiness between them. Or the emptiness may be filled occasionally with an unexpected sound, the sound effect as non sequitur which takes place in *The Cherry Orchard* in act 2 when the sound of a breaking string is heard, inexplicably, in the distance. Chekhov attempted to insert such an absurd sound into *The Three Sisters*. Stanislavski reports that the playwright personally oversaw the sound effects used to create the fire alarm in act 3: in violation of the play's naturalistic mise-en-scène, Chekhov's fire alarm consisted of cacophonous noises produced by the banging together of pots, pans, and various bits of debris. Chekhov was dismayed that neither the director nor the audience appreciated the fact that the playwright's sound effect drowned out his characters' words.

Realizing that he could not change Stanislavski's limited assumptions about his writing, Chekhov retreated into the ambiguous hints he made to the actors, which they mulled over for years, and into inexplicable laughter. Stanislavski reports that Chekhov roared with laughter when he first saw the detailed drawings for the sets for *The Three Sisters*, and then bemoans Chekhov's inability to specify the contents of the rooms in the Prosorov household, even though Stanislavski was convinced that Chekhov "knew it himself in detail, had been there, but had taken absolutely no note of what rooms there were, or furniture, or objects contained in them"[53] Although Chekhov never commented on the contemporary work of Gordon Craig and Adolphe Appia in designing nonrepresentative stage scenery consisting of geometrical shapes and columns of light, perhaps he would have preferred this extreme absence of detail to the interior decoration practiced by the Moscow Art designers.

As the director suggested, "Only Chekhov was able to laugh unexpectedly at a time when laughter was the last thing expected of him."[54] Chekhov's laughter points to his belief in absurdity as a governing principle of existence, an absurdity realized more fully in the theater of Beckett and Pinter, for which Chekhov paves the way. If we share in his laughter, we indict ourselves. Chekhov interpreters from Stanislavski to the present have believed that the process of identification between actor and audience that they find in the play prevents such laughter. For example, Maurice Valency writes that "The principal characters in Chekhov's later plays are all conceived in such a way as to invite a very high degree of identification on the part of the spectator. One can laugh at them only by laughing at oneself."[55] On the contrary, Chekhov's contribution to comedy and to drama is to combine the genres, so that his audience may distance itself from his plays and laugh at his characters; but to the extent that the audience empathizes with these characters, because of their fallacious vision, the audience laughs at itself.

In spite of the playwright's fear that the Moscow Art Theater consistently misinterpreted his plays, Chekhov continued to entrust each of his new works to Stanislavski. Eventually the director became convinced that he had conceived his system of acting out of an understanding of Chekhov's work. In this study we have examined the limitations of his further claim that the Stanislavski system can serve as a bridge to the approach of Chekhov. But the similarities between the philosophy of playwriting and the philosophy of acting espoused by Chekhov and Stanislavski do indicate the ground from which Stanislavski could develop his system, even though it does deviate from Chekhov's intention. A brief examination of common assumptions and contrasts between the two philosophies indicates, perhaps, Chekhov's reasons for accepting Stanislavski's work, however begrudgingly; his grounds for believing that he could influence the director to conform more closely to his own vision; and finally, his realistic acknowledgment that no other style of staging currently available in Russian or European theater could accommodate his work so well as the style of the Moscow Art Theater.

Stanislavski's debt to Chekhov begins with the process by which the playwright presents his characters as coming to know themselves and their world. Chekhov cannot believe that men possess an essence before they have experienced an existence, or a governing "humour" or stereotypical vision before they have lived that life. His characters are coming to be, and stand before life, but ironically Chekhov denies them what existentialism concedes a man at the end of his life, an essence which is the sum of his acts as seen from the point of view of death—for Chekhov's characters rarely die, and even more seldom do they take action. (One result of Chekhov's placing of the plot events outside the action, in intermissions or offstage, is the implication that while the nonevents happening on stage are absolutely real, the more major off-stage events do not occur at all. This implication is heightened by the lack of causal connection between the two series of events: those we see happening on stage in no way have to happen because of the offstage events—which further discredits their existence.)

Chekhov's elaborate time-schemes allow him to slay time and to pay homage to the moment in which man is living now, or the moment in which the recipient of his artwork is living when he receives it. But Chekhov finds no salvation in this moment, merely eternity: he dooms his characters and his audience alike to a potentiality. Stanislavski will not accept the rejection of both meaning and meaninglessness which this vision assumes. He converts Chekhov's sentence of potentiality to a blessing of potentiality. His actor comes to know his own person and constantly renews the sources of this knowledge (through affective memory) as a means of imitating the process by which Chekhov's characters are brought into such a knowledge. The active and passive verb constructions of the preceding sentence reflect the different orientations of the two thinkers. Stanislavski's actors pursue the process of self-discovery consciously, by means of technique and reflective thought, while Chekhov's characters avoid the discovery, at the same time they are being manipulated into making it by the comic mechanism of the plays' structures. Since Stanislavski's actors will their self-discovery, they avoid the despair of Chekhov's characters who possess "nothing but" a future, outside of which they stand. Stanislavski's actors renew each present moment in the process of experiencing a work of art. They change, re-create, and make unique each presentation of the work (each performance and each moment of performance) by varying the sources of their psychological technique, and thereby renew the moment of "now" in which they always exist. Instead of standing outside the future in an empty "now," as do Chekhov's characters, they expand the "now" to encompass all time, and banish the need for a future.

The implication of this attitude for the question of change reveals a similarity between Chekhov and Stanislavski which Stanislavski could never expunge as a defect from his system. Chekhov concludes that change does not exist, and the future (defined as different from the "now") can never enter the present because it will never be different—there will never be a future, only more "now," or as Chebutykin says, denying any distinctions, "What's the difference?" Although Stanislavski's goal in his actor training is nothing less than the salvation of the whole man, his body, emotions, intellect, and sensitivity, and even a restructuring of his social world so that performance occurs within a "temple of art," nevertheless, a contradiction in his understanding of affective psychology forces him to limit his actor to reliving his past, not, in Schechner's term, pre-living his future. By living a character through an affective memory technique which gradually exhausts his own past of emotional trauma and emotional motivation alike, Stanislavski's actor becomes a prisoner of his past: he may be able to live his character, but he cannot live on stage, or prepare a future. Ironically, he stands outside this future just as does Chekhov's character: this similarity between the two systems may have led Chekhov to believe that he could manipulate Stanislavski's methods to serve his own ends.

Chekhov and Stanislavski differ in their intuition of catharsis. In terms of their assumptions about drama and the techniques they will apply to it (from which we may derive philosophical implications), we may say that Chekhov and Stanislavski begin their work with the same "art object," which Chekhov will neutrally label "a drama." But all of Chekhov's additions, alterations, suggestions during production, and interpretive reflections outside of the theater, will lead him to see the work as a vaudeville, while all of Stanislavski's efforts move it toward the pole of tragedy. Through his comic mechanism Chekhov withholds or averts self-knowledge from his characters, and prevents them from ridding themselves of the trauma behind this knowledge, which would amount to catharsis in the purgative sense; he also prevents his characters from reconciling themselves to the inevitability of trauma (by coming to know that there will be no change, only more potentiality), which would be catharsis in the sense of purification. Stanislavski's system plays against Chekhov's comic control mechanism. As we have seen, he replaces this form of control with motivation, logically deduced from the characters' unstated offstage lives, and through affective memory, invented from the actors' own stores of emotions. Thus his productions give the appearance of characters achieving self-knowledge and reconciling themselves to it, for his actors have recognized parts of their selves within the characters, and make penance for these aspects by revealing them in public. But since Stanislavksi insists that any act of self-exposure on stage be oriented toward the goal of living and portraying a character, he removes this catharsis of purification from the actor who would logically be expected to experience it (and from his audience, who would experience it through empathy), and burdens the play's characters with it. In the case of Chekhov, the burden is undeserved, for it transforms Chekhov's unredeemed comic vision into a sentimental tragedy, "redeemed" but unilluminated by the weight of Stanislavski's optimism.

Stanislavski's assumption that a play's characters live offstage as well as on, that their unstated lives may be deduced logically from what the playwright has given them to say, and that this unstated material provides appropriate motivation for all details of a mise-en-scène indicates his radical alignment with naturalism, or at least with the "spiritual naturalism" which the director felt lay at the heart of his theater. He rationalizes each gap or lack in the play—all the absences of physical detail, emotion, motivation, and even of words (the pauses)—and fills them with psychological content taken from the actor's self. By rationalizing the play's characters, he gives them tragic stature, and by creating this rationality out of his actor's self, he causes the actor to participate in the artwork both as creator and as work itself. For his time, this contributes a unique innovation to the theory of mediation between work and recipient, and by linking aesthetics and affective memory it gives significance to the act of performance in theater. It is Stanislavski's most important contribution, but it does not quite fit the plays from which his innovations emerged, especially plays like *The Three Sisters*.

Chekhov's theory of participation in the art process and mediation between work and recipient is more ironic and intellectualized than Stanislavski's approach. Chekhov felt that he had written it *all* down, and throughout rehearsals he refused to elaborate the details of production which would contribute to a naturalistic reading of his plays. He inserts gaps and pauses into his texts not so that they may be filled but so that their emptiness may be acknowledged by actor and audience. Both participate by a negation: not by adding to the work's content but by actively refraining from inserting meaning which is not there. Chekhov uses comic mechanisms to "set up" his actor and audience, brings them to the verge of a gap which they might be expected to fill in a different aesthetic theory, and then leaves them stranded, confronting the lacuna. This process causes the nervous laughter which accompanies performances of his plays, laughter which is accompanied by a shudder. Chekhov's contribution to participation theory in performance lies in his blending of "drama" and "vaudeville" so that his actors and audience experience both empathy with and distance from the play's characters and events. An apparently naturalistic psychology allows them to enter into, live, and empathize with these characters, until actor and audience recognize the unmediable abyss within and around them, and the comic mechanisms which control them. Recognition of the comic machinery incites laughter, but since it has resulted from an initial empathy, the laughter reflects back from the limited character to the recipient (actor or spectator) newly aware of his own limitation—he laughs at himself. If Stanislavski breaks new ground in his development of connections between affectivity and aesthetics, Chekhov's innovation lies in his radical critique of the effectiveness of affectivity. His doctrine of the impossibility of change creates an ideal and unbreached distance between work and recipient, instead of the identity sought by Stanislavski. Each party remains alone, pure but incomplete, acknowledging the failure of mediation which lies between him and the others: if Stanislavski creates a presence in performance, Chekhov creates a concrete absence.

Stanislavski's influence on the modern stage has had two legacies. The lesser of these has been the direct application of his theories, beginning with his own productions. Through his belief in the reality of physical and psychological detail, his honest but limited concept of the "sincerity" of the actor's emotions, his creation of a lifelike process by which the actor gradually can come to know and inhabit his character on the stage, and his faith in the role of the audience in participating in catharsis by means of empathy, he contributed an important staging technique to a subgenre of drama, the naturalistic play. Ironically, he did not stage the plays which respond most directly to his acting style—in fact, these plays were written after his great work and in response to it, especially the psychological melodramas of the American and British realistic movements in the decades between 1930 and 1960. The canon ranges from O'Neill to soap opera; this latter pole indicates the media in which a strict application of Stanislavski's technique has most often flourished, television and film.

But we are still assessing Stanislavski's second legacy, the philosophical implications of his theory. His discoveries in regard to the actor in the act of living on the stage, the role of the mediator vis-à-vis the artwork in theater performance, the necessity of constant renewal of the art experience by means of the recipient's participation in its creation, the formulation of an affective aesthetics, and his dream of a life in art—these discoveries lie behind all subsequent experimentation in modern theater. We all have had to acknowledge or refute them.

PART II

**Beyond Catharsis
of Incident in
Presentational
Acting
and Epic
Dramaturgy**

3. Brecht's Epic Theater and Visionary Dialectics

While Stanislavski developed his theory of acting in reaction to the drama of Chekhov, Bertolt Brecht created a style of staging in reaction and opposition to the idea of theater dominant in his time: the idea derived from the practice of Stanislavski and the theory of Aristotle. Of all the theoreticians of theater writing in this century, Brecht has been most conscious and explicit about his understanding of catharsis: Brecht wrote in 1935 that what he calls "Aristotle's recipe" for achieving catharsis results in "the spiritual cleansing of the spectator,"[1] purification not only of emotions like pity and fear but, more important, of any will or willingness to change the world represented (and, for Brecht, validated) by Aristotelian tragedy. And he links the theory of catharsis with the practice of empathy, upon which Stanislavski founded his psychologically realistic style of acting, only to reject them both. He said in 1933 that the epic theater

> makes nothing like such a free use as does the Aristotelian of the passive empathy of the spectator; it also relates differently to certain psychological effects, such as catharsis. Just as it refrains from handing its hero over to the world as if it were his inescapable fate, so it would not dream of handing the spectator over to an inspiring theatrical experience.[2]

Throughout his early writings Brecht describes his own epic theater as "non-Aristotelian," by which he means "not depending upon empathy."[3] However, Aristotle does not mention empathy in the *Poetics*, nor does he dwell on the psychological realism of the acting style employed in Greek staging (for none was employed); apart from the controversial catharsis-clause in his definition of tragedy, Aristotle does not discuss the psychological effect of theater performance on its audience.[4] Brecht was certainly aware of this, yet he continually used such polemical overstatements as "non-Aristotelian dramaturgy" throughout his early writings. He does not retract them in his longest and most complete elaboration of theater theory, the "Short Organum for the Theater" (*Kleines Organon für das Theater*) written in 1948. Instead, he qualifies and refines earlier scattered remarks into an aesthetic system, discarding terms and extreme opinions which have outlived their use-

fulness in his thought, while acknowledging that they served as necessary steps in a dialectic which resulted in his present understanding
(itself not yet complete), still preserving their importance in terms of
theory. In the "Short Organum" Brecht even avoids the term "epic
theater," after having spent twenty years writing essays to promulgate
the concept. He abandoned none of its techniques or aims, but at the end
of his life he wrote that in itself epic theater did not give rise to the
mutability of society he desired; in 1956 he speculated about replacing
the concept with a theory of "dialectical theater."[5]

Likewise, his treatment of Aristotle mellows in the "Short Organum," a work which pays homage to the Greek aesthetician in its
form of numbered paragraphs and in its intent to be a new, Marxist
poetics. He does not retract his earlier polemical reading of Aristotle's
catharsis-clause, even though he indicates his awareness of the
philological crux which he exploited to coin the term "non-
Aristotelian." In paragraph 4 of the "Organum" he defines catharsis
alternately as "cleansing by fear and pity, or from fear and pity" ("die
Reinigung durch Furcht und Mitleid, oder von Furcht und Mitleid"),
but he does not speculate which definition Aristotle meant; he has cited
the term only to emphasize that whatever purification is intended in the
Poetics, it is performed "for the purpose of pleasure,"[6] a function which
Brecht applauds in Aristotle. Although this citation suggests that
Brecht's scorn of catharsis depended upon a definition of the term
which Aristotle did not share, Brecht never bothered to investigate the
contending claims of "purgative" and "purificatory" catharsis to determine what Aristotle had actually intended; instead he exploited a
common assumption about catharsis to derive the polemical counter-
assumption inherent in the term "anti-Aristotelian," and then dropped
the term when the polemical point had been established.

Keeping in mind this assumption that Brecht evolved his theory
through a series of polemical essays, I shall draw on the whole range of
his writings to investigate the stance of the dramatic text toward its
audience in epic theater, and the contribution to the work's meaning
and affectivity made by the actor, who no longer represents a character
but presents it. The final cause of Brecht's theater is to determine and to
effect an understanding of social process in its recipients—actors and
audience, whom Brecht merges in his Lehrstücke ("didactic" plays) like
The Measures Taken (Die Massnahme). If we follow modern interpretations of the Poetics which take catharsis to mean the clarification of
pitiable and fearful incidents in a social context, then Brecht's concern
with clarifying the social process which underlies such incidents stands
as an elaboration of Aristotle, not as a rejection.

Much has been written by Brecht and the Brechtians about "epic thea-

ter," a phrase which Brecht did not invent. Erwin Piscator first coined
the phrase as the director of Berlin's Volksbühne around 1924; the
young Brecht assisted Piscator during his staging of several productions
there, most notably Håsek's *Adventures of the Good Soldier Schweik*
which Brecht later rewrote as *Schweyk im zweiten Weltkrieg*. By "epic"
qualities, Piscator referred to both the magnitude of the plays he staged
(their many episodic scenes, large casts, and the quantity of factual and
statistical detail they introduced), and to the *narrative* method by which
much information is presented to the audience, as opposed to strictly
dramatic representation in which everything the audience learns about
the play emerges from characters exchanging realistically motivated dialogue. Narrative methods employed by Piscator included projections
of films, photographs, and charts, placards bearing plot information or
political slogans, and enormous and costly settings which displayed
several locations simultaneously, or which involved turntables and
treadmills so that a character like Schweik could be shown "marching
across Europe." Brecht delighted in all this machinery (which he called
"electrification"),[7] but he came to demand that all the devices be sub-
ordinated to a philosophical position more lofty than the presentation
of large amounts of information, "sensory input," and leftist spectacle.

Piscator never progressed beyond being an engineer of the theater, a
manipulator of technological devices to confirm the technological and
political assumptions of an already-convinced audience; unlike Brecht,
he did not write plays, and he came to prefer the staging of novels,
newspaper accounts, and political pageants to actual plays. There is a
comfortable quality about Piscator's discussion of the role of technology
in epic theater:

> the Epic Theatre director ... should be a good engineer of the
> theatre. The modern playgoer responds positively to the new
> theatre construction of glass and metal and the technical in-
> ventions. He likes to have confirmed on stage what surrounds him
> in his daily life—the machinery of civilization. He is proud, in this
> way, to share the alpha and omega of the newest creations.[8]

Brecht did not believe in confirming his audience's beliefs but in
changing them. His contribution to the epic theater, the contribution
which makes it more than a collection of mechanical aids to staging, is
the development of a style of acting which, combined with these mechanical aids, makes strange and unfamiliar the machinations as well as
the machinery of society which surround the modern playgoer in his
daily life, so that the playgoer will *notice* these machinations and
criticize and change them, not simply accept them as inevitable. While
Piscator coined the phrase "epic theater" as a descriptive noun, Brecht
was more interested in how such a theater actively affected its audience,

and so he preferred to employ the term as if it were a verb—hence his neologism "epicize" (*episieren*) (and, later, "dialecticize" [*dialek-tisieren*]).

Hence Brecht's concept of epic theater is connected with his theory of *Verfremdung*, the making strange or de-familiarizing of events, actions, and relationships which we fail to notice in daily life because they have become too habitual; they seem to be a fixed part of the human condition. Brecht argues that no aspect of the human condition should be considered fixed except its ability to be changed: "Only the dead are beyond being altered by their fellow-men."[9] For Brecht, naturalistic acting styles which encourage the audience to empathize with the character *as it is* at the moment of presentation by the actor have to be swept from the theater, along with what Stanislavski called "the illusion of the first time," the pretense that what is happening to the character during the course of the play is happening at the present moment. Because naturalistic acting makes the character appear to be contemporaneous with the audience, it suggests that the character's behavior and fate are shared by the audience, and that the two will always be bound together, the character's condition representing the inevitable condition of the spectator. But defamiliarized (or "epicized") acting emphasizes the historicity of the event portrayed, the uniqueness rather than the universality of the character; not "what happens" but what *has* happened, could have been avoided, and ought to be changed.

Paradoxically, the representational style of Stanislavski's actor causes him to posit his character in an eternal and immutable present, while Brecht's "historical" theater replaces the character's presence "now" with the *actor's*, by the following process. Brecht's actor does not attempt to resemble his character or to feel his character's emotions: he does not represent but simply presents certain characteristics and traits by which a particular man or kind of man *who is not the actor* can be recognized and judged. Although Brecht's actor does not represent his character, the character is "re-presented" (made present again, seen as historical and not "always present"). In fact, what *is* always present in Brechtian characterization is the presence of the actor on the stage, conscious of himself during each moment of performance and causing the audience to be conscious of his performance and its contemporaneity; or as Brecht puts it, the artist's object is "to appear strange," which he achieves "by looking strangely at himself."[10] Together, actor and audience look back on the historical character (whereas in Stanislavski's theater the audience looks across to the eternal character in which the actor has effaced himself). But their contemporaneity implies no mutual confirmation of each other's values;

through *Verfremdungseffekte* Brecht's actor points out that the audience's assumptions about itself (as well as about the character) are not necessarily natural and are certainly not inevitable. Hence the actor stands permanently in opposition to his audience, and "solutions" to the problems raised by Brecht's plays do not take effect within the plays or during the performances.

This becomes complicated in Brecht's *Lehrstücke*, which he intended to be performed by school groups and choral societies for their own edification, not for presentation to an audience. In cases like the play *The Measures Taken*, the spectator and the actor are one and the same person, but his two functions are separate and at odds with one another. Such self-division suggests schizophrenia, and in a valuable essay the critic Walter H. Sokel has used this psychopathological term to describe Brecht's split characters.[11] Sokel's term reflects Brecht's delight in estranging our ordinary understanding of things through an unexpected usage, and I shall adopt this notion of "schizophrenia" in my discussion. This schizophrenia of function is Brecht's most sophisticated paradigm of a schizophrenia within human nature which he portrays in several plays involving split personalities—for example, Shen Te and Shui Ta in *The Good Woman of Setzuan*, or Herr Puntila while drunk and while sober. It relates to Brecht's important contribution to Piscator's epic theater, the "estranged" or "alienated" actor. Brecht summarized his position late in his career in the "Short Organum," in which he discusses all the devices of epic theater but avoids that term, preferring to employ and therefore to parody Wagner's term *Gesamtkunstwerk* (which the opera composer coined to describe an utterly different kind of "total" or "integrated work of art," one which used similar spectacular elements to involve and drain its audience emotionally):

> So let us invite all the sister arts of the drama, not in order to create an "integrated work of art" [*Gesamtkunstwerk*] in which they all offer themselves up and are lost, but so that together with the drama they may further the common task in their different ways; and their relations with one another consist in this: that they lead to mutual alienation [*sie sich gegenseitig verfremden*].[12]

But the end of this mutual *Verfremdung* in Brecht's theory and art does not lie in a confession of the world's absurdity or irrationality; ultimately Brecht does not estrange us simply to confront us with visions of ourselves as grotesque schizoids, self-divided men. Throughout his theoretical writing, Brecht argues from the side of reason, from the position that something in life can be understood (not merely accepted), and that theater can be a tool for such understanding. The detached and ironic tone of his essays stands in sharp contrast to the hysterical lyricism of his early expressionistic plays, whose monstrous protagonists (Baal, Garga, Schlink) seem insusceptible to any rational system of understanding, be it from the point of view of naturalistic psychology or economic determinism. Brecht's subsequent acceptance of Marxism alters his playwriting greatly, from the destructively individualistic stance of the early plays through the almost fanatic anti-individualism of the *Lehrstücke* to the "mixed" (or schizoid) mode of what have been called his mature plays, which involve characters divided against themselves either figuratively (Mother Courage living off and falling victim to the war, the Gruscha-Azdak "dual protagonist" of *The Caucasian Chalk Circle*) or literally (Shen Te–Shui Ta, Herr Puntila drunk and sober). Despite great changes in Brecht's style of writing and in the particular ideology he espouses from play to play, no Brecht play presents a view of society in a perfected state, or characters who are completely available to rational understanding (let alone to emulation, as with the "positive heroes" so sought by communist aestheticians). But all the time Brecht is writing plays in which no solution to the social problem being analyzed is presented, he is arguing in his essays that solutions are possible, and that the world can be understood through the employment of reason. If despite stylistic differences his plays all portray a world whose problems are irrational and insoluble within the context of the play, all his theoretical writings (despite differences of emphasis) argue for a world which is reasonable.

How do we reconcile this contradiction? First, we must recognize that Brecht did not oppose the idea of contradiction per se. As a Marxist, he believed that the antithetical conflicts between opposing social forces bespoke the existence of history as a dialectical process, and that such clashes or "contradictions" were essential not only for desirable change but for existence itself. As John Willett points out, contradiction becomes "at once the motive force and the social-aesthetic justification of his later work."[13] So we must reject the shallow views of critics who profess to admire Brecht's plays but find his theoretical writings in opposition to the effect the plays have on an audience. For example, Martin Esslin holds the curious view that although Brecht was wrong to banish the audience's empathy with his characters (because empathy is one of "the basic mechanisms by which one human being communicates with another"), fortunately for Brecht his audience went right on "being moved to pity and terror"; for Esslin, Brecht's effect lies in the conflict between his theoretical opposition to empathy and his audience's stubborn emotional involvement in his plays, or his success "lies in his partial failure to realize his own intentions."[14] Such statements reduce Brecht's concept of contradiction to the level of inconsistency. These critics assume mistakenly that the object being discussed in Brecht's theory is the literary work of art, the play's text and the meaning which emerges from reading it. They correctly conclude that his theories have little to do with such a reading, that the plays as texts are to a certain degree self-explanatory, and that further analysis is better provided by other literary critics, not by the author of the plays.

Brecht would have to agree, for he was not very interested in the literary analysis of his own works. He believed so little in the sanctity of his texts that he constantly rewrote and revised them to correspond to party dictates, current events, and the audience responses which he wished to elicit. Brecht's theory has less to do with his plays as literature than as theater event. He investigates the philosophical implications of the act of presenting his texts to an audience, the meaning which emerges from performance. To a large extent, this meaning does not lie within the plays' lines themselves (lines which Brecht viewed to be as mutable as the world they reflect). The chaos and irrationality registered in Brecht's plays reflect the world of historical events, while the reason and appeals for understanding voiced in his theoretical statements can be explained by the fact that they reflect the artistically controlled world of the stage. But Brecht was not content to effect solutions and understanding *within the theater* alone, as does Piscator's "theater as tribunal" which resolves social problems through the audience's "vote" and offers social programs from the stage, or the self-congratulatory left-wing staging which believes that it satisfies its obligation toward creating a collective consciousness by transforming its audience into an artificial collectivity during the time it sits in the theater. Brecht divided his audience into conflicting individuals rather than uniting them into "the collective individual," and he left his plays unresolved so that his audience would seek to solve problems outside the theater, in the world. To progress beyond the contradiction of his plays' chaos and his theory's reason, we shall have to discuss the role of *clarification* in Brecht's theater (a concept which, I have argued, is the most likely meaning of Aristotle's "catharsis"). What can be rationally understood in Brecht's theater, and to what extent is the understanding effected by means of theatrical performance?

Characteristically for Brecht's evolving theory, his emphasis on what is to be clarified changes several times in his writings. Brecht first held that the *character* could be so understood. In an early interview with Bernard Guillemin (in *Die Literarische Welt*, Berlin, 1926) Brecht first proposed that plays can only be understood when performed, and that the portrayal of characters is not a matter for empathy but for understanding; this interview contains Brecht's first public announcement of "epic theater," identified with the reason as opposed to empathy.[15] The idea of understanding a play through its performance underlies all the epic theater devices and *Verfremdungseffekte* which Brecht is to invent or to borrow from other theater traditions (notably the cabaret stage and Chinese acting); all of them call attention to the theatricality of performance as opposed to its naturalness, and break down the empathy which audiences conventionally share with characters portrayed on stage. This confirmation and acceptance of the character's experience through empathy with the character's emotions had been the audience's chief connection with the play in earlier "Aristotelian" theater, Brecht thought; he was determined to create another kind of connection with the artwork, through detachment and rational evaluation, and to this end he does not banish emotions (and empathy) from his stage but changes their function.

Perhaps, then (Brecht argues), what can be rationally understood beyond characters is our emotional response to their enactment—if emotions are properly "refunctioned" (Brechtian *Umfunktionerung*). For example, if spectators tend to fall into empathic relationships with characters, Brecht will exploit this fact by writing an emotional speech or employing sentimental music to draw the audience into unthinking sympathetic involvement; but then he will employ *Verfremdungseffekte* such as enclosing the emotional speech in quotation marks (adding "he said" to it) by which the actor "shows the showing" ("zeigt das Zeigen") to confront the audience with the inadequacy of identification and the need to take a more critical position. On certain occasions, empathy may even be appropriate apart from this ironic and critical usage: the most obvious example is Kattrin's heroic death in *Mother Courage*, which Brecht consistently refused to "de-familiarize" of its emotional content, even when his wife, the actress Helene Weigel, pointed out the superficial theoretical inconsistency. Writing in 1949, Brecht tempered what had been interpreted as a negative stance toward the arousing of emotion in his theory, and suggested that certain emotions are appropriate to it, such as "the sense of justice, the urge to freedom, and righteous anger"; Brecht does not even take their presence for granted, but says that he seeks "to arouse or to reinforce them. The 'attitude of criticism' which [epic theater] tries to awaken in its audience cannot be passionate enough."[16] Although it can be argued that only one of the terms on Brecht's list (anger) is actually an emotion, Brecht's statement indicates his basic agreement with Stanislavski about the affective potentiality of theater performance. However, Brecht is more selective about the emotions he wants to affect. As early as 1935 he wrote that the epic theater does not simply eliminate emotional effects; rather, "emotions are only clarified in it" ("tatsächlich sind ihre Emotionen nur geklärt").[17] This is another instance in which Brecht's language reflects the recent reinterpretation of Aristotle's "catharsis" as "clarification."

Edward M. Berckman has expanded on Brecht's choice of desirable emotions, and speculates that his drama arouses "the revolutionary emotions of anger and hope":

> One becomes angry when, in the action of the plays, hopes are frustrated. But hope is sustained because an alternate possibility has been displayed, and because the "Truth of utopia," the vision of what man essentially is and is meant to be, once glimpsed remains with the spectator.[18]

When he posits the complementary nature of anger and hope, Berckman recalls the mutual interdependence of pity and fear in the *Poetics*: in section 13 Aristotle explains that we pity the misfortunes of others because we fear that they may befall ourselves. Berckman's theory of a re-functioned, Marxist catharsis is appealing, but he limits his revolutionary emotions of anger and hope to their connection with actions in the plays. But Brecht has not simply replaced one set of emotions with another set more worthy of our empathy, he has expanded the concept of empathy to extend away from emotions, characters, and even actions in the plays, toward the act of performance itself.

The "attitude of criticism" mentioned in Brecht's 1949 statement cited above, which Brecht wants to provoke in his audience through "passionate" means, does not belong to the character in Brecht's play but to the actor who presents it to the audience. Brecht wants his audience to empathize with *the acting of the role*. As he says in his famous essay "Alienation Effects in Chinese Acting":

> The performer's self-observation [*Sich-selber-Zusehen*], an artful and artistic act of self-alienation, stopped the spectator from losing himself in the character completely, i.e. to the point of giving up his own identity, and lent a splendid remoteness to the events. Yet the spectator's empathy was not entirely rejected. The audience identifies itself with the actor as being an observer [*fühlt sich in den Schauspieler als in einen Betrachtenden ein*], and accordingly develops his attitude of observing or looking on.[19]

Brecht's final opinion on empathy appeared in a posthumous appendix to the "Short Organum." In a continuation of the Organum's fifty-third paragraph, he links acting with demonstration (*Zeigen*) and opposes these two to the pair of experience and empathy. Brecht qualifies the implication made in the "Short Organum" that, because the two pairs stand in opposition, only one pair or the other may appear in the actor's work. He says that the actor in epic theater cannot exclude all tendencies toward experience and empathy, even if he should try to do so, which Brecht does not recommend. In fact, it is Brecht's intention to fuse the pairs of "mutually hostile processes"—here, "experience and portrayal, empathy and demonstration, justification and criticism"—a fusion which results in the desirable showing of contradiction.[20]

What emerges from Brecht's continuing discussion of empathy and emotions in theater is the general conclusion that he neither banned them nor overestimated their importance. In fact, he answers his own call to clarify emotions with a theory that the audience should empathize with the actor's intellectual observation of his character (not with that character's emotions and certainly not with the actor's sympathetic probing of his own emotions, as in Stanislavski's theater). When Brecht rechannels empathy toward acting technique, he suggests that what we are to understand in his theater lies beyond emotions. Are Brecht's characters accessible to rational understanding, or are the incidents of their lives, the events they perform? In the early "Dialogue about Acting" (1929), Brecht asks himself whether the actor ought to make the man he is representing understandable, and decides that this is not so important as understanding "what takes place."[21] Brecht does not define this phrase more specifically here, but it clearly stands beyond and even in opposition to an isolated or intrinsic understanding of the character cut off from his relationship with other men. Hence the Brechtian actor comes to understand his character not through an examination of the character's internal psychology but through the amassing of social "gests" (Brecht's term *gestus*, a combination of the English sense of "gesture" and "gist") which show his social relationship to other men. In terms of rehearsal techniques, Brecht's actor does not employ affective memory but rather learns and plays during rehearsal all the other parts in the play. In Walter H. Sokel's apt phrase, Brecht's character disappears in the web of the interpersonal "deals" which constitute the play's action.[22] But we cannot view these "deals" as simple equivalents of the play's incidents. Brecht had acknowledged as early as 1926 that he failed to make clear the incidents of his plots "so that the audience can think for itself": "That's why I need a quick-witted audience that knows how to observe, and gets it enjoyment from setting its reason to work.... The sense of my plays is immanent. You have to fish it out for yourself."[23]

By the time he composed the "Short Organum," Brecht had decided what could be clarified by means of reason in his theater: "the connection of events" can be told clearly ("deutlich zu erzählen die Verknupfüng der Geschehnisse").[24] By "connection of events," Brecht means an understanding of historical process which does not collapse in the face of contradictory incidents, characters, and emotions, all of which Brecht had sought to clarify in his theoretical writings, and all of which he had had to view as unreconciled constituent elements. In paragraph 45 he identifies this process with dialectical materialism:

> The technique [i.e., *Verfremdung*] allows the theatre to make use in its representations of the new social scientific method known as dialectical materialism. In order to unearth society's laws of motion this method treats social situations as processes, and traces out all their inconsistencies. It regards nothing as existing except in so far as it changes, in other words as in disharmony with itself. This also goes for those human feelings, opinions and attitudes through which at any time the form of men's life together finds its expression.[25]

By taking the dialectical process (which by its very nature is not to be concluded or finished) as the "final cause" of his aesthetic theory, Brecht resolves the many apparent contradictions within the theory: he turns contradiction into a constituent of rational analysis. And, fittingly for an aesthetic theory, when the spectator gains understanding of the dialectical process, he should experience aesthetic pleasure—in the theater vocabulary which Brecht employs, the spectator is thus "entertained."[26] We are entertained with the presentation of what would be no source for joy outside of an artistic context—the solution of problems ("Organum," Paragraph 24) and knowledge of our own mutability (which Brecht calls the "terrible and never-ending labor" which ensures our maintenance, "the terror of [our] unceasing transformation").[27] Even contradiction itself Brecht can refer to as "a joke," as he says in a note appended to the Organum, which concludes with the belief that knowledge of all these terrors cited above brings "ways of enjoying the liveliness of men, things, and processes, and they heighten both our capacity for life and our pleasure in it."[28] Of course, earlier aesthetic theories have similarly noted that art makes pleasurable the contemplation of the ugly or the frightening, because of the aspect of learning which accompanies it. In section 4 of the *Poetics*, in his general discussion of imitation (which directly anticipates the catharsis clause of section 6), Aristotle notes the pleasure we derive from skillful imitation of even despised animals and of corpses. And in the "Short Organum," Aristotle is never far from Brecht's mind. We might also recall Aristotle's dictum that tragedy should not provide its spectators with every pleasure but only with that pleasure which is proper to it (section 14); for Brecht, the proper pleasure is derived from the clarification of dialectical connections between events.

However, it is important to note Brecht's insistence upon the *performing* of his plays through the media of *Verfremdungseffekte* as being the primary means of effecting an understanding of them upon their audience. For Brecht, as I shall demonstrate, it is primarily the idealized function of the actor which provides this desired clarification. We might normally expect a playwright who claimed to instruct us through reason to believe that he had incorporated rational logic into his characters' verbal arguments. But Brecht knows that his characters' words are contradictory. Instead, he has placed his *actor* in the position of reasonable understanding. At any given point in the play, Brecht's actor behaves as if he were aware of not only the events which have already transpired (the character's limited knowledge), but also of the events which come afterwards, even of events and "solutions" which occur outside and beyond the world of the play. He speaks from what Sokel calls "the vantage point of the end of time," looking back upon the character and the play from the perspective of an ideal future, in "the position of a judge seeking a verdict concerning the character."[29] (Note that this is—to continue Sokel's metaphor—another example of a schizoid state: the particular actor himself does not necessarily have the knowledge to make such a judgment, but he plays the part of "the Brechtian actor who knows," along with playing a specific character, and thus imparts the possibility of such knowledge to the audience.)

Sokel goes on to connect the actor's role of judge and his degree of knowledge with the understanding achieved by the spectator as a consequence of the actor's employment of *Verfremdungseffekte*. But the equation is not so exact. Brecht's actor—by *playing* the Brechtian actor who is also creating a character—speaks from beyond the understanding of both the character and the audience. If he spoke only from the position of knowledge achieved at the end of the play—in other words, if he behaved as if he had already lived through all the events within the play at any given moment during the performance of the play—then he would speak from a position identical with that of the audience. For the audience will likewise observe all these events during the course of performance. Brecht's production style (unlike Stanislavski's) does not ask the members of the audience to forget that conceivably they may have read the play in advance (like the actor) or have seen an earlier performance; in any event, the titles which precede most of the scenes in Brecht's plays, which the audience reads from projections or placards before the scenes are performed, place the audience in the position of knowing the outcome of the scenes, an equivalent of the knowledge possessed by the actor, who speaks from knowledge of the whole play. But the actor's knowledge goes further: in principle, he speaks from the position of a Marxist utopia in which the problems of the play that Brecht suggests *can* be solved *have been* solved. The actor's *confidence* in the fact that "for him," in this idealized future, the problems have been solved, and his *refusal* to elaborate the details of the solution must both be considered as constituent elements of the work of art which Brecht creates. Neither of them is "in the play" proper: the audience receives them through performance (or, in reading, through familiarity with Brecht's staging style and theoretical writings). Brecht's insistence that these factors which are "outside the work of art" be considered as constituent parts of the experience of the work reflects one of the most symptomatic aspects of the modern artwork: its disappearance as an intrinsic object which possesses an objective reality outside of the fact of its being perceived or received by human consciousness.

Characteristically, Brecht does not simply accept this aspect of his work as an inevitable and neutral aesthetic quality but refunctions it and puts it to a particular social use. He does not want his audience to share his actor's confidence in the *fact* of the play's solution of its problem, only in the possibility of such a solution. Otherwise, the play's problem would be solved "in the theater," instead of outside it, in the world, where Brecht hopes the watching of his plays will have an effect. Aristotelian aesthetics assumes that the resolution of the questions raised by the artwork lies within the work. From this perspective, parallels exist among all the conflicting translations of "catharsis," and on these grounds Brecht would indeed have rejected all of them. If we accept the view of catharsis as an intellectual clarification of incidents and problems which arise within the play through the exposure of certain knowledge which is also accessible within the realm of the play, we can describe a purgative or purificatory catharsis in parallel terms which extend it from the realm of self-contained text to the realm of self-contained performance. (This is Stanislavski's understanding.) Thus the performance would arouse certain emotions during the time spectators spent within the theater, only to purge them of these emotions by the time the performance ended, or to inure them to the emotions within the same limits of performance. In either case, the actors and the audience experience catharsis at the same time, the actors using techniques of affective memory to excite and then resolve emotions within themselves, and the audience depending upon empathy to share this performance-contained rhythm of excitation and resolution. From this point of view, purgative and purificatory catharsis do not contradict Aristotle's attempt to demonstrate the intrinsic quality of the literary work, they simply extend the intrinsic quality to the theatrical performance (and to the perception and the reception of the artwork).

Brecht counters all this with the stipulation that the resolution of the artwork be moved outside the closed circuit of work and recipient, into a larger circuit of recipient and world. The superior knowledge which Brecht's actor feigns to possess, coupled with his refusal to reveal the source of this knowledge (which lies in the future, outside of and "after" the action of the play, which is all that is available to the audience), both insure that whatever kinds of catharsis Brecht's actor and audience achieve will not be achieved simultaneously. From a schematic point of view, in Aristotelian dramaturgy actor and audience experience catharsis at the same time during the apprehension of the play; Brecht really is "non-Aristotelian" in that, according to this scheme, his actor would have to have achieved catharsis before the play or the performance began, while his audience cannot experience it until after the play has ended. We can observe a correspondence between the confidence and superiority of knowledge which Brecht's actor holds over both the character he plays and his audience during performance, and the confident and positive tone with which Brecht's theoretical writings hold sway over problems which arise in the "realities" of his plays and in their audiences' lives. Whether one considers Brecht on the stage or on the page, one must keep in mind the agent (ideal actor or theory) by which Brecht argues for the potential understandability of social process, given our acceptance of the dialectical process, a process which, when we engage ourselves in it, will bring about not only understanding but also a changed world.

Brechtian acting, in which the performer feigns to inhabit a position of knowledge that is superior to that of the audience, is essentially ironic, which may account for the response of naive spectators who sometimes accuse Brecht's actors of being "cold" or "haughty." It should be noted that Brecht does not ask his actors to live this part, only to play it. Still, his actor's refusal to elucidate the source of his superior confidence can be viewed as a calculated hostility inherent within Brecht's artwork. In this sense, the actor's employment of *Verfremdung* can rightly be translated as "alienation" in the psychological (non-Marxist) sense of the English word. I have avoided using this common translation until this time because I did not wish to introduce the emotional coloring which it inevitably entails, the suggestion that Brecht wished us to dislike or display hostility toward his characters or works. Brecht performs a more sophisticated feat when he provokes our hostility. By shifting our emotional engagement away from our usual sympathy or hostility toward the play's character and onto the actor who is the specifically theatrical manifestation of the character, Brecht insists that the understanding we achieve through *Verfremdung* is gained through conscious awareness of the theatrical context in which it is given. This understanding is a means, a dialectical process for knowing and making a future and not the end product of an analysis of what has happened in the past (in this case, in the play) and hence not something already known. So Brecht's actor will evince hostility toward the audience whenever it attempts to empathize with the actor's assumption that the future is already known to him, at the same time that he encourages empathy with his means of knowing. The germ of this conclusion lies in Brecht's statement in the passage cited from his essay on Chinese acting, that the audience identifies with the actor's act of self-observation, that it identifies with this most primary *Verfremdungseffekt*![30]

Brecht sets up such a paradoxical situation to convince his audience that the sighting of a perfected future is the inevitable outcome of an engagement in dialectical process (the actor's position of inevitable knowledge) but that for the dialectic to commence we must postpone this visionary solution, inevitably, until the future (his withholding of knowledge from the audience, by which he makes that knowledge *inevitable but inevitably not yet*). Such an orientation toward the future sets Brecht apart from Stanislavski in terms of philosophical implication as well as acting technique. In fact, Brecht uses an opposite technique to demonstrate and effect a different philosophical conclusion. When Stanislavski solicited the empathy of his audience with what had occurred in the fictional past of the play's characters and the personal past of his actors, he limited his audience to a view of life which sees it as a simultaneous summary of these past moments. Brecht opposes this with a technique based on calculated hostility, which orients his audience toward the future in two complementary ways. First, he uses *Verfremdung* as defamiliarization to show that a perfected future is knowable (by estranging us from a common acceptance of social situations which does not even notice their problematic nature, Brecht suggests that we will come to accept certain solutions as the right ones just as completely as we now accept as inevitable the situation for which the solutions are needed). Second, he uses *Verfremdung* as alienation from the state of knowledge to activate us toward seeking these solutions in the future and not to be content with an aesthetic solution within the present context of the art experience (which is always in "the present" when we are speaking of an artist's work); he wants to *affect us* into moving beyond the work into the world (engagement with which always lies in the future from the point of view of the art experience).

Only in this last aspect, his belief in the affective nature of the art experience, does Brecht betray his debt to Stanislavski. Stanislavski employed affective memory to reconcile the recipients of his artwork—actor and audience—with their past lives. Rather than seeking verbal contexts (didactic play texts) which inform these recipients of this end, Stanislavski sought to structure intellectual relationships and emotional transactions between work and recipient so that this reconciliation would inevitably take place, a reconciliation which he believed would clear the ground for a new "life in art" after the experience of the artwork had purified the past of trauma. Brecht questions the possibility of a new future emerging from this conciliatory position, yet he exploits the same affective potentiality to incite the recipients of his artwork to begin a progress toward a perfectible future which lies beyond the horizons of the artwork (and hence outside merely aesthetic perfection)—a world nevertheless made knowable through awareness of the work's artificial nature (its theatricality, the fact that the actor-as-theatrical-mediator speaks from this future). Brecht uses Stanislavski's theory of affective art not to prepare the ground for a life in art but to move by means of art away from it and into a new life.

One danger is inherent in both Stanislavski's and Brecht's use of affectivity. We may wish to limit our understanding of either man's thinking to the kind of understanding achieved by the recipients of his artworks—that is, by his audiences. Then it follows that according to our prejudices we may wish to enter into the affective relationship Stanislavski or Brecht initiates and be manipulated by it; or, because we possess a prior conception of how an artwork "ought" to move us, we may decide to reject it entirely. But the critic of affective theory must speak from a more neutral position, viewing the affective strategies of works of modern art as intrinsic components of the works, which must be considered along with their other formal attributes when any explication of such works is attempted.

Brecht complicates such an explication by subdividing the terms within the circuit of artwork and recipient. Stanislavski had already complicated our notion of "artwork" by stipulating that what the interpreter of the work (the actor) brought to it constituted part of the work's content. But he used the conciliatory emotional transaction of empathy to insure that actor and audience (seen here as recipients of the playwright's initial creation) experienced a pattern of aroused and reconciled sentiments which paralleled the feelings of the character (here, the playwright's character constitutes the artwork). This consolidates (rather than complicates) the notion of "recipient." Brecht further complicates the affective circuit by assigning separate functions and positions of knowledge to two categories of recipient, actor and spectator. A spectator irritated by the hauteur of the Brechtian actor's superior knowledge, which views yet withholds from view the perfected future, might well wonder why the actor does not simply describe the nature of the perfection to his audience, along with specific methods of achieving it. But Brecht does not imply that the historical person who happens to work as a Brechtian actor possesses this knowledge himself, and could reveal it to audience members outside of the context of a performance of the play. Acting in Brecht's theater guarantees no necessary therapy and imparts no necessary wisdom to the man who undertakes the profession. I mention this fanciful possibility because it suggests a further refinement of the affectivity circuit between work and recipient that Artaud and Grotowski introduce, a refinement that complicates the notion of the recipient until we can hardly separate the artwork from our notion of the man who receives it. Brecht does not carry the argument so far. He does not make the easily refuted claim that the historical person who acts in his play benefits from being "the actor" by achieving knowledge superior to that of the historical spectator. Instead, Brecht separates the historical man who acts from the aesthetic function of the actor. Brecht's actor exists in a schizoid state that is instructive. The part of him which Brecht can control—the actor's ideal aesthetic *function* within a theory of performance—is said to achieve a superior knowledge of social evolution (i.e., Brecht asks his actor to *feign* such knowledge). But the part beyond Brecht's control—the contingent, historical *man* who happens to be an actor in Brecht's theater—remains instructively ignorant of these future solutions, along with the audience, but both have been given the dialectical means by which they may achieve knowledge. The acting *man* who fleshes out the aesthetic *function* is a recipient for the artwork, as is the audience, but the aesthetic function of actor becomes part of the artwork itself.

This kind of split personality ought to be the appropriate medium for portraying the bifurcated characters who people Brecht's plays, as I suggested earlier in this chapter. These roles make the Brechtian actor's self-division an appropriate technique for character portrayal, but they suggest another implication as well. As I noted earlier, Brecht's essay on Chinese acting calls for the audience to empathize with the fact of the actor's self-alienation, that is, with his self-observation or split into aesthetic function of actor (his aspect as artwork) and acting man (his aspect as recipient). In other words, Brecht asks his audience to share the schizoid state entered into by the people who act in his plays. Though the audience may not be consciously aware of the schizoid role it has undertaken with (or taken over from) the Brechtian actor (for Brecht never announces this aim in his texts), nevertheless this self-division serves as the central means by which Brecht initiates within his spectators the dialectical process which will lead to the knowledge and creation of a perfected future. As we noticed earlier in the examination of Brecht's theoretical writings, such a clarification of dialectical process (which for Brecht combines the aspects of making the process known and making it *take place*) subsumed all the partial clarifications of the constituent elements, like emotion, character, and plot incident.

Indeed, the fact that he only partially clarified these elements and was forced to recognize them as essentially contradictory and hence as constituents of a dialectical process themselves suggests the importance of the dialectic to Brecht's aesthetic.

While many of the great roles in Brecht's canon present examples of this complicated and creative kind of "schizophrenia," no play explores the idea so single-mindedly as does the short *Lehrstück*, *The Measures Taken*, which Brecht wrote in 1930. Within the plot of this play-within-a-play four characters are made to reenact within a courtroom context transpired events (within the play's fiction) in which they actually took part. Brecht has thus set up a literary paradigm for the theatrical reality of Brechtian actors observing and commenting upon the characters they play before a critical audience which judges rather than empathizes. But, of course, the entire self-criticism inherent in the play-within-a-play structure elaborated above *is itself played* according to the dictates of epic theater, so that the play-characters' self-observation is observed in turn by the Brechtian actors, and the play-jury's critical judgment of the characters' self-observation is judged and criticized by the historical audience. Within the framed play, each of the four characters in succession acts the central role of the Young Comrade, who thus comes into our consciousness as a composite of four self-alienated personalities. And as if all these levels were not complex enough, Brecht stipulates that *The Measures Taken* not be played before an audience which has no function other than to watch its performance; instead he assigns the choral role of the play's jury to all the *spectators*, who in their part of the Control Chorus watch and judge in the context of the play-within-a-play but who in the context of the historical performance cease to exist (as audience). The didactic element of such a *Lehrstück* has as much to do with our apprehending of Brecht's aesthetic strategies, the means by which he would effect dialectical knowledge and process, as it does with the extrinsic ideological teaching that he would have us learn. In this play Brecht comes as close as he ever will to the belief of Artaud and Grotowski that change and learning—or therapy and super-intellectual knowledge—can take place *within* the theater (as opposed to the world outside it), but Brecht's relentless complication of the functions of the artwork and recipient prevent him from arriving at such a purely aesthetic conclusion.

4. *The Measures Taken* and the Schizoid Actor

Considering how infrequently *The Measures Taken* is performed, Brecht's didactic play has proved to be a surprising litmus test of the playwright's critical reception.

Between the composition of his last major opera, *Rise and Fall of the City of Mahagonny*, in 1929 and his great plays *Galileo* and *Mother Courage and Her Children* (both finished in 1939), Brecht devoted most of his creative energy to writing half a dozen short schematic plays which he called *Lehrstücke* ("didactic," "learning," or "teaching" plays), which were to be performed in schools and workers' assembly halls, not in formal theaters. During this period, he wrote only one full-length play that has gained lasting critical appreciation and widespread performance, *Saint Joan of the Stockyards*, which resembles the *Lehrstücke*, although he intended it to be performed from a formal stage without the audience participation in choral sequences that characterizes the short didactic pieces. His adaptation of Gorki's novel *The Mother* was played on various left-wing stages, including the Theater Union of New York in 1935, in Brecht's first important American production; his other major play from this decade, *Fear and Agony of the Third Reich*, is really a collection of twenty-seven simple anti-Nazi sketches, many of which are slighter than the so-called *Lehrstücke*.

In general, critical opinion, not to mention infrequency of performance, suggests that these works reflect a dry period in Brecht's development. Most critics prefer to divide his writing into periods, finding him an existentialist in the twenties, a communist in the thirties, and, finally, a Marxist humanist in the forties. Darko Suvin labels the three decades "anarchist," "rationalist," and "mature," respectively, in his influential essay "The Mirror and the Dynamo,"[1] and contrasts the "absolute non-consent" of early heroes like Baal to conform to any social strictures with the "absolute consenting" of heroes like the Young Comrade in *The Measures Taken* to subjugate their individual identity to the social will (here, of course, the party); Brecht's own term for this consent, *Einverständnis*, constantly crops up in the texts of the *Lehrstücke*. Useful as these distinctions can be when employed descriptively, Brecht's critics have applied them shortsightedly to a chronological evolution which they wish to perceive within his work:

since they want to be able to acclaim late plays like *Galileo* and *Mother Courage* as his masterpieces, they see his earlier works as necessary phases which he had to transcend in order to produce the great plays. So in the typical study of Brecht, much space is devoted to discussion of his earliest plays, which in their characters' personal contradictions apparently lay the ground for all the contradictions that will follow and that are extended into the social sphere in Brecht's masterpieces; in such a scheme, the exclusive acquiesence to the social will manifested by the didactic plays serves as a necessary if unfortunate transition between two bodies of favored works.

But even in such a discussion, *The Measures Taken* gets more notice than the other *Lehrstücke*: it is seen as the paradigm of the lot. The play even possesses the honor of having been cited against Brecht during his investigation by the House Un-American Activities Committee in 1947. In a comparative study by Julian H. Wulbern titled *Brecht and Ionesco*, Wulbern devotes half his section on Brecht to a discussion of *The Meaures Taken* as an example of the limitations of "engaged drama." Wulbern opposes the didactic play to *Galileo*, which he favors and refers to as an example of "concerns beyond engagement," but even so he acknowledges that "*The Measures Taken* stands at the epic extreme of theatre."[2]

Critics who speak for the Communist party have not treated the play more kindly. After the first performance in 1930, Brecht was so chastised by party critics like Alfred Kurella that he withdrew and rewrote the play, but even this measure did not suffice.[3] In 1955, a year before Brecht died, the East German critic Ernst Schumacher was still attacking the play's didactic content and failure to conform to what Schumacher called the "historical situation" which stands behind the play.[4] Schumacher's attack in *Die dramatischen Versuche Bertolt Brechts 1918– 1933* probably directly anticipated Brecht's brief note on *The Measures Taken* (published after his death) which explains why the playwright had always turned down requests to perform the play: "only the actor of the Young Comrade can learn from it and he only if he has also acted one of the Party workers and taken part in the Control Chorus."[5]

Brecht's note reminds us of his belief that his plays are not to be understood outside of the circumstances of their performance, and that the didactic element which we learn from them is no mere paraphrasable statement of ideology. In the case of *The Measures Taken*, Brecht's dictum leads him to the position of apparently stating that no actor can learn from this most extreme of epic plays, because no one actor portrays the part of the Young Comrade. But in another sense, everyone who takes part in a production of the play participates in the acting of the Young Comrade: the actors playing the Four Agitators share his part collectively, and they also take part in the Control Chorus, which is augmented by the voices of what normally would be called the audience. In this sense the Control Chorus subsumes all the participants in the theater event entitled *The Measures Taken*, the characters, actors, and spectators; it speaks from the position of humanity as a collectivity, not from that of some local entity such as the Communist party. The Control Chorus does not exist simply to stand in opposition to "the individual" (the Young Comrade) and to judge and execute him. Rather, at the intellectual level (toward which all Brecht's epic devices direct our consciousness of the work) the Control Chorus exists as the primal entity from which the Young Comrade emerges into being, serves a dialectical function in differentiation from the collectivity but not in opposition to it, and then merges again with that Chorus when the Young Comrade's function is fulfilled—significantly, the play's first words are an injunction by the Chorus to "Step forward!" (as if from out of their midst). Such a reading suggests Brecht's reason for insisting that the part of the Young Comrade be played collectively by actors who also belong to the Control Chorus: so that audience sympathies do not gravitate to the character who appears to have the most individually defined personality, displays the most emotions, and becomes the underdog in that he has to be executed. Brecht cuts off such empathy not to suggest that the Four Agitators are "right" and the Young Comrade "wrong," but to compel us to recognize that *all* of them take their being from the prior existence of the Control Chorus, which is the real hero of this play and, in fact, its only character.

But, in another sense, Brecht is equally right in claiming that no one can learn from *The Measures Taken*, since he forbids any one actor from playing the part of the Young Comrade. Contradicting the reading of Brecht's note which suggests that every recipient of his work is in a position to learn from it, this counterclaim refers to the way in which Brecht's actor (and, by extension, his acting audience) must be divided into two components: his function as actor, standing aloof from the play's problem in a position of knowledge which exceeds what can be learned from the play, and his historical identity as the man who receives Brecht's artwork by acting in his play, the man who must engage in a dialectical relationship with the play's problem in the hope that this will affect his understanding of the world outside the play.

Only a few of this play's many critics have given much credence to Brecht's note that links an understanding of his play with the way in which it should be produced. The best of these critics is Reiner Steinweg, whose study *Das Lehrstück* provides an exhaustive compendium of these plays' textual variations and Brecht's own statements about the *Lehrstück* form; indeed, Steinweg designates as the *Basisregel* Brecht's idea that they were written for the participants, not for uninvolved spectators.[6] Too many critics have dismissed Brecht's "retraction" of *The Measures Taken* as a bitter remark to justify the poor reception of an equally poor play, and one writer even treats the statement as a joke, using the words "leg-pulling" and "irony."[7] But Brecht had been making similar statements about his didactic plays for years. In 1936 he called the *Lehrstück* "a type of theatrical performance that could influence the thinking of all the people engaged in it" and spoke of "experiments . . . meant not so much for the spectators as for those who were engaged in the performances;"[8] even earlier, in 1929, he had said that the form "envisage[s] the collective practice of art" and is designed "to clarify the ideas of the authors and of all those taking part, not to provide anybody with an emotional experience."[9] In a conversation with his French translator, Pierre Abraham, in 1956, Brecht referred to his plays as "limbering-up exercises for those athletes of the spirit that good dialecticians must be," and disclaims any particular ideology or "learning" which may be extracted from them as an element which he had not introduced into the plays at all.[10] And a week before his death in August, 1956, Brecht was still thinking about *The Measures Taken;* in a conversation with his directorial heir at the Berliner Ensemble, Manfred Wekwerth, when he was asked which of his plays he took to be an example of the form of the theater of the future, he immediately answered: *The Measures Taken.*[11] Common elements emerge from all these remarks scattered over twenty-five years of Brecht's thinking: the orientation of the plays away from emotional apprehension toward intellectual clarification of a *process* (not a particular idea or meaning), the affective implication of taking part in their performance, the necessity for such participation if the plays are to be understood.

A reading which ignores this aspect of performance still expects a "learning" play to teach something, and if its author is foolish enough to use the weighted term "didactic" in reference to his play, this reader will take the most obvious ideology which can be extracted from the play to be its "learning," and judge or condemn it accordingly. The most obvious conflict in *The Measures Taken* lies between what Lionel Abel calls "the individual, moral experience as such" and "absolute authority."[12] The play's simple plot then follows the line of a martyr-play. A provincial communist youth, ordered by four professional agitators from Moscow to help them secretly plant the seeds for revolution in the Chinese city of Mukden, continually endangers the mission's secrecy by emotional reactions which indicate his purity of motive and innocence of the agitators' pragmatism; finally, he announces a premature revolution and reveals his identity, thus breaking the group's "cover" and endangering their mission—a crime for which he must be shot. Of course, this summary simplifies Brecht's already skeletal play, and fails to reflect the metallic poetry of its verse sections (devoted to such unlikely "lyrical" topics as praise of the party and of illegal party work, and analysis of the law of supply and demand). And it fails to note the formal purity of the play's construction, the brevity with which all the incidents are presented to the judging audience as evidence, largely in declarative sentences (epic narration) yet still exploiting the devices of dramatic exchange during heightened moments in the action.

These aesthetic qualities which so clearly set *The Measures Taken* above the other *Lehrstücke* and seem to be wrongheadedly employed in defense of a pernicious argument prevent most of Brecht's critics from condemning the play out of hand, but these same qualities also inspire them to seek categories which defuse the play of its dangerous "learning." Thus Robert Brustein understands the play as a psychological manifestation of the playwright's attempt to "punish" (as Brustein puts it) Brecht's own "subjective, instinctual and individual qualities" which however he never manages to extinguish; the newly converted communist writes the *Lehrstücke* as "self-disciplinary" measures, "the 'Aves' of a novitiate, paying penance for a recurrent sin."[13]

The critics who echo this psychological-religious language can be less charitable: Peter Demetz thinks that the play's "vile philosophy" will appeal only those who prefer "to have artistic pleasures flavored with masochism";[14] Herbert Luthy speaks of the play's author as "a monk—though a false one—rather such for the sake of the style and cassock, than for belief,"[15] while Willy Haas simply speaks of Brecht "unroll[ing] the whole panorama of Jesuitical Machiavellianism."[16] There is a sense in which these readings do accurately reflect the play's fervent, near-hysterical language and its resemblance to a religious exercise which has to do more with initiating a process of discovery (the dialectic) than discovering any particular ideological truth; even Demetz's suggestion of sado-masochism on Brecht's part reflects the play's aggressiveness towards its audience, though Brecht introduces this hostility as calculated alienation toward an artistic end, not simply to assuage his neuroses.

Brecht's interpreters also attempt to fit him into the role of unwitting political prophet. Martin Esslin imagines *The Measures Taken* to be "an exact and horrifying anticipation of the great confession trials of the Stalinist era."[17] Hannah Arendt does not attempt to justify the play's accuracy in term of events which come after its performance but merely states that the work "told the truth about the basic rules of a totalitarian party."[18] Both writers go on to acknowledge the play's brilliance, but lest we assume that they merely represent a syndrome which could be

called "saving Brecht for the West," we must note that Brecht's communist critics take the same approach: they assume that he has
unwittingly vilified the party, and go on to explain how he should have
restructured his play to avoid such implications. Hence Alfred Kurella
objects that, like the Young Comrade, Lenin had prematurely encouraged revolutionary uprisings before all the proper grounds had been
laid, complains that the fictional plot deviates from historical events
surrounding the German Communist party's activities in Saxony in
1923 which Kurella takes to be the play's inspiration, and ends up
labeling the Agitators as "right opportunists."[19] And Ernst Schumacher
agrees about the Agitators' guilt, suggesting that it would have been
more appropriate for Brecht to have removed them from leadership "as
reformists and opportunists."[20]

Such rewriting of Brecht does not occur only in East Germany.
Brecht's English interpreter Ronald Gray suggests a whole series of
alternatives to the Young Comrade's execution, alternatives which he
accuses Brecht of deliberately overlooking. The Agitators could have
delayed their revolutionary activity to smuggle the Comrade out of
China, or sent him out with one member of their cell, or hidden him,
or let him be killed by the Chinese police rather than taking the
responsibility and guilt onto their own hands. Gray protests:

> The shoddiness of the reasons offered, the complete lack of any
> attempt at envisaging a situation in real life, can only lead one to
> suspect that Brecht had determined before ever writing the play to
> bring it to this conclusion, and that he was indifferent to the
> means by which its harshness was defended.[21]

Gray has overlooked a direct statement in the play's text which explains
why the Young Comrade must be liquidated once he breaks his
cover—the fact that gunboats and armed trains are waiting at the bor-
ders of both Russia and China and will attack the revolutionary government in Russia on the provocation of the sighting of a revolutionary
agitator in imperalist China. But beyond this, he errs in his attempt to
ground the plot in what he calls "a situation in real life," just as Kurella
errs when he links the plot with historical events in Saxony. As
"limbering-up exercises" of the dialectical spirit, Brecht's *Lehrstücke* do
not attempt to clarify events taken from historical reality. They clarify
only a process by which such a reality can be dealt with, and they
should not be measured against such events.

Despite the prevalence of such interpretations, Brecht's play has been
discussed sympathetically by a few sophisticated critics, among them
Frederic Ewen, Reinhold Grimm, and Walter H. Sokel. They recognize
the art with which Brecht elicits audience sympathy for the position of

the Four Agitators and the Control Chorus, a sympathy which Brecht intends to be as strongly felt as the attraction to the Young Comrade. If these readings mislead us, they err on the side of justice, for in pleading the cases of both the Comrade and the Agitators, they suggest that an insoluble conflict between two "rights"emerges, which, since Hegel at least, has been viewed as a criterion for tragedy. But before we question this "tragic" reading of *The Measures Taken,* which is clearly an attempt to redeem a much-maligned play, we should examine the play's text more closely, with an eye toward how certain lines might "read" to an audience which is aware of the complex dynamics of performance which operate among character, actor as function and as historical man, and the "acting" audience.

Any reader of *The Measures Taken* immediately notices that, from a technical point of view, the play is a compendium of the epic theater devices and *Verfremdungseffekte* which so fascinated Brecht the theoretician in the early thirties. These include projected titles, masks, epic narrative, and songs (with music by Hanns Eisler). None of the *Verfremdungseffekte* are employed merely as epic theater "decorations," and each contributes a specific aspect in terms of affecting the audience into an awareness of the play's self-referential nature (as theater event to participate in). The play consists of eight episodic scenes, each of which bears a title; a production photograph from the first performance shows several lines of verse projected on a huge screen which hangs over the audience, so presumably Brecht intended parts of the text to be projected, in addition to the titles.[22] Some of these titles summarize the events which will take place in the forthcoming scene, a favorite Brechtian device to destroy suspense. For example, scene 6 is titled "Rebellion Against the Teaching,"[23] which is exactly what the Young Comrade does in this scene; his rebellion comes after a series of provocations, arguments with the Agitators, and references to supporters of the Comrade's premature revolution who are waiting in the next room for the Agitators' decision. This title reflects in miniature the major suspense-destroying device employed in the play's second line, the Agitators' announcement that they have already killed the Comrade; Brecht immediately eliminates any possibility that he will survive the events which the Agitators recall through flashbacks, thus eliminating the audience's emotional involvement in the character's personal survival and putting it in a position to judge whether the measures taken by the Agitators can be justified.

Other titles simply point to symbolic elements which figure in the scenes they serve to describe: the first title, "The Classical Writings," refers to the "teachings of the classic writers and the propagandists, the ABC of communism,"[24] which the Agitators bring to Mukden in place of much-needed material aid; the third title, "The Stone," refers to the Young Comrade's first tactical error when he lays a stone under the feet of a faltering Coolie and arouses the suspicion of the Overseer. The seventh title, "Final Pursuit and Analysis," refers both to an "elapsed" event of the play-within-a-play (the pursuit of the Agitators by the police once the Comrade breaks their cover), and to the "contemporary" analysis of this event which in the fiction of the frame play is being made at the present moment by the Control Chorus; of course, the participating audience is also making its own analysis.

Another epic device employed in the play is the use of masks, which enables the four actors playing the Four Agitators to play the Comrade and several minor roles as well. Brecht integrates the masks into the play's fiction in one of the more poetic scenes of this play, entitled "The Blotting Out." The leader of the Russian frontier outpost from which the Young Comrade is conscripted informs the Agitators and the Comrade that they must disguise their faces and their personalities as Chinese, perhaps permanently, to avoid the disaster of being detected as Russian provocateurs in imperialist China:

> Then you are yourselves no longer. You are not Karl Schmitt from Berlin, you are not Anna Kjersk from Kazan, and you are not Peter Sawitch from Moscow. One and all of you are nameless and motherless, blank pages on which the revolution writes its in-structions . . . (*gives them masks; they put them on*). Then, from this time on, you are no one [*Niemand*] no longer. From this time on, and probably until you disappear, you are unknown workers, fighters, Chinese, born of Chinese mothers, with yellow skin, speaking Chinese in fever and in sleep.[25]

By covering up and perhaps obliterating their historical identities, Schmitt, Kjersk, and Sawitch have not simply lost their precious indi-viduality: they have ceased being "no one." (The German *Niemand* is stronger.) Instead of the personal finitude which Brecht associates with bearing a particular name, the Agitators' new anonymity allows them to merge with a collective entity whose namelessness is a virtue, an entity which suggests a merging with all of humanity and all being. White European Brecht represents this entity emblematically by reference to the exotic yellow race; in addition he views it during the moments when the defenses of our consciousness and ego are traditionally most open to penetration from outside the self—fever and sleep. Brecht transforms a harsh scene in which men lose their unique human identities into a dream of merging with an undifferentiated yet more permanent extra-human or rather inter-human entity. Again, the participating audience represents in microcosm this human family.

This position of strength allows the Four Agitators to succeed during their revolutionary mission, while the Young Comrade fails. It also justifies their playing all the parts in the play, including the part of the Comrade. At the practical level, this device eliminates audience identification with a particular actor who might be playing the role, an identification which would then extend to the character played; this is particularly true in *The Measures Taken*, for one of the Agitators who plays the Comrade is a woman (played by Helene Weigel in the first production). Because of Brecht's equation between namelessness and pan-humanity, as opposed to the position of being "no one" which he associates with bearing a name, the Comrade's act of ripping off his mask in defiance of the Agitators does not so much serve to demonstrate that he is the only unique individual amongst a chorus of automatons as it exposes the degree to which he is now "no one." In Brecht's 1931 revision of his play, he added a line to one of the speeches of the First Agitator in the last scene which indicates the weakness and transience of the individual man or "no one" when he separates himself from the inter-human entity in which the Agitators have submerged themselves:

> I confess that the face which came out from under the mask was another from that which we had covered with the mask, and the face which the lime will devour another from the face which first greeted us at the border.[26]

After the use of masks, probably the most prominent epic device in the play is narrative statement addressed directly to the Control Chorus (which is also the audience). The Agitators tell the story of the measures they have taken largely in the past-tense, third-person voice. Brief interludes of dialogue interrupt this reportage, during which they play events from the Young Comrade's career. His initial meeting with the Agitators at the frontier outpost and his four tactical errors made during the Mukden propaganda campaign are all played in the dramatic present, the characters talking to one another as if the events were taking place at the present moment. To the extent that no distancing device intrudes into the text during these scenes, Brecht allows the audience to empathize with the Young Comrade's actions, all of which spring from his pity for the Chinese workers' wretched conditions, and the pride which prevents him from collaborating with profiteers for a revolutionary end. (Even though narrative devices do not disturb dramatic empathy during these early scenes, an interlude of "analysis" or "discussion" of the scene's significance *follows* each scene, in which the Control Chorus weighs the evidence presented "dramatically" by the Agitators and decides that in each instance the Comrade has erred. These analytical interruptions disturb and alienate any dramatic continuity *between* the early scenes.)

In the final scene of the Comrade's cross-examination and execution, Brecht makes his dialogue even more "narrative" in quality by adding phrases like "he said" and "we asked" to nearly all the speeches which the characters exchange with each other:

> THREE AGITATORS: Where shall we put you, we asked him.
> YOUNG COMRADE: In the lime pit, he said.
> AGITATORS: We asked: Will you do it alone?
> COMRADE: Help me.
> AGITATORS: We said: Lean your head on our arms
>   Close your eyes
>   We will carry you.
> COMRADE (unseen): He then said:
>   "In the interests of communism
>   Agreeing to [*Einverstanden mit*]
>   the advance of the proletarian
>   masses of all lands
>   Saying Yes to the revolutionizing
>   of the world."[27]

Notice that each "dramatically present" speech is distanced into an elapsed "narrative past" except the Comrade's call for help: if the audience empathizes with the character momentarily, as if he and his predicament were actually present, it empathizes with his acquiesence to the death sentence. By asking for the Agitators' help in the act which will bring about his own death, he has for the first time joined them in a deed which will further the revolutionizing of the world, the cause that he espouses. (In terms of the plot, the Agitators' primary reason for haste in this scene is to return to Mukden to salvage the revolution which the Comrade precipitates prematurely.) The Comrade has not merely agreed to snuff out his own individual existence to aid a collective cause which he had unwittingly obstructed, he actively re-merges with the collectivity and contributes to it through his act of self-sacrifice. Of course, this is better understood generally, on the abstract and ideational level, than it is when viewed by the separate observers as the personal fate of another man. It is a measure of Brecht's artistic skill, not his icy ruthlessness, that he structures the spectator's response to spring from abstract thought rather than felt passion: we see the Comrade at this point as more of a term within a dialectic than as a man who bleeds and weeps. From the perspective of the participating audience at this moment, we examine the Young Comrade's *behavior*, not an individuated man who is to be snuffed out.

We should notice that while Brecht's writing in the execution scene works against our empathy with the Comrade, it actually fosters our sympathy for the Agitators, who for the first time are shown to suffer, doubt, and bewail the fact that they must execute not only a man but a part of their collective entity:

Also beschlossen wir: jetzt
Abzuschneiden den eigenen Fuss vom Körper.
Fruchtbar ist es, zu töten.[28]

("So we decided: forthwith
To cut a foot from the body.
It is a terrible thing to kill.")

Ironically, not until they reach the decision to execute the Comrade do the Agitators display what we conventionally call "emotions," or gain a unique "personality."

But in general in the scene of the Comrade's death, Brecht directs his spectators away from empathy by means of several devices: he does not show the death scene but has his Four Agitators narrate it in four rapid lines of verse; his stage direction instructs the Young Comrade to speak his last words from an unseen position, so that they become disembodied thought and not the dramatic gesture of a hero at the stake. The words themselves do not refer to the Comrade's individuality as character or man but to a system of belief—in fact, they quote the charge given to the Agitators and the Comrade by the leader of the Russian frontier outpost (in scene 2), but in that scene the words are printed as prose, while here Brecht elevates them by printing them in verse form.

Indeed, the finest writing in the play is found in the hymns to communism sung by the Control Chorus (i.e., by the audience). In comparison, the characters' bits of dialogue seem stilted and schematic, appropriate to the "speech patterns" of abstract elements in an argument (which, after all, the characters *are*), but hardly an imitation of men talking. While this style sticks in the mouths of separate characters, it suits the dithyrambic choral passages perfectly. These arias spring from the tradition of the patriotic anthem and the religious hymn; in them Brecht counters abstract hortatory appeals with his particular concreteness of detail, graphic language, and occasional use of his own artificial slang, all of which "stop short" his listeners, break the narcotic effect that abstract diatribe invariably has on its auditors, and force the listeners to examine critically the ideas contained within such exhortations.[29]

Brecht thought highly of the songs he wrote for *The Measures Taken*, and reprinted several of them in collections of his verse. One of the songs, "Praise of Illegal Work," acknowledges the work of the word as weapon of revolution:

Schön ist es
Das Wort zu ergreifen im Klassenkampf.

> Laut and schallend aufzurufen zum Kampf die Massen
> Zu zerstampfen die Unterdrucker, zu befreien die
> Unterdrücken.[30]

> ("It is splendid
> To take up the word as a weapon in the class war
> To rouse the masses to the fight in a loud and ringing voice
> To crush the oppressors
> To free the oppressed.")

The song reflects the conviction that the real work of the Russian team in Mukden is one of education, preparing the intellectual ground from which revolution may spring, and not the autonomous and un-connected offers of material assistance which the Comrade makes to suffering individuals:

> In the city of Mukden, we made propaganda among the workers. We had no bread for the hungry but only knowledge for the igno-rant. Therefore we spoke of the root cause of poverty, did not abolish poverty, but spoke of the abolition of the root cause.[31]

By enclosing the "propagandistic" elements of his play in the heightened language of verse, Brecht implies that "the teachings of the classic writ-ers" and "the ABC of communism" to which the Agitators and Control Chorus constantly refer are "classic" not merely in their ideological content but in their linguistic style as well—that they are works of art, as well as propaganda. (The fullest expression of this belief came in the late forties, when Brecht translated the first paragraphs of *The Com-munist Manifesto* into stirring verse.) In the play's system of values, it is the *word* which acts, not the Comrade's nominal deeds. In fact, his greatest error, the one which directly precedes his unmasking, is not his premature revolution but his rejection of the classic writings: he tears them up and declares that he, not they, constitutes both action and revolution:

> That's no good any more. Looking at the struggle as it is now, I throw away all that was good yesterday, I reject every agreement *with* everybody and do what alone is human. Here is action. I place myself at the head of it. My heart beats for the revolution, and the revolution is here.[32]

In this speech Brecht combines several themes: the Comrade's individ-uality, seen in his repeated use of the pronoun "I" here and in the surrounding speeches, a pronoun which the rest of the play virtually bans;[33] his existence in opposition to the collectivity, rejecting "every agreement with everybody" and believing that he "alone" is human (and that, in this context, it is desirable to be uniquely human); the

Comrade's submission to emotions ("my heart beats for the revolution") and not to rational thought.

But perhaps the Comrade's greatest shortcoming lies in his erroneous
belief that the revolution can be made at this particular moment, that
the revolution "is here," as he puts it. Within the fiction of the plot, this
"moment" and this "here" refer to some time a few weeks or months
short of the ideal time for revolution according to the Agitators' calen-
dar. And within the fiction, it is not so premature that the Agitators
cannot salvage it immediately following the Comrade's death; in fact
the last lines of the play praise the Agitators for taking measures which
brought about a successful revolution.[34] But by using epic distancing
devices which call attention to the theatrical context within which the
Comrade debates with the Agitators about the appropriate time for
revolution, Brecht forces us to see the terms of the argument in a larger
theoretical context. He clarifies them in terms of dialectical process, not
in terms of the history of the Mukden revolution or any other particular
revolution for which we may take this one to be an allegory. Hence
revolution becomes a concretization for that which in Brecht's theater *is
not today*, that which *is not yet*. Earlier in the discussion, we examined
the way in which Brecht's schizoid actor separates himself into
function-as-actor and reality-as-man, and the way in which the "acting" audience participates in this division by extension. The actor-as-
function speaks from the position of the clarified, changed, and "rev-
olutionized" world, a future utopia which is not to be achieved (even
symbolically) within the context of the theater. If it were enacted in the
theater "at this moment" of performance, "here," to quote the Comrade, it would last only as long as the performance lasted: it would be an
artificial solution within the realm of artifice. Brecht wants it to be
enacted in the streets outside his theater. It is from this point of view
that we should examine the response of the Agitators to the Comrade's
statement that the revolution is "here":

> Take a look at reality!
> Your revolution is quickly made and lasts one day
> And is strangled the morning after
> But our revolution begins tomorrow
> Conquers and changes the world.
> Your revolution stops when you stop.
> When you have stopped
> Our revolution marches on.[35]

The Agitators are not just talking tactics—they are speaking from the
position of actor-as-function who stands permanently distanced from
the spectator or recipient of Brecht's artwork, the function from whose
point of view revolution is *always* tomorrow (that is, *not here* in the

theater) and inevitably changes the world. As usual, Brecht counters the Comrade's prose with the Agitators' verse—characteristically, he titles another of their songs "Change the World, It Needs It."

From this closer examination of the play's epic devices we can conclude that Brecht presents the Comrade's weaknesses and the Agitators' virtues more explicitly than his hostile critics have been willing to grant. But should we conclude that Brecht is balancing his arguments so that both antagonistic sides appear in a favorable light, that in fact Brecht has written "the one classic tragedy of Communism which world literature possesses," as Walter H. Sokel puts it?[36] Several of Brecht's best critics have interpreted *The Measures Taken* as a tragedy. For example, Frederic Ewen speculates that many of our reservations about the play stem from political origins, the fact that it is an explicitly communist play. He suggests that the play be "considered abstractly"[37] instead of being seen through the light of a particular ideology (a thought I would like to extend by proposing that the play be seen as an abstract discussion of dialectical process, not as a commentary on any particular political system of values). But Ewen prefers to abstract from the play the Young Comrade's martyrdom, a reading which contributes to the theory of two opposing "good forces" in irreconcilable collision:

> Is not self-sacrifice of the individual in the name of the communal good in a great emergency (say on the battlefield) or in the name of some great religious, social, political or ethical ideal, taken for granted in our society, and eulogized as a high "moral" imperative? Are we not all tacit worshippers of saints? Why then should martyrdom in the name of one cause lead to canonization, and in another to obloquy?[38]

Ewen's rhetorical questions emphasize the uniqueness and virtue of the Young Comrade as opposed to the "communal good" represented by the Agitators and Control Chorus. But Ewen does not take note of the sense in which the Comrade's identity and individuality spring from the pervasive communal entity represented in the play text by the Control Chorus and in the circumstances of performance by the audience—the sense in which, as I have suggested, the Control Chorus is the only character in the play.

Reinhold Grimm carries this reading even further than Ewen, and suggests that the play, in its "contradiction of two absolute values," is tragic in the German classical sense of the word.[39] Grimm concludes that Brecht's unwitting composition of a tragedy of antitheses contributes an irrational element to the play, which cannot be tolerated within a Marxist framework that postulates the rational perfectibility of the world:

[Whereas] Brecht . . . meant to write a purely Marxist drama, he had fallen victim to the dialectics of his own creativity: as a Communist *Lehrstück, The Measures Taken* should have demonstrated the absolute feasibility of the right attitude, yet instead of that it proved, as a tragedy of conflicting duties, the impossibility of doing that which was absolutely just. Since by the nature of its formal structure it will always function to instruct, it provides the spectator either foreground details without meaning, or on the other hand perceptions which must seem highly suspect from the viewpoint of the teaching propounded.[40]

I agree that the play will always function to instruct, but this testifies not so much to the quality of Brecht's writing as it acknowledges that the intellectual implications of the structure of the artwork, and the reception of that work by an audience conscious of itself *as audience,* inevitably lead such an audience into a position of being instructed. Grimm's admission that because of its formal structure the play will always function to instruct is crucial, for if he based his claim for the inevitability of the play's instruction on purely aesthetic grounds, saying that we "have" to learn something from the play because it is so "well-written," hostile audiences could respond that in fact they have learned nothing from the play, just as any critic of the affective aspect of theater performance can always claim that he was not affected by an author's device in the way in which the author intended him to be.

Instead, Grimm implies that the affective potentiality of an artwork must be interpreted as it lies within the exchange between work and recipient which the author structures into the work's ideal presentation to an audience. This separates the work's affective potentiality from the actual effect it has on any particular audience member, who may refuse to be moved by the work or may take an idiosyncratic meaning from the work and hence be instructed incorrectly. But Grimm does not realize that if we assign this affective potentiality to the exchange between work and recipient, we likewise cannot posit it as lying entirely within the *work's* intentionality: it cannot be reduced to an ideological exemplum which can be paraphrased from an examination of the text in isolation. For both these *exclusive* assignments of affective potentiality (exclusively to the work, or exclusively to the recipient) open the doors to a rampant plurality of readings: we should have to acknowledge as equally valid every particular impression the work makes upon audience members, who differ greatly in their attentiveness to the work, their knowledge of its author and its background, and the filtering devices of consciousness which allow different people to notice different aspects of the work as being prominent. We should also have to acknowledge as equally valid the variety of implicit and explicit statements about

behavior in the world proposed within the work (which are often contradictory) and conclude that the affective content of the work (if di-
vorced from its receiving audience) is to instruct us in any one of these
exhortations to action.

Since Grimm does not separate the play's "instruction" from the exclusive realm of the play's text, he extracts what he calls a "teaching"
from this text which, he says, contradicts the antitheses which underlie
the play (the conflicting duties and the opposition of two absolute
values); this contradictory "teaching," he asserts, undermines the rationality of Brecht's world and the degree to which it can be understood
and changed. This is to imply that for Brecht the world which is to be
understood rationally is synonymous with the world of the play's
events—that is, that the alternatives open to us, what we may take as
"teaching," are the same choices open to the characters of his play. But
as we discovered earlier in the examination of Brecht's theoretical
writings, what he believed could be clarified in his theater lies beyond
or between particular events or alternatives within his plays—that is, it
lies in the dialectical process which connects events and alternatives.
The principles of contradiction and antithesis are essential to such a
process; as such, they do not represent an irrational or a tragic element
within *The Measures Taken*. The play's instruction lies less in specific
exhortations about the subjugation of the individual will to the collective good than in a celebration of the process of understanding whereby
such a subjugation is clarified: a process which removes the protagonists from the concrete human realm which can interpret this subjugation as a tragedy, to the realm of abstract thought which sees it as
pure intellectual pattern. Far from falling victim to the dialectics of his
own creativity, as Grimm suggests he does, Brecht uses dialectics to
rescue himself from the position of "instructing us" in the unpalatable
necessity of subjugating our individuality to the collective will. The
circumstances of the *instructing* in Brecht's work—that is, the circumstances of performance, the schizoid split between actor as instructing
function and historical man who acts as learning recipient—these circumstances transmute the individual's subjugation from the status of a
piece of instruction, something to be learned, to the status of a term
within a larger process which leads beyond it. That is to say, we recipients of Brecht's artwork (the actors and audience) are not merely
taught to subjugate our individuality, nor is this subjugation simply
discredited within an ironic or a tragic framework; but we are taught to
come to grips with the contradictory aspects of this subjugation, so that
we may engage our thinking in the larger process of dialectic. Since
Brecht wants this dialectic to extend from the theater into the world and
from thought into action, it is essential that he not conclude it or resolve

it within the terms of the play; hence he never puts us in the position of concluding a judgment about the absolute worth or worthlessness of the terms within this dialectic.

We can notice some indication of this dialectic within the text itself. At the end of the play, the Control Chorus does not express its agreement with and favorable judgment of the Agitators' *completed* act of the Comrade's execution—in fact, the Chorus offers no explicit judgment of it—but instead the Chorus expresses its *Einverständnis* with the *ongoing* process of education into class consciousness and revolution which the Agitators have brought about, the "ABC of communism." (Brecht's subsequent addition of a chorus emphasizing the need to learn from reality in order to change reality strengthens this shift in focus from the Comrade's fate to the ongoing process—see note 34 for this chapter.) Another indication of this shift in emphasis from judgment to instruction can be seen in a textual change which Brecht introduces into the later version of *The Measures Taken*. In Eric Bentley's translation of the version of 1930, Brecht ends the song "Change the World, It Needs It" with the harsh thought that if the dedicated fighter for change must resort to base means to eradicate evil and effect desired change, the final evil which he must eradicate is himself for having stooped to baseness:

> If, finally, you could change the world
> What task would you be too good for?
> Sink down in the filth
> Embrace the butcher
> But change the world: it needs it!
> Who are you?
> Stinking, be gone from
> The room that has been cleaned! Would that
> You were the last of the filth which
> You had to remove![41]

In this version, the Control Chorus rhetorically asks the Agitators who they are in order to suggest that their identities have become inextricably combined with their necessarily base means. And critics who take the play's instruction to lie in the various exhortations within the text might rightly interpret this self-destructive contradiction as tragic. But when he rewrote the play in 1931, following its unfavorable reception, Brecht eliminated the last five lines of this song and substituted lines which indicate an understanding of the Agitators' means, not a condemnation of them:

> No longer do we listen to you as
> Judges. Already
> As Learners.

(Lange nicht mehr hören wir euch zu als
Urteilende. Schon
Als Lernende.)[42]

Both passages are linguistically brilliant and poetically multivalent, and it would be hard to choose between them on purely aesthetic grounds. But Brecht wisely alters this passage to remove the sense of completion of the dialectic of change inherent in the earlier version, the sense in which the dialectic of the eradication of baseness requires the Agitators to eradicate themselves, and substitutes an ongoing educative process by which the dialectic results in the Agitators being remade, not eliminated.

The sense in which Brecht uses circumstances which could be viewed as tragic *within the play* to contribute to a dialectical process which moves beyond tragic *in the play's ideal performance* suggests an avenue beyond the conclusions of Walter H. Sokel in his important essay, "Brecht's Split Characters and His Sense of the Tragic." There, Sokel concludes that "Communism is not exempt from the tragic contradiction between ends and means; it cannot overcome the tragic condition of man. On the contrary, Communism is for Brecht the tragic hero par excellence."[43] Sokel arrives at this conclusion through an insightful examination of the contradictions inherent in the many split characters in Brecht's plays and adds the useful suggestion that the "hero" of *The Measures Taken*, Communism, is another schizophrenic assemblage consisting of the Young Comrade's natural and spontaneous aspects (analogous to Shen Te of *The Good Woman of Setzuan*) and the Four Agitators' deliberate and planning aspects (analogous in Sokel's parallel to Shui Ta). Accordingly, Sokel says, the Agitators " must suppress and kill goodness in order to prepare its actualization."[44] Within the framework of the play, this is so. But we have already seen that Brecht demands that we understand his plays from the circumstances of their performance. By extending Sokel's concept of split or schizophrenic character to the idea of the schizoid actor, we discovered that tragic contradiction within a given character becomes translated in a Brechtian production into generative contradiction in the future-directed opposition between actor and audience. That is, the act of portraying through divisive means (*Verfremdungseffekte*) a character divided within himself serves to initiate within an audience watching this portrayal a translation of the audience's understanding of contradiction as "tragic"—fixed, inevitable, part of the human condition which must be accepted—into the concept of contradiction as dialectical—changing and changeable, in a future which extends beyond the artwork and the theater in which this understanding is initiated, not completed.

Sokel concludes that the essence of tragedy in Brecht's work lies in his split characters, in the paradoxical relationship "in which the pseudo-self must destroy the true self in order to fulfill it . . . . It is primarily the tragedy of those who, like Brecht himself, seek to eliminate tragedy from this world."[45] Sokel derives his concepts "true self" and "pseudo-self" directly from *The Measures Taken:* he claims that the Young Comrade has to hide his "true face" under a mask, and the "pseudo-self" of the Agitators and Control Chorus (the self implied by the mask or the emblem of yellow skin) is inferior to this true face beneath the mask, which it eventually denies, opposes, and finally kills. In other words, Sokel equates the pseudo-self or the mask with base means, which conspire to destroy good ends, and he equates these good ends with the true self or face under the mask. We have already noticed that Brecht's description of the anonymous yellow faces which mask the Agitators is far more ambiguous and seductive than Sokel's formula suggests, and that Brecht's description of the mutability of the Comrade's face when he unmasks himself undercuts the "trueness" of this face in Sokel's scheme. But beyond this, the discussion of mask and face points toward the theatricalist understanding which we have argued for in Brecht. Mask and face are paradigms for the two aspects of the self-divided Brechtian actor, and, in *The Measures Taken*, every audience member is also an actor. Brecht did not attempt to choose between the antitheses, but instead subsumed them into a larger dialectic that does not resolve the fact that they are in conflict but freezes them into a permanent and creative tension, oriented toward the future, the world, continuing revolution, the *not yet.* He was not interested in eliminating tragedy from the world, only from the theater—in his affective theater, *that* measure suffices—and his use of the schizoid actor was his primary means of accomplishing this.

And yet the fact remains that after Brecht wrote *The Measures Taken* and a few lesser *Lehrstücke,* he retreated from the extreme kind of audience participation in which the acting audience is considered to be co-equal with the actor in terms of creation of the artwork and engagement in the dialectic of "schizophrenia." In his later and most admired plays Brecht confines the split of personality and function to the character within the play and the actor portraying it, and consequently creates his "most rounded" and "fullest" characters—Galileo, Mother Courage, Azdak, and the like. And it must be admitted that fascinating as the patterns of abstract thought are in *The Measures Taken*, they are created at the expense of individualized and memorable characterizations; indeed, these would tend to make the thought-pattern repulsive. We can only speculate about why Brecht abandoned the epic extreme of the *Lehrstücke*, but one explanation may lie in the difficulty inherent in the "learning" to be taken from them. Contrary to the assertions of most of the hostile readers of *The Measures Taken*, the "ABC of communism" which as a theater event the play attempts to instruct and effect upon its audience is not a fanatical or simplistic homily about the individual's noble martyrdom to the collective, but a complicated dialectic among all the constituent terms within the phenomenology of performance: character, actor, audience; artwork and recipient—all self-divided in creative schizophrenia, or as Brecht put it at the end of his "Short Organum for the Theatre," all interacting within a relationship of "mutual alienation."[46] If something is to be learned from a didactic play, Brecht might have concluded, it must be incorporated into a dramatic form which is simpler to understand as a dynamic entity than the complex machinery of *The Measures Taken*. Otherwise, the play's learning is open to misinterpretation, as the history of its status among the critics manifests. One direction beyond the *Lehrstück* is the kind of drama found in Brecht's last plays, in which the complicated division of function once demanded of the acting audience becomes internalized in richer and more complex characters. Another direction is the elaboration of performance theory which educates the reading public about its role within Brecht's theater and speculates on the ideal audiences which it seeks to create as recipients for his artwork; this is the direction of the "Short Organum" and the model-books which provide historical documentation of the elaborately rehearsed productions undertaken by the Berliner Ensemble.

Another direction is inherent within Brecht's philosophical reasons for eliminating tragedy from the theater, along with solutions to the problems which his plays pose. It is inherent within his radical but partial examination of the actor's and audience's function within creation and reception of the artwork, and inherent within his experimentation with affective theater, with didactic plays which are so complicated in terms of the contradictions of the components within their performance that we do not seek a rational understanding from their verbal texts but trust in our being "affected into" an understanding by engaging in their performance. This is the direction of Artaud and Grotowski, who attempt to lead their audiences into a new understanding of themselves strictly by means of engagement in and contemplation of theatrical performance, not from examination of plays as texts from which we may extract rational understanding or "meaning." Artaud refers to this affective education as our need to absorb metaphysics through the skin. His disciple Grotowski arrives at a performance theory which attempts to understand the phenomenon (and artworks which attempt to personify and instigate it) by completing Brecht's partial incorporation of the audience into the artwork as creative component. Just as Brecht posits a theory of alienated acting which often stands in contradiction to the apparent "meaning" of his written works, and demands that we accommodate both of these into our understanding of his creation, Grotowski posits a theater which stands in creative confrontation with the play texts which it selects from the repertories of the past. And like Brecht in his deliberate introduction of hostility toward the audience by means of alienation effects and the schizoid actor, Grotowski explores to its logical conclusion the implications of conflict between actor and audience. (Indeed, the Grotowski-inspired "performance theater" of the last two decades, depending as it often does on audience co-creation of the theater event, overt didactic content with "guerilla theater" intervention into public affairs, and performances springing out of unique social/political subcultures, is strong evidence for the fecundity of the *Lehrstück* idea, and its legitimate heir; in some ways, it has proved to be—as Brecht predicted just before he died—the form of the theater of the future.) Finally, we shall see that Brecht's intellectual attempt to eliminate tragedy from the theater stands behind a more recent attempt to exhaust and eliminate through this exhaustion the function of theater itself.

PART III

**Toward Catharsis
of Actor and
Audience in the
Theater of Cruelty
and the
Poor Theater**

5. Artaud and Grotowski
The Theater as Separate Reality

The evolution of modern acting theory can be traced through the degree to which an acting style addresses its audience. Stanislavski grants his actor and audience a share in the creative process through affective memory, but his actor remains oblivious to the audience, disguising his theatrical context in an attempt to further the illusion of the character's reality. Brecht's actor turns toward his audience: addressing it from the position of *Verfremdung*, the actor acknowledges that participation by actor and audience in the theater event constitutes their creative share in it. Most recently, theoreticians of theater have suggested that this participation constitutes the core of theater. Far from admitting actor and audience into their theories in a partial or begrudging way, they argue that actor and audience, in essence, are all there is. Instead of speaking from within a character, as in Stanislavskian acting, or stepping outside of it, as in Brecht's theater, their actors stand in place of traditional characters, and address the audience directly. Conservative critics may view these phenomena as fatal to mimetic art, and the student of dramatic literature probably still gasps when he examines Artaud's polemics against written texts or Grotowski's radical reshaping of classic dramas. Despite these fears, the directness of address of actor to audience in modern theater and the primacy of actor and audience in its creation and meaning are logical conclusions of tendencies inherent in modern theater tradition; even total rejection of the tradition is well within the tradition. In spite of much confrontation with the classics and calls for no more masterpieces, provocative aesthetic theory and multivalent new works continue to emerge—"art objects" if not proper "texts" of dramatic literature.

Another gauge of modern acting is its temporal orientation. We noted that Stanislavski's technique of affective memory evoked the past of character, actor, and audience, while Brecht's defamiliarization oriented them toward the future. Both orientations suggest a dissatisfaction with the present and a belief that theater's affective or even "therapeutic" value lies somewhere other than in the here and now. Stanislavski's actor recapitulates the process of psychoanalysis in the belief that formative and authentic reality lies behind him, and that art is part homage to what has gone before, part manipulation of it to rid it

111

of trauma and thus permit contentment in the present. Brecht's actor believes conversely that authentic life is yet to come; he recapitulates the process of dialectic so that art may point out and even move us away from present discontentment toward liberation in the future. The new theoreticians, however, posit both theater's temporal orientation and its affectivity in the present, in its "presence." The fact that the theater event takes place and exists here and now becomes central to their thinking, and they react against any imitation of a reality which might have transpired before, and even against theoretical speculation about the direction of the future.

The new theater creates an uncomfortable situation for the historian of aesthetics. First of all, the movement is far from over, and it may produce additional theoretical works which will supplant the writings which I take to be most indicative and central, those of Artaud and Grotowski. And it would certainly be a premature judgment to give the status of classic to any artwork within this movement. Although I will discuss two theater pieces by Grotowski and Peter Handke as exemplary works, I recognize that both men have years of creative work before them and may surpass these early achievements. Another critical problem lies in these artists' orientation toward the present. It would be folly to inquire into a projected outcome for this experimentation, and, aside from the impossibility of predicting the future evolution of an art movement, its leaders, particularly Grotowski, refuse on principle to speculate about the nature of their coming work. A historical placing of this movement within its tradition does not yield much enlightenment either, other than the discovery that the movement is conscious of and stands at least in confrontation with all that has gone before in theater history, beginning with primitive ritual—a facile observation which the movement's leaders acknowledge anyway.

Yet because of this theater movement's resistance to speculation about its past and future, the theater historian should feel a responsibility toward documenting it; taking place as they do in a present which is constantly renewed and yet repeatedly effaced by the act of performance, both "meaning" and "art object" vanish from the record. In the case of Grotowski's *Apocalypsis cum figuris,* no independent text exists; after the work is dropped from the Laboratory Theater repertory, it can never be reproduced by another company. And although a play like Handke's *Offending the Audience* possesses a full text—indeed, having abandoned character, plot, and action, it consists of nothing but words—still, the work's meaning emerges only from a consideration of what actually transpires between an actor reciting these words and an audience receiving them. The fact that most audiences have been offended by Handke and have occasionally stopped the performance of his play must be considered as part of the theater event he created: in this sense, although Handke's play theoretically "has the same words" in every production, the theater event governed by these words should be seen as a composite of all performances.

Michael Kirby has suggested that the theater historian creates a "surrogate performance," through which a reader may construct what his own experience would have been had he been a spectator of the performance.[1] Aside from fulfilling the need for objective documentation of transient artworks, the critic has a more creative function. Since, more and more, theater art takes meaning from and comes into existence because of the circumstance of its being performed in the presence of an audience, the critic's creation of a "surrogate performance" turns him into something of a "surrogate audience" as well, an "audience" which can bring about and feel an artwork's ideal effect, and which can further this affectivity in others, the critic's readers, even after the work (in the sense of it being an "art object") has ceased to exist. Ironically, the fragile entity of affectivity, at the core of modern art and yet always in danger of not being felt, not being understood, and not being recorded, emerges as the permanent aspect of the theater event, surviving long after the work's presence in performance, and its creators and its auditors, have vanished.

What shall we call this new theater?—for we certainly cannot call it that. Naming this theater proves to be more of a problem than in the cases of Stanislavski and Brecht; in fact, because of its newness and its problematic nature, no single descriptive name for it has become widely accepted. A critic can be comfortable with conventional appelations like "naturalism" and "epic theater." Both terms had been established in literary history before theater directors took them over. Naturalism as a movement was known throughout Europe from the theoretical statements and novels of Zola, Strindberg, and many others; although never bound by any terminology, Stanislavski tentatively referred to his work as "spiritual naturalism." And before Brecht "refunctioned" the concept of epic for theater, Goethe and Schiller had attempted to distinguish between the epic and dramatic genres in their theoretical writings, while more recently Piscator and Döblin tended to merge them. Both Stanislavski and Brecht eventually moved beyond their own terminologies, and in my analysis of their thought I have found it convenient to coin a phrase to indicate Stanislavski's main direction—the theater of affective memory—and to inflate a late notion of Brecht's to indicate the ultimate direction of his work—the dialectical theater. But no single "conventional" or "creative" term serves for the new theater.

Many terms have been offered as partial descriptions. Artaud named both a theory and a short-lived production company "the theater of cruelty," a widely misunderstood metaphor which its creator himself failed to define. Yet one of its associations points us toward this theater's aggressive effect upon its audience and its demand that the audience participate in an almost masochistic way to achieve both enlightenment and therapy. Grotowski calls his producing unit an "Institute of Actor's Research" and a "Laboratory Theater," terms which refer to the experimental nature of his work—an aspect common to all avant-garde activity since the nineteenth century—and to the centrality of mediation by means of the actor's performance, an aspect particularly characteristic of this movement we are trying to name. The term Grotowski used to designate his activity described in his theoretical book *Towards a Poor Theatre* also suggests this concern with performance, for a "poor theater" is one which is stripped of any element not deemed essential to the theater event, which for Grotowski consists of the confrontation between actor and audience.

"Poor theater" also suggests the minimalist tendency or *reductio* quality which is being felt in the plastic arts, music, film, and literature—notably, through the work of Beckett, Pinter, and Handke, to mention only playwrights. This striving after a minimum of the essential qualities of theater results in a phrase like "the empty space," which Peter Brook used to title both a book and a production company. "I can take any empty space and call it a bare stage," claimed Brook in the book's first (and best) sentence;[2] he points to a phenomenon of theater architecture which has broader implications for our understanding of space in dramaturgy and in general aesthetics. Concern with empty space suggests the disavowal of an autonomous site of theatrical activity—a rejection of both the stage setting and of the auditorium, if the setting be understood as a scenic mimesis of some place other than what it is (a stage with decorations), and the auditorium be understood as an assembly hall set apart from the world and having no other function than that of paying homage to such mimesis. Instead of this separation, the empty space asks for a continuity between theater event and life event—that is, it claims that the theater event is a *kind* of life event, not a *copy* of one. And its more general aesthetic implication is to require us to pay as close attention to the empty space surrounding and shaped by the art object as we pay to the object itself; this tendency was initiated much earlier in poetry (Mallarmé), music (silences, dodecaphony), and the plastic arts (impressionism, minimalism, environmental sculpture), yet the theater's belated concern with space has had the benefit of building on these earlier discoveries to produce a theory which links a work's affectivity with its spatiality, a concretization of the intangible quality of affectivity.

The antimimetic nature of theater space suggests an argument with Aristotle, who initiated literary and theater criticism with the contention that tragedy is an imitation of an action. Much of the new terminology argues specifically with Aristotle's vocabulary. Rejecting the formal and aesthetically completable concept of dramatic *action*, recent theoreticians have called for the centrality of *activity*; not, as Aristotle had it, "what might happen," a probable and universally applicable action, but "what happens," the fragmentary, contingent, time-bound, and unrepeatable activities which have the advantage of being real, not ideal. Opposing Aristotelian action, Richard Schechner terms these unique happenings "actuals";[3] Allan Kaprow simply calls them "Happenings." For Schechner, theatrical space is actual space found in life and not in auditoriums, which the director and performers shape into a significant environment which is unique for the given production and yet still partakes of its nontheatrical function "in life." Schechner's own work ranges from examination of village space which is transformed into theatrical space during certain aboriginal rituals—one kind of "actual"—to his own transformation of a New York garage into the Performing Garage, the space in which his company, the Performance Group, plays its rather different "actuals"; more recently, Schechner has referred to this work as "environmental theater," a term which embraces both the theatricalizing of spaces-at-hand and the holistic overtones of the enviromental movement (the social community at one with the biosphere, a concept stemming in part from the belief systems of primitive cultures, another of Schechner's interests).[4] Kaprow's Happening movement, which flourished in the early sixties, emphasized the environmental setting surrounding both performers and spectators, a setting partially "found" in life and partially constructed by both parties during the course of the Happening. The Happenings were also paradigms of nonrepeatability in theater performance, for they had no texts, and their massive, often self-destructive spectacular effects necessitated their being done only once; but beyond this technical limitation, other nonrepeatable phenomena were intrinsic to the genre, especially improvisation, chance, use of found settings and found objects, and spectator participation which resulted on occasion in the use of "found performers."

The participial construction of the term "happening" points to this theater's concern with the present moment of performance, what is happening "now." This radical contemporaneity informed both the name of America's most prominent experimental theater during the fifties and sixties—the Living Theater—and the title of its most extreme attempt at involving the audience in performance and even saving it by participation—*Paradise Now*.

The term "living theater"—another participial construction—refers to the actuality of contingent activity as opposed to the imitativeness of ideal action; on another level, it refers to Stanislavski's goal of a life in and through art. At its height, the communal nature of the company's life-style probably achieved the Russian director's goal of a theatrical commune, even though Stanislavski would have shunned the particular shape that commune took. The Living Theater's didactic ends and confrontational tactics also indicate Brecht's influence: its directors, Julian Beck and Judith Malina, had been students of Piscator, and they shaped *Paradise Now* as a dialectical progression through various stages of consciousness which should engage the audience's participation and cause it literally to move the play's ideology out of the theater and into the streets—where audience members were sometimes arrested by the police, which is one tangible instance of affectivity in modern theater! Though Beck and Malina employed certain *Verfremdungseffekte* and the form of the dialectic in their work, the mystical content which fleshed out this form partook more of Artaud's spirit and language than of Marxism or dialectical materialism. In his book *The Life of the Theatre*, Beck acknowledges that his theater's therapeutic and affective qualities were more spiritual than intellectual or ideological.[5] The title of the book points to the aesthetic quality of contemporaneity and to an assumption that theater is a part of life—not an ideally typical imitation of some aspect of life, but a particular and separate aspect of life itself. It is a part (not a representation) of reality, but, in effect, a separate reality.

If the Living Theater attempted to realize the impossible project of Artaud, another company working in the sixties provided an American translation of the more realizable goals of Grotowski. Joseph Chaikin left the Living Theater before the creation of *Paradise Now* to found the Open Theater, a company which Grotowski has publicly admired (and which he briefly instructed in his techniques). An "open" theater suggests experimentation and sensitivity to the concept of space, typical traits of the avant-garde, but the term also may refer to the actor's stance toward his audience—in proscenium staging, an "open" acting position means that the actor faces the audience directly; but Chaikin's term is metaphoric, implying beyond a scenographic position the actor's openness of self toward his audience, his addressing of the audience directly in his own personality, as well as through the fact that he is an actor. The title of Chaikin's theater memoirs, *The Presence of the Actor*,[6] reflects Grotowski's *reductio* of theater event to confrontation between actors and audience, contemporaneity (in that "presence" indicates "present-ness"), and the therapeutic, even messianic aspect of what Grotowski calls "the holy theater," fraught not with background but with "presence."

All these theoretical terms, metaphoric names for acting companies, and visionary book titles provide partial descriptions of the new genre. They travel through different avenues of thought—contemplation of scenic and aesthetic space; orientation toward play-time, stage-time, and the time during which affectivity occurs; investigation of actual activity and mimetic action—but the catchphrases all argue with Aristotle (or our misassumptions about him) to propose a concept of theater event which finds its meaning and being in performance, not in literary encapsulation, the preservation of which has prompted the writing of so many poetics. Since its spokesmen find performance so central, this theater might well be called "performance theater." Some critics have used the phrase, yet none has provided a thorough discussion of the term's implications;[7] I will adopt it occasionally but try to avoid the schematic comparisons which make such terms necessary. Perhaps we will have to wait for the movement's demise to learn its name—and, in fact, the potential demise of theater as such is one of the theoretical assumptions behind much of this new activity.

If "performance theater" must serve for this discussion, our wariness of the term indicates another aspect of the phenomena it encompasses—its antiliterary orientation. The term "naturalism" was promulgated by literary critics and novelists, and the theater took it over relatively later; talking about the "epic" qualities of theater connects it with a specifically literary and specifically nondramatic genre, the epic, a genre discussed as such by Aristotle and also standing conveniently at the very beginning of Western literature. But performance theater wants no canonization by means of association with the classical genres; its cry is "no more masterpieces," in Artaud's words, and if Grotowski's behavior subsequent to his theoretical books sets a trend, this cry may be expanded to "no more poetics, either."

In the mid-sixties, we might have referred (perhaps uncomfortably) to all the new activity as "theater of the absurd."[8] But today Martin Esslin's provocative phrase brings to mind a school of playwriting which seems to have receded if not terminated with the publication of his study. The metaphor behind Esslin's term comes from existentialism in general and Camus's essay *The Myth of Sisyphus* in particular. "Absurd" theater still referred to literary theater, or at least to a philosophical movement whose greatest documents are imaginative works, not books of technical philosophy—and we ought to recall that "naturalism" first referred to a philosophical movement, too. But "absurdist" is far less neutral a descriptive word than "naturalistic." Although the word has a technical meaning to Camus and Esslin, its ironic and provocative connotations suggest the orientation of absurdist theater to aggressivity toward its audience. This trait brings it closer to performance theater, the aggressivity of which demands a reaction from— that is, participation by—its audience. But when we reflect upon the great "absurd" plays, we notice that, although they discuss the problems faced by performance theater, such as being-on-the-stage (*Waiting for Godot*) or the creation of an interhuman church by means of profanation of sacraments (Gombrowicz's *The Marriage*), their formal innovations are literary, not theatrical, and they are enshrined in lasting texts which have already become part of the canon of masterpieces. We should note that absurdist playwrights occasionally incorporate their ideas about life-as-performance in new literary forms which are objective correlatives of the ideas themselves (Beckett, Genet, and Pinter do this; Camus and Sartre do not). But the formal innovation is as much literary as it is theatrical. Moreover, the theater of the absurd has provided no innovative theory of dramaturgy or of acting style. This is not so surprising when we consider that most of the plays in its canon are extreme parodies of naturalism (Ionesco sends up Strindberg's "arranged naturalism," while Beckett parodies the extreme concept of *tranche de vie* suggested but never realized by Zola, which was to document each minute and banal occurrence of daily life)—or they are parodies of epic dramaturgy and ideology, as in the case of Genet's more political plays. But before we depart from the theater of the absurd, I should note that my description does not disparage a canon of fascinating texts which is the outcome and to a certain extent the combination of two literary movements but is not a new kind of "theater event" in itself. It must be recalled that "the theater of the absurd" received its name and status as a movement from a literary critic, not a writer—which was not the case with "naturalism" and "epic theater"—and that all the leading playwrights within this reluctant "movement" deny that they belong to any particular school.

Returning to performance theater, I would contend that it is the new theatrical movement which succeeds naturalism and epic theater, if we agree that a new theatrical movement results in a new dramaturgy and acting style as well as a new subgenre of literary texts. For though "absurd theater" has produced more great works of literature while still preserving aggressivity toward and doubt of the literary artifact, performance theater has done more than to provide an extreme exploration of the *reductio* which calls for the abolition of literary texts and finally of the theater itself. Paradoxically, there has begun to emerge a canon of literary texts *within* performance theater, and at least Peter Handke's dramas should survive the movement as classics, not just exemplary works. Is it a coincidence that he begins his playwriting career with the most extreme *reductio* of the play as both dramatic literature and theater event, and then proceeds beyond *Offending the Audience* to write a series of plays which all deal with theatrical life reduced to its reality of being-on-the-stage (the position reached at the end of the *reductio*), each of which is richer and more expansive than the last?

I have discussed performance theater at this length because the movement is still ongoing and largely unrecorded—which is not the case with naturalism and epic theater—and because the central texts of an ongoing movement are not as apparent as are the landmarks of a spent period of cultural history. I believe that the seminal theories and exemplary works have emerged or will emerge from the creators discussed in this introduction. To narrow my discussion, I will make some critical and some arbitrary choices. It would certainly be folly to imply that so diverse a movement could be traced to the inspiration of one man. It would also be folly to deny that if performance theater were to have one saint, one exemplar, one central actor whose life was affected by and even merged with the project and *oeuvre* of performance theater, this holy actor's name would be Antonin Artaud.

The Theater of Antonin Artaud

Artaud, poet and madman. To date, more has been made of his madness than his poetry, even in the theater, the field in which his suggestions are most concrete. Pehaps the programmatic nature of *The Theater and Its Double* (*Le Théâtre et son double*, 1936) accounts for this phenomenon in which theater groups stage his scenarios, laboriously reconstruct the plastic and scenographic effects he described, and in general "apply" Artaud rather than respond to him as a poetic inspiration. And his critics further the popular image of mad Artaud, reveling in his troubled life, or, when they become specific, recounting his assaults upon the Paris avant-garde and its audience during the twenties and thirties, as if to suggest that the particular "shock techniques" Artaud invented for theater, poetry, and film could still startle an audience today. In their small way, monograph writers and theater archivists contribute to current tendencies to apply Artaud literally, rather than to demonstrate how his thought might inspire philosophical speculation. I cannot argue with the value of this historical scholarship when it documents an art movement which is both "modern" and rapidly fading from our memory. But since the work of Jerzy Grotowski, the position of "applying Artaud" rather than being inspired by him has become unacceptable, for the Polish director, in his essays and in his stage practice, has demonstrated how Artaud's thought may be continued. Grotowski is Artaud's best critic in both aspects of theater work, although he had laid the grounds for his own theory and practice before he first read *The Theater and Its Double* (in 1964, according to Raymonde Temkine).[9] Clearly, he would understand Peter Brook, who argues:

> Artaud applied is Artaud betrayed: betrayed because it is always just a portion of his thought that is exploited, betrayed because it is easier to apply rules to the work of a handful of dedicated actors

than to the lives of the unknown spectators who happened by chance to come through the theatre door.[10]

Grotowski has not written a synoptic study of Artaud's thought which maps out its overarching implications for performance in general; instead, his writing demonstrates that he has internalized this overview and worked out from it. So, though I shall pay some attention to his fine essay on Artaud entitled "He Wasn't Entirely Himself," I proceed on the assumption that his study has more significance for his own theater work than for our objective and historical knowledge of Artaud's own project.

Grotowski is in agreement with Brook's argument in two other respects. He has refrained from a partial application of Artaud's technical innovations; in fact, he rejects the eclecticism which turns to Artaud or any theater theorist to see what it can "use." Grotowski even manages to demonstrate the flaw behind all of Artaud's frantic barrage of technological effects, the impulse toward "total theater," while he isolates the sense in which Artaud's thought is a total coming-to-grips with the essential elements of theatrical experience. And, perhaps more important, Grotowski's theoretical work with audience involvement has pointed out the way in which a *metteur-en-scène*—a director who oversees all the production elements, scenography, text, and audience configuration—can structure and ideally affect the being if not the behavior of those "unknown spectators" who chance to come through his theater door. My discussion of Artaud and Grotowski will emphasize Grotowski's elaboration of Artaudian catharsis, the way he has made the French poet's intuitive notion of affectivity concrete and local by linking it to an idea of spatiality—a sense of space which itself has roots in Artaud. The Polish theater thinker asks us to turn our attention away from historical considerations of influence, such as the particular technical application he himself makes of Artaud (or of Stanislavski or Brecht, all of whom he acknowledges), and to contemplate, very intellectually but also passionately, the essence of an affirmation Artaud thought so much of that he had it printed in bold-face type: **"Inspiration certainly exists."**[11]

Artaud compiled *The Theater and Its Double* in 1936 at the very end of his engagement in practical theater production. He wrote the essays collected in this volume over the preceding six years, which spanned the founding and dissolution of two theater companies and his most famous production, *The Cenci*. Both the Theater Alfred Jarry and the Theater of Cruelty company exhausted their funds after a few productions; Artaud thought *The Cenci* was only a partial exploration of the concept of theater of cruelty, but it concluded the activity of the company of that name after only seventeen performances. Artaud managed to antagonize his co-workers and his audiences long before he ran out of money. But from the point of view of *The Theater and Its Double*, we are led to a more neutral evaluation of his practical achievement: his companies ran their course rather than failing; or, their failure in actuality and the impossibility of deriving a concrete practice from his theoretical assumptions resulted in Artaud's finding a way to incorporate failure and impossibility in a positive theory of art. After *The Theater and Its Double*, he abandoned theater for other pursuits. He wrote poetry, lectured, cultivated drug hallucinations in Mexico, where he studied the Tarahumara Indians, and spent the war years in an insane asylum. Some would say that through public behavior—lectures, readings, and life-style itself—he found the purest concretization for the theater of cruelty in his own life. Others simply note that he went mad.

No matter what kind of inspiration we take from his later career, I think we can agree that his theater work stops with *The Theater and Its Double*. After this book, Artaud loses interest in any concrete sense of theater, and he loses contact with his concept of "the double," a force in life (perhaps an ideal audience) which exists outside of and apart from the artwork and the actor considered as work of art, a double which the actor-as-artwork confronts and from which he takes meaning and existence. In short, Artaud loses a sense of audience and of "the Other," and focuses all his attention upon himself. He writes poems in an invented glossolalic language. When he uses denotative language, he discusses his bodily organs and functions in graphic detail, while he protests that man is ruled by so vile a thing as the human body. Meantime, he coins a metaphor for this self-inspiration: creativity is growing inside him, like a new organ; in fact, Artaud is dying painfully of a cancer of the rectum. Finally he writes a long and bitter poem called "I hate and renounce as a coward . . ." in which he contends:

> I do not consent to not having created my body myself, and I hate and renounce as a coward every being who consents to live without first having created himself . . . who agrees with the idea of a god, at the origin of his being as at the origin of his thought.[12]

Days later, he was dead.

Artaud valued the idea of the double enough to incorporate it into the title of his most lucid book, and when he abandoned the idea, his work and his life changed considerably. The double lies behind all his theater work and, as an ideal, it results in a theater which exists only as a mental act. Having come to an idealistic conclusion on theater practice, Artaud proceded to explore the implications of completely internalized thought and activity—an exploration which can bear fruit for a study of extremism in avant-garde art theory (this is the route of A. Alvarez in *The Savage God: A Study of Suicide*), or it can motivate a study of mental derangement (the route of moralistic critics who find that Artaud confuses cruelty with evil, or who note that his theory of homeopathic catharsis is a psychological and philosophical error).[13] Neither avenue is open to the theater worker: if he is committed to an ideal sense of audience which emerges from repeated confrontations with concrete audiences, and to a sense of performance which gives meaning and existence itself to that entity known as "dramatic literature," then he remains on the earlier side of the chronological watershed marked by Artaud's concept of the double. Seeking the double, he finds theater.

But nowhere in *The Theater and Its Double* does he find a definition of the concept. Artaud in his evolution had already moved so far away from the double that he neglected to elaborate upon it in his book. His most specific statement about the double comes from a letter written to Jean Paulhan in 1936, in which Artaud explains his choice of a title for his collection of essays about theater. "If the theatre is the double of life," he writes, "life is the double of the true theatre."[14] Platonism permeates this aphorism, just as it runs through all his notions that result in an ideal, nonconcrete, and impossible theater—and underlies his violent animus against any "possible theater" that tells lies or, as Susan Sontag points out, *becomes* a lie by becoming a masterpiece consecrated by society.[15] But when we analyze the aphorism which motivates his intuition of the double, we note that it only appears to fall into the idealized three-level hierarchy of Platonic rejection of imitation. Artaud might have followed the logic of Book 10 of *The Republic*, and stated that life is an imitation at one remove of an ideal form ("true theater"), and that mere "theater" introduces another level of removal by imitating life. Instead, Artaud introduces the double to convert the three terms into a dialectical process which moves from theater to life back to theater, and by this process returns to a theater renewed and made "true" by the encounter with life.

Artaud would have to agree with Aristotle, who posited his *Poetics* on the assumption that we know the ideal forms, and that they come into existence, only through a contemplation of concrete instances—in this case, plays. But he resists Aristotle's tendency to deduce categories for the classification of these instances, which in turn results in canonizing certain plays which fit these categories as "masterpieces." Artaud's interest lies completely in the moment in which the theater comes into authentic existence, the moment in which it shares or "doubles" the authenticity of life, which in turn causes our consciousness of authentic life to acknowledge or "to double" the "truth" of theater, that is, to recognize that our consciousness of authentic life has come about through participation in theater.

I admit that this is a highly idiosyncratic understanding of the word "double," and no evidence exists to prove that Artaud intended the word to function as a verb which bears two such diverse meanings. Contemplating such a crux as Artaud's aphorism about the double, a critic echoes with relief Grotowski's caveat that "Artaud explains the unknown by the unknown, the magic by the magic";[16] we shall see that Artaud's alogical impulse causes Grotowski to make a similarly asemantic (and highly fruitful) reading of another crux, Artaud's suggestion that we be like sacrificial victims, burnt at the stake but still signalling through the flames. But maddening (or inspiring) as a careful analysis of any Artaud phrase may be, a general sense of the phrase about the double emerges from *The Theater and Its Double*. In the case of "the double," the process of experiencing authenticity through participation in theater has something to do with affectivity—variously referred to as "catharsis," "purgation," "purification," and even linked by metaphor to the "infective" quality of the plague. If we ask what is affected, and by whom, the aphorism about the double responds that engagement in theater is one means of authenticating life, and that the achievement of authenticity in life is a means of discerning that which is "true" about theater. Each affects the other, and the operation is simultaneous, not progressive. The fact that this conversion of affectivity into authenticity must be instantaneous accounts for Artaud's maddening, circular argument, his nearly solipsistic form which serves as a concrete embodiment of a nonlinear process (at the expense of violating the linear quality of syntax). And since the process is instantaneous, it immediately falls into inauthenticity and must be renewed. In terms of mental activity, Artaud does not allow his thought as it is expressed in the linear progress of words to complete its journey along that route before he forces it to return to and renew its origins, to double back upon itself before it has played itself out, at the same time as he sets up the possibility of an *uncompleted* thought-route whose *potential* shape and *actual* emptiness both give meaning to the necessity of doubling back. In the more concrete terms of actual artworks, Artaud resists any impulse to argue through an Aristotelian "hierarchy of actualizations"[17] of the elements of dramatic poetry that would result in his acknowledging an artwork as a masterpiece: as soon as our consciousness of the artwork reaches this stage, it loses authenticity, and he rejects the work with the cry of "no more masterpieces."

Yet Artaud realizes that the temptation towards canonization is inherent in our orientation toward *any* artwork, not just the standard classics (he mentions, of course, *Oedipus*) and not even the "counter-tradition" of plays which in his more prosaic moments he proposes to produce (*Ubu roi, Woyzeck, Arden of Ferversham, The Revenger's Tragedy*, all plays which his epigones have recently revived). The temptation towards "finalizing" a work as a classic exists in relation to *every* artwork, a discovery which motivates Artaud's contention that written poetry should be read once and then be destroyed. It also motivates the fact that as *metteur-en-scène* Artaud produced no play which completely satisfied his idea of a theater of cruelty, and that as playwright he left no "imaginative work" which fully embodied his theories. Ultimately, it accounts for his rejection of theater altogether, but at the same time it accounts for something more creative: through a curious process of habitual negating of each proposition which he throws up for examination, the thought of Artaud manages to make concrete and permanent a concept of potentiality which he leaves *unimpinged upon*. It is as if his negations clear a space for us in which we may exist, and even if we do not inhabit that space the contemplation of its pure emptiness from a distance is enough to effect both a degree of self-knowledge and inner peace. That is, through use of theater he clears a space in which we might experience authentic existence providing we do not inhabit that space: this act of clearing ground, performed at enormous personal expense to Artaud and to ourselves when we truly engage in it, manages to affect us as long as we do not finish the process, or terminate the engagement, or enter the forbidden space of potentiality. As we shall see, it has been Grotowski's genius to flesh out this central yet fragmentary suggestion of Artaud and to incorporate it into his own concept of scenographic space. Moreover, beyond the importance space has to Grotowski's plastic design-scheme, he transforms his homage to potentiality into a metaphor within his artworks and into an actual experience that results from participating in them.

In the following discussion, I will analyze the main elements of Artaud's theater theory in terms of this ground-clearing which results in a space of potentiality (and potency). Artaud makes original interpretations of the place of the literary text, the role of literary and gestural languages in theater, and of the actor himself, and each element contributes to an overarching theory of the way the theater should affect its audience. But in a certain way, each element has to be superseded and almost "eliminated" (through Artaud's radical redefinitions) for the space of potentiality to emerge.

In one of the central essays of *The Theater and Its Double*, "Metaphysics and the *mise-en-scène*," Artaud asserts that "the stage is a concrete physical place which asks to be filled, and to be given its own concrete language to speak."[18] A large part of Artaud's book consists of specifying the elements of this concrete stage language. The "Theatre of Cruelty Manifestos" record his concerns with staging technology, architecture, lighting, musical instruments, costumes, properties, and repertoires, all of which seemed innovative in 1936 but which look rather dated today, given the expanded technologies of cinema, television, and mixed media. Two essays devoted to the actor, "On the Balinese Theatre" and "An Affective Athleticism," argue for the creation of a fixed language of hieroglyphic gestures on the Balinese model, which are to be accompanied by rigidly controlled breathing patterns—in "An Affective Athleticism," Artaud claims these patterns are derived from the Cabala and consist of masculine, feminine, and neuter breaths. He seems to be quite unaware that these exotic borrowed semiologies contain no intrinsic meaning for Western practitioners or observers, and that in effect he substitutes another frozen code of meanings for what he thinks is ossified and repetitive behavior in the Western "theater of masterpieces." From a historical perspective, Artaud appears to have been singularly unsuccessful in elaborating a "concrete language" in which the stage might speak.

But a resonance remains in Artaud's assertion that the stage is a concrete physical place which asks to be filled, even though it has been the task of others to complete the Artaudian project and successfully fill the empty space. If we attempt to reconstruct a phenomenology of the theater event in the thinking of Artaud, it begins with his contemplation of this potential space. With this act, Artaud at once achieves the goal sought by anyone who voices the cry "no more masterpieces": he negates the idea that dramatic art is known through a canon of classic texts, the assumption that the contents of this canon never change except through addition of new masterpieces, the belief that each item within the canon retains an unaltered existence and meaning over time that are controlled by its being transmitted through the medium of print, and the supposition that a structural dissection of any category of items within the canon—i.e., a genre study—can isolate the criteria by which works of this type may be known and created. In other words, Artaud repeals the *Poetics* and subsequent theories which share its assumptions.

As we have observed of the *Poetics*, the order of Aristotle's arguments suggests his belief in an idealistic arrangement of the elements which make up drama. Artaud might say of Aristotle, "He begins with the knowledge of certain plays (Greek tragedies), then determines that each of these embodies an idea of action (that is, a conventional assumption taken from the realm of moral philosophy) in a plot (best found in the annals of 'certain families,' i.e., Homer's favorites) which is peopled by consistent characters (out of Theophrastus) who speak appropriate thoughts (Aristotle means they parrot received knowledge) phrased in felicitous diction (he prescribes the acceptable meters) set to appropriate music (the scores are no longer extant) and recited by actors whose visual appearance, movements, and scenic groupings also conform to preordained expectations—the stage designs are also lacking, but Aristotle devotes very little attention to *melos* and *opsis*, anyway." This unflattering anatomy of Aristotle's arrangement of the parts of tragedy fails to do justice to the uniqueness and greatness Aristotle manages to demonstrate in those works which confirm his ideal arrangement. But Hellenic balance and fairness were not among Artaud's virtues. Artaud's project reverses Aristotle's order and posits a phenomenology of theatrical perception which begins with visual and aural observation of spectacular elements which have no meaning *as yet*. But even before these sensory perceptions begin, we contemplate the empty stage conceived of as place waiting and asking to be filled. No kind of "received" or "fixed" knowledge will be permitted to occupy this perceptual space *in advance*—that is, we come into Artaud's theater with no concept of "masterpiece" or of a "poetics" which would allow us to conceive of one. This primacy of space accounts for Artaud's obsession with shocking spectacular elements (a technology bold in its time but now obsolete), and more important, it accounts for the brilliance with which he manipulates language for shock value, and coins incandescent metaphors like "theater and plague," "alchemical theater," and "theater of cruelty," metaphors which Artaud "explains" by employing *further* metaphors rather than using discursive language (as Grotowski points out). Artaud wants his unlocalizable metaphors to affect us so that we cease looking for a kernel of paraphrasable wisdom within them, and return to a mode of "space" of potentiality in which they may *make us wise* rather than *convey a wisdom* that was already ours. As Artaud says in his essay "Oriental and Occidental Theater," the purely theatrical language with which he seeks to fill the potential space "has the power, not to define thoughts but *to cause thinking* . . . ."[19]

Space, then, becomes linked with affectivity in Artaud's project: it becomes a means of achieving catharsis. As we saw in Peter Brook's warning that Artaud applied was Artaud betrayed, the Artaudian work's affectivity toward its audience is its final justification, and, leaving evaluation aside, it is its final actualization: the work *comes to be* as and because it affects, or achieves, catharsis. In an ironic way, Artaud's aesthetics is the first to realize that commonplace assumption derived from Aristotle, "catharsis is the final cause of tragedy." After the work of Else, Golden, and Hardison (which I discussed in the Introduction), we are confronted with a modern reading of the *Poetics* which *begins* with an idea of catharsis, rather than ends with it. This reading translates the Greek crux to mean "clarification of incident" rather than "purgation of emotion," and offers the unromantic picture of the Greek tragedian consciously selecting and arranging plot incidents so that they rationally justify an otherwise pitiable and fearful incident—like parricide or incest. This catharsis of clarification can be seen as "final" in the order of actualizations which makes up the writing or the experiencing of a play only because the tragedian employs the time-honored device of suspense. The playwright withholds his audience's knowledge of the logical justification of the pitiable and fearful incident until the play's end, so that the completion of the mental action which hovers above the play, the plot action which is spun out within it, and the experiential action of the audience outside of it and watching it, all coincide, about five minutes before the curtain call. This sense that Aristotelian catharsis "finally" results in the creation of a high-class thriller has probably been the historical motivation for the many attempts to read something different into the catharsis clause. It remained for Artaud to propose an aesthetics of the art experience which makes catharsis its final cause.

But before Artaud arrived at this point, he was obliged to perform a massive ground-clearing of detritus occupying and in effect "polluting" the potentially empty space with which, he contended, we begin our experiential participation in the theater event. The thoroughness of this *reductio* is confused by the fact that Artaud's various manifestos and programs also contributed to the congestion of this space by calling for many specific and time-bound scenic and gestural elements which we, today, have to see as dated and extraneous (which, in effect, we have to clear away if we are to complete the more essential Artaudian project). As Romain Weingarten notes in his essay "Re-read Artaud": "In this profusion and hammering of explosive images, and even in this literary sumptuousness, there is the danger that we will be diverted from the care for absolute *stripping down* that evoked it all."[20] After we perform the surgeon's task of separating what is essential from what is contingent in Artaud, we note the rigor (if not the success) with which he applied the same *reductio* to the theater as it had come down to him, and to his own thinking. For literary critics and for the French tradition which links authentic thought with the success with which one expresses it in words, the most shocking aspect of Artaud's *reductio* lies in his assertions that "dialogue—a thing written and spoken—does not belong specifically to the stage, it belongs to books," and as far as books are concerned, "written poetry is worth reading once, and then should be destroyed."[21] Artaud supports the first contention with historical

evidence from various theaters which dispense with written texts—
Eastern, aboriginal, commedia dell'arte—and qualifies the book-
burning overtones of the second statement by acknowledging that
"fixed" written poetry attests (however inadequately) to the existence
of something more essential beyond the written texts, to what he
metaphorically calls "actual poetry, without form and without text."[22]
As usual, Artaud refuses to elaborate the specific qualities of this non-
verbal "actual poetry"; instead, he sets up the *possibility* of it since it is
unspecified and unwritten. He has performed an operation similar to his
initial operation with space, in which, as we noted, the assertion of
space's affectivity remains potentially possible as long as the space remains potential and unoccupied. (Bettina Knapp has noted the paradox
of Artaud's communicating his antiverbal thoughts through writing:
Artaud was forced to use words to describe his expansive and associative ideas, but words are inherently limiting agents. "The *term terminated* the thought, he maintained, rather than described or represented
it; it paralyzed his efforts, confined, limited, 'localized' and strangled
his every action and breath."[23] This fear partially accounts for Artaud's
obsessive refusal to define key terms like "cruelty," "plague," and so
on; instead, in additive fashion, he expands the variety of metaphoric
meanings the terms may have).

Artaud's treatment of words is not consistently condemnatory, however. In the first "Theatre of Cruelty Manifesto," he specifies that his
project does not consist of "suppressing the spoken language, but of
giving words approximately the importance they have in dreams."[24]
We can see the result of this dictum in contemporary dramaturgy,
which in its treatment of words has rejected the assumption of both
naturalistic and epic dramaturgy that narrative elements must be "read
into the record" somehow, either through realistically motivated dialogue, as in naturalism, or through direct address to the audience, as
in epic narrative. Performance theater dispenses with words which
have no function beyond exposition, and presents "narrative" material
through pantomime or through an assumption that the audience brings
a certain knowledge of the play's plot and conventional meaning with it
to the theater. (Both Grotowski's treatment of classic texts and the
collective creations based on contemporary history make such an
assumption—for example, see the Performance Group's treatment of
the Vietnamese War and the Manson murders in *Commune*.) But beyond this stripping down of the function of language in theater, which
is really an emulation of that "purifying of the dialect of the tribe"
which the symbolists already performed on lyric poetry, there remains
the affinity Artaud says theater language should have with dream language, which suggests its obsessiveness, associative quality, re-

petitiveness, tendency toward being a semiotic code, and, finally, our inability to resolve it into rational and discursive elements, which, were we successful, would free us of the power of inscrutable language to haunt and affect us. Essential theater language becomes solid for Artaud, an object, with the quality of spatial dimension and therefore intimately connected with his theory of space. In "Metaphysics and the *mise-en-scène*," he expands his notion of the concrete language with which the stage as place asks to be filled:

> It consists of everything that occupies the stage, everything that can be manifested and expressed materially on a stage and that is addressed first of all to the senses instead of addressed primarily to the mind as in the language of words.... This does not prevent [language] from developing later its full intellectual effect on all possible levels and in every direction. But it permits the substitution, for the poetry of language, of a poetry in space which will be resolved in precisely the domain which does not belong strictly to words.[25]

Note here that this language addresses the senses "first of all," and that "later" it may develop its full intellectual effect: Artaud is observing the phenomenological priority of our sensory perception of the artwork, a priority which, as we noted, reverses Aristotle's ideal ordering of the actualizations. The sense in which language "materially" occupies the stage and becomes a "poetry in space" is developed by Artaud in "Oriental and Occidental Theatre," where he links language, spatiality, and affectivity, voicing the desire

> to change the role of speech in theatre ... to make use of it in a concrete and spatial sense, combining it with everything in the theatre that is spatial and significant in the concrete domain—to manipulate it like a solid object, one which overturns and disturbs things.[26]

Beyond language, what other codes of meaning does Artaud examine, in his attempt to collate a vocabulary for that "concrete language" his stage will speak? Gestural languages have attracted European and American avant-garde artists since the turn of the century, and Artaud's longing glances toward the Orient are not unique in modern theater. Artaud responds to the intricate gestural code of Balinese dancers much as Pound does to Chinese ideograms: both forms combine a matrix of intangible thoughts and emotions in a concrete sign which has spatial extension and is also a "picture" of what it signifies. Perhaps the degree of abstraction by which the sign is distorted from being an "illustration" and by which it takes on a conventional aspect even reflects the emotional qualities which infuse the denotative nature of the sign, on an analogy with abstract expressionist painting, which is not a picture of a "thing" but of a "feeling." At least, Artaud and Pound thought that ideograms and hieroglyphs convey these qualities. A pictorial language also seems more immediate and simultaneous—at least to the theoretician who cannot actually read it—for the ideogram combines shape and meaning at once, and supposedly those who read it are immediately struck by all its components in one epiphanic glance. The pictorial sign is immediately and thoroughly perceptible, as is not the case with phonetic and linear languages which yield their denotative, connotative, and emotive contents serially, after a certain amount of mental labor. Of course, valuable as the theory of ideograms has been for modern art, it has not stood up under investigation, either from the point of view of linguistics or psychology of perception. To a large extent, the elements within ideograms and gestural languages can be as abstract as, say, the letters of the Phoenician alphabet, and rather than connoting a vast web of associations, gestural language may be rather fixed and simplistic, its elements "standing for" localized and limited denotations.

This error permeates Artaud's discussions of Balinese dance and Cabalistic breathing patterns, but it leads him to an important intuition about the nature of the actor's gestures in performance. The actor's gesture cannot be repeated, Artaud says: "the theatre is the only place in the world where a gesture, once made, can never be made the same way twice."[27] This statement comes from "No More Masterpieces," but Artaud had voiced this opinion as early as 1926, in the manifesto "The Alfred Jarry Theatre, First Year—1926–1927 Season." Here he writes:

> We can no longer subscribe to theatre which repeats itself every night according to the same, ever the same, identical rites. The show we are watching must be unique and give us the impression of being as unexpected and as incapable of being repeated as any act in life, any occurrence whatsoever brought about by events.[28]

Artaud is doing more here than arguing for the appearance of freshness at each performance. He is denying the mimetic impulse which sees theater as representation of life event—for him, it *is* life event. But if theater partakes of reality rather than imitates it, it is a very special and separate reality for Artaud. He believes that the theater is the only place left in the world where making a gesture exhausts it, uses it up—and this becomes central to his theory of purgative catharsis, in which the performing and observing of certain violent actions purges us of the will to perform them outside of the theater. Moreover, we should notice that although Artaud attempts to build up a vocabulary for a concrete stage language in all his discussions of gesture, he actually succeeds in furthering his *reductio:* after their single performances, gestures are used up for him; in effect, discarded. He systematically strips his actor of texts, words, even gestures, in his attempt to isolate something more essential inherent in the theater event.

After such a process, it should not surprise us to note that Artaud devotes relatively little attention to how the actor behaves in his theater. Artaud has no interest in the actor's autonomous personality and what he may create out of it; he rejects the actor's inspiration and says that the actor will be "rigorously denied all personal initiative."[29] (Grotowski differs considerably from Artaud in this respect, and shows more of Stanislavski's influence.) Artaud devotes more attention to the role and the almost religious vocation of the *metteur-en-scène,* who has a shamanistic function in the creation of theater of cruelty, and who uses actors along with plastic and musical elements as vehicles for *his* creation. To a certain extent, the director replaces the actor in Artaud's thinking, and when he calls for the direct creation of plays on stage, the two roles are fused.

When he does speak of the autonomous actor, Artaud seeks ways to allow some creation beyond the actor to shine through him. This demands a high degree of physical training and prowess, and Artaud calls his actor "an athlete of the heart";[30] Grotowski later develops this premise to posit an actor whose elimination of the physical resistance of his body leaves him open to impulses and feelings which cannot be described physically, yet are somehow transmitted by means of the physically perfected vehicle. Artaud's actor is equally diaphanous: he will use his body "like a screen through which pass the will and the relaxation of will," and he possesses "a kind of affective musculature which corresponds to the physical localizations of feelings."[31] Artaud links his theory of affective athleticism with his almost mystical concept of the double, and it is at this point in *The Theater and Its Double* that he offers the most thorough description of that term.

> To make use of his emotions as a wrestler makes use of his muscles, [the actor] has to see the human being as a Double . . . like a perpetual specter from which the affective powers radiate.
>
> The plastic and never completed specter, whose forms the true actor apes, on which he imposes the forms and image of his own sensibility.
>
> It is this double which the theatre influences, this spectral effigy which it shapes, and like all specters, this double has a long memory. The heart's memory endures and it is certainly with his heart that the actor thinks; here the heart holds sway.
>
> This means that in the theatre more than anywhere else it is the affective world of which the actor must be aware, ascribing to it virtues which are not those of an image but carry a material sense.[32]

This passage emphasizes Artaud's distance from Platonism, for he calls his spectral double "plastic and never completed"; it is no fixed ideal form but a fluid source which is itself shaped and changed by the true actor's influence, just as it shapes and changes him. And characteristic for Artaud's dual and contradictory impulses toward amassing a vocabulary as he is conducting a purification of its elements, his linking of affective acting with the double performs a *reductio* of the actor himself. Seeking to expose the plastic forms behind the vehicle of the actor, Artaud effectively eliminates him as an essential component of theater. His theater will concern and will be peopled by forces beyond their individual manifestation in the shape of dramatic characters; having eliminated characters, he eliminates men, and leaves the actor no function beyond becoming diaphanous and attesting to something beyond his self by his very act of self-obliteration. As Artaud says of the theater of cruelty, "it will stage events, not men."[33] In one of his "Letters on Cruelty," Artaud writes to Jean Paulhan:

> The theatre must make itself the equal of life—not an individual life, that individual aspect of life in which CHARACTERS triumph, but the sort of liberated life which sweeps away human individuality and in which man is only a reflection.[34]

This entity of which the individual man is only a reflection Artaud will refer to as the double in subsequent essays. As he performs his *reductio* of the inessential elements through and beyond which he must work to expose true theater, Artaud constantly approaches this double, and constantly draws back from defining it, partially in fear that definition of the term would freeze and "terminate" it as a source of affectivity, partially in conviction that it constantly renews and reshapes itself; that, like theatrical gesture, it can never be repeated identically.

Before we move beyond Artaud's theories about gesture as language of signs, about repeatability, and about the function of the actor, we should examine one final metaphor from which each reader of *The Theater and Its Double* takes a personal meaning and inspiration. Artaud appends a preface to *The Theater and Its Double* entitled "The Theatre and Culture," in which he distinguishes between an authentic idea of "culture"—a realm of forces capable of affecting us, what he calls "the idea of culture-in-action, of culture growing within us like a new organ"[35]—and "civilization," a collection of objects, artifacts, and masterpieces within which culture is fixed and frozen. He asserts that theater is the only art form left which can free "culture" from the constraints of "civilization," because it uses what he calls "living instruments" and because the gestures of its actors cannot be repeated:

> For the theatre as for culture, it remains a question of naming and directing shadows: and the theatre, not confined to a fixed lan-

guage and form, not only destroys false shadows but prepares the way for a new generation of shadows, around which assembles the true spectacle of life.[36]

He concludes the preface with a qualification which links this "true spectacle of life" with his concept of the double:

Furthermore, when we speak the word "life," it must be understood we are not referring to life as we know it from its surface of fact, but to that fragile, fluctuating center which forms never reach. And if there is still one hellish, truly accursed thing in our time, it is our artistic dallying with forms, instead of being like victims [suppliciés] burnt at the stake, signalling through the flames.[37]

The "fragile, fluctuating center" which Artaud opposes to surface life refers us to the aphorism from which Artaud derives his book's title, the thought that "life is the double of the true theatre." But who are these "living instruments" who give theater as an art form its only criterion for being linked with vital "culture" rather than fixed and dead "civilization"? Artaud does not identify them. Their true mission is to be like victims of torture "burnt at the stake, signalling through the flames." This rich metaphor tempts many readers to associate these tortured ones with the actor: his priestlike function in a holy theater has now fallen to that of being a victim, and he is like a martyr or scapegoat sacrificed for the community of onlookers, to whom he signals, that is, speaks in the gestural language Artaud proposes, while the very flames consume him, that is, as he becomes diaphanous and is eventually eliminated through Artaud's relentless *reductio*. Grotowski interprets the metaphor this way, and translates the phrase thus: "Actors should be like martyrs burnt alive, still signalling to us from their stakes."[38] His substitution of "martyrs" for *suppliciés* tells us much about the secular *sacrum* which permeates his theater, and creatively expands upon the latent aggression and sado-masochism in Artaud's writings. And he specifies the direction of the "signalling" by adding the phrase "to us," since, for Grotowski, the essence of theater lies in the creative confrontation of actor and audience.

But Artaud's metaphor is more open-ended than any particular "use" of it can be. He does not identify his victims with "actors," instead he points to "us." "We" should be like the victims, we who participate in the theater event. Part of the reason for this lack of focus lies in Artaud's desire to substitute the *metteur-en-scène* for the actor as the true creator *and* realizer of theater. Part stems from his desire to acknowledge the actor as conveyor of this creativity at the same time as he renders him diaphanous, that is, burns him away so that something may shine through him. But most important, Artaud wishes to involve his

audience—"us"—in the process of creating and being affected by theater. Even when he feels compelled to discuss the transitional elements
by which he comes to know and to isolate theater's essence—text, language, gesture, the actor himself—Artaud's focus turns toward the
audience, and toward the problem of affectivity. His *reductio* results in
a confrontation with catharsis.

"The theatre, utilized in the highest and most difficult sense possible,
has the power to influence the aspect and formation of things," Artaud
writes in the pivotal essay "No More Masterpieces."[39] Throughout *The
Theater and Its Double*, Artaud develops metaphors which suggest how
theater may affect and change its participants. He devotes a chapter to
"The Alchemical Theatre" because both theater and alchemy are "mi-
rages" yet both are symbols "which provide the spiritual means of de-
canting and transfusing matters," of effecting change.[40] In "The Theatre
and the Plague," Artaud devotes some of his most brilliant writing to
equating the two, for he believes that "the theatre, like the plague, is a
delirium and is communicative":[41]

> The theatre, like the plague ... releases conflicts, disengages
> powers, liberates possibilities, and if these possibilities and these
> powers are dark, it is not the fault of the plague nor of the theatre,
> but of life.
> ... It appears that by means of the plague, a gigantic abscess, as
> much moral as social, has been collectively drained; and that like
> the plague, the theatre has been created to drain abscesses collec-
> tively.
> ... The theatre like the plague is a crisis which is resolved by
> death or cure. And the plague is a superior disease because it is a
> total crisis after which nothing remains except death or an extreme
> purification.[42]

Besides being the perfect manifestation of the violent but invisible force
which causes upheaval and alteration in society, Artaud's plague infects
and transforms "the collectivity," each member of society, whether he
contracts the disease or not; as a metaphor, it is the opposite of the
internal and private disease of cancer, whose specter motivates Artaud's late poetry. And unlike self-consuming cancer, the plague offers
an alternative: death or cure. The "extreme purification" offered by
Artaud's plague is the most striking interpretation of medicinal catharsis in modern literary criticism.

But an "application" of Artaud's cathartic plague, like any other application of Artaud, is dangerous. The Living Theater's actors "staged"
this chapter of *The Theater and Its Double* with great success in their
montage *Mysteries and Smaller Pieces*. But if we extend this "extreme
purification" to affective theory, we are left with a simplistic theory of

homeopathic catharsis which says that the performance or observation of violent and undesirable actions in art "cures" us of the desire to perform them in life. Modern philology has demonstrated that Aristotle really said nothing of the kind in the *Poetics;* even if he had, few would believe him today. Artaud's advocates tend to gloss over his tendency toward this discredited position, and his detractors leap on it when they spot it. We can ascribe some of Artaud's extremism on the subject of purgative catharsis to the traditional reading of Aristotle which he inherited, a tradition which includes Castelvetro, Corneille, Milton, and Lessing; we can partially ascribe it to his desire to refunction and transform the inherent aggression and sado-masochism he sensed in the act of theater performance; and we must trace a good part of it to the poet's immaturity and sensationalism.

Artaud was aware of these conflicting tendencies, and he discussed them in the essay which contains his own catharsis clause, "No More Masterpieces." The essay is a compendium of all his thought, and it deserves close analysis. He begins with his attack on "masterpieces," which he takes as a metaphor for the pervasive conflict between "culture" and "civilization" lying behind all his discontent. After condemning Shakespeare for having introduced limited naturalistic "psychology" into the theater, he proceeds to vilify all written poetry and propose its destruction. Only the theater can be salvaged, because the same gesture cannot be made twice in it. This leads Artaud to assert that only the theater has retained its power to affect us:

> The theatre is the only place in the world, the last general means we still possess of directly affecting the organism and, in periods of neurosis and petty sensuality like the one in which we are immersed, of attacking this sensuality by physical means it cannot withstand.[43]

Therefore, Artaud calls for a theater of cruelty, by which he does not mean "blood" or barbarism, but an extreme rigor, purity, and self-discipline, since, as *metteur-en-scène*, he will be its chief creator and actor—"'*theatre of cruelty*' means a theatre difficult and cruel for myself first of all."[44]

These ideas, brilliantly stated here, may all be found in other essays in *The Theater and Its Double.* But his conclusion in "No More Masterpieces" is unique. He proceeds from the thought that the theater of cruelty will reintroduce into theater an idea which Artaud traces to the psychoanalytic theory of his decade: "effecting a patient's cure by making him assume the apparent and exterior attitudes of the desired condition."[45] Artaud is not referring to a behavioral conditioning which reinforces desired behavior through compulsory repetition of it. He does not specify here the activity to be performed in the theater of cruelty, but the violence of the cure effected and the tendencies he claims to purge—"war, riot, and blatant murder"—suggest that the repertoire of gestures in the theater of cruelty tends more toward the Grand Guignol than to pastoral. The psychotherapeutic method he has in mind is more Freud's than Skinner's; in its simplest and least creditable form, it can be reduced to a mental reenactment of primal scenes and primal offenses to rid the patients of their trauma in the present.

Next, Artaud recapitulates the process by which we experience these formative scenes in this theater. This progress is a phenomenology of sensory experience: we are impinged upon by "sounds, noises, and cries" until we assemble them into words and syntax, and we perceive flickers and bursts of light until we combine them into significant images. Ultimately, after sound and light, comes the perception of action. Artaud has reversed the order of actualization of the "parts" of theater which Aristotle listed in the *Poetics;* curiously enough, the progression of his actualizations parallels the process by which Stanislavski's actor uses affective memory to relive the past—but Artaud's affectivity contains no memory, it is a means of perceiving the present.

Having arrived at the level of action, Artaud reveals that the "cruelty" of his theater is no mere metaphor, and he exposes himself to the attack of rationalists who have demonstrated the scientific error of "purgative catharsis":

> A violent and concentrated action is a kind of lyricism: it summons up supernatural images, a bloodstream of images, a bleeding spurt of images in the poet's head and in the spectator's as well.
>
> Whatever the conflicts that haunt the mind of a given period, I defy the spectator to whom such violent scenes will have transferred their blood, who will have felt in himself the transit of a superior action, who will have seen the extraordinary and essential movements of his thought illuminated in extraordinary deeds—the violence and blood having been placed at the service of the violence of the thought—I defy that spectator to give himself up, once outside the theatre, to ideas of war, riot, and blatant murder.[46]

The optimism underlying Artaud's purgative catharsis is unfounded, and he knows it. He immediately calls his idea "dangerous and sophomoric," and reminds us that "example breeds example."

But the whole project of Artaudian *reductio,* resulting in catharsis, does not end in ruin. Artaud salvages it by returning us to the concepts of space and potentiality with which he began:

Everything depends upon the manner and purity with which the thing is done. There is a risk. But let it not be forgotten that though a theatrical gesture is violent, it is disinterested: and that the theatre teaches precisely the uselessness of the action which, once done, is not to be done, and the superior use of the state unused by the action and which, *restored*, produces a purification.[47]

This is Artaud's catharsis clause, and though the passage is infrequently cited, it may be his most important statement. On the one hand, Artaud posits violent deeds whose uselessness is demonstrated through their performance. In this realm "cruelty" refers to sensory shock, and this realm has been discredited by Artaud's utilitarian critics, and strongly qualified by Artaud himself. On the other hand, Artaud posits empty space, an unused state of potentiality which is *restored* through the violent activity in the other realm, restored because that activity does not impinge upon it, because Artaud's actors do not enter into it nor do they induce us to enter into it. This restoration results in a purification of the space itself, and of our selves by bestowing its potentiality upon us. Artaud's massive *reductio* ends in his purification and restoration of the stage as a space; as a result, in the process of returning us to a potential state *before* theater and, ironically, beyond it as well, he eliminates each concrete element which we have traditionally believed to be essential to theater. In his own case, Artaud found himself beyond theater, and abandoned it for other pursuits. In our case, we may respond to his inspiration by acknowledging the potentiality bestowed upon us, the space restored to us. And though we may not move into that space and "use" it, we may let it use us, and move us to a recognition of that true theater which is the double of life.

THE THEATER OF JERZY GROTOWSKI

For his time, Artaud envisioned the most radical degree of theater turning toward its audience, acknowledging its presence, taking its meaning from and finding its affective end in audience participation. But almost exclusively, Artaud spoke in terms of his *theater's* implications for its audience, not the stance which his *actor* takes toward the spectator. This sets Artaud apart from Stanislavski and Brecht, who both devoted considerable attention to the training of actors and to theoretical implications behind the training. Hence we have no "Artaudian" acting style today. And from the documentation which exists of Artaud's own productions, it appears that he had little talent for coaching actors. The sense of an "acting which glows" emerges from certain essays in *The Theater and Its Double*, and some find it embodied in Artaud's own screen performances (he played Marat in Gance's *Napoleon* and the Young Monk in Dreyer's *Passion of Joan of Arc*, but had ceased acting for films before composing his major essays). By contrast, still photographs of productions he directed only indicate the Theater of Cruelty company's indulgence in mugging and expressionistic posturing.[48] His lack of rehearsal time and funds accounts for some of his actors' inadequacies: he mounted amateur productions in a matter of weeks, whereas Stanislavski, Brecht (and now Grotowski) were able to rehearse their plays hundreds of times (four hundred rehearsals for *Apocalypsis cum figuris*, nine hundred for one of Stanislavski's Chekhov productions). But even if Artaud had possessed the ideal circumstance of a subsidized laboratory theater, we can doubt that he would have contributed significantly to acting theory. For in an important sense, he eliminated the actor from his essential theater in the course of his *reductio*, which resulted in an ideal and empty space to which both actor and audience were forbidden entry. In the end, this empty space cannot be used by later theater workers as anything but a poetic inspiration; concrete application violates its spirit.

But inspiration does exist, as Artaud was fond of saying. At the beginning of this discussion, we glanced briefly at some of the contemporary ensembles which have responded to it: the Living Theater, the Open Theater, Performance Group, Peter Brook's ad hoc companies such as the Theater of Cruelty Project (which resulted in the more "West End—oriented" production of *Marat/Sade*) and, more recently, his Empty Space Company, experiments with Ted Hughes's Orgast language, and now the Paris-based International Center of Theater Research. But only Jerzy Grotowski of Poland has created an acting *praxis* accompanied by cogent theoretical speculation which attempts to respond to and continue Artaud's speculations, and to place itself within the tradition originated by Stanislavski, Meyerhold, and Brecht. Within a decade, theater companies all over the world have felt the influence of his three productions which have toured outside Poland, his half-dozen actors, and his handful of theater essays. Grotowski has already begun to disavow his epigones, and he is now only in his forties.

Unlike Artaud, whose writings over several years possess a consistency which does not lend itself to chronological speculation, Grotowski's thought has evolved through several distinct yet logical stages. He acknowledges this progression, and warns us not to assess his current thinking and activity in terms of his earlier writings and productions. So, to a large extent, all my "conclusions" about Grotowski will be contingent and temporary ones. Although his work contains themes, thoughts, and gestural motifs which unite all of it, and mark it as his own, what I respect in it, beyond its unity, is Grotowski's ability to surprise me with unprecedented innovation. It is this quality of personal surprise, which results in a renewal of the person, that characterizes Grotowski's theory of catharsis and also the affectivity of his theater company. Postponing theoretical discussions for the moment, I have to attest that viewing his actors perform *Apocalypsis cum figuris* has been the most profoundly moving and disturbing of my experiences in the theater: Grotowski has marked my life, if not changed it. Many noted theater workers and as many anonymous audience members have made the same testimony, and it is significant that most people enter Grotowski's auditorium with a considerable amount of advance knowledge, preconceptions, and resistances—his company is one of the most well documented and well publicized in the world— yet they emerge from the Grotowski experience struck by the newness and personal affectivity of the work *to them*, not just by its intellectual and technical brilliance.

So, out of respect for Grotowski's constant and ongoing evolution as an artist and thinker, and because of the centrality of surprise and renewal in his work, we must keep the chronology of his productions and essays in mind. For the purposes of my discussion, Grotowski's career to date falls into three phases (as he has acknowledged himself in his more autobiographical statements).

His student years and early productions reflect the eclecticism of a young artist who wants to sample and synthesize as many influences as possible. This period finds Grotowski studying at the Advanced School of Dramatic Art in Krakow, where he received his diploma as a director in 1956; significantly, he interrupted this study to travel to Moscow in 1955, where he observed the aging practitioners of the Stanislavski era and researched Meyerhold's production of *The Inspector General*. A trip to China in 1962 allowed Grotowski to familiarize himself with Peking Opera, and by extension, the traditions of Indian Kathakali (the oldest "epic theater" extant), and Japanese Nōh and Kabuki. During these years Grotowski directed plays at Krakow's Stary Teatr and was given his first company, the Teatr 13 Rzedów in Opole (1959)—or "Theater of 13 Rows," a name which attests to the intimate chamber-nature of all his ventures, although he did not keep the seating arrangement in rows for long. Grotowski's productions reflect this eclecticism—*Uncle Vanya*, absurdist plays like Ionesco's *The Chairs*, Cocteau's surrealistic *Orpheus*, and Mayakovsky's constructivist play *Mystery-Bouffe*. At the same time we see the director beginning to grapple with major plays from several traditions, the reworked "national classics" (written in verse) with which he eventually established his reputation as a producer. This is the period during which Grotowski staged adaptations of Byron's *Cain*, Kalidasa's ancient Kathakali play *Siakuntala,* an adaptation of Dostoyevsky's *The Idiot,* an abbreviated production of the Polish national drama *Forefathers* by Adam Mickiewicz, Słowacki's *Kordian,* and even a series of *Exercises on Hamlet.* The range of languages, theater traditions, and dramatic themes encompassed by these productions suggests that Grotowski was still searching for his own path among the routes taken by many masters. And his theoretical speculation which dates from this period, an account of actor's training in the years 1959-62,[49] suggests that his actors were still amassing a series of techniques in the absence of a central purpose relating to audience affectivity or even mutual contact: these are solo exercises. (To be more exact, Grotowski has never trained actors in techniques of "how to do something"; even in this early period he had developed his *via negativa* which trains actors to remove vocal, physical, intellectual, and psychic resistances to what Grotowski wants "done." His actors "resign from not doing" something, rather than learn "how to do" it, even in the exercises of 1959–62, but they do this *alone,* so in a sense they are still working on their own persons, not opening themselves to change through interpersonal or "ensemble" relations.)

Already in his Opole period, Grotowski began to experiment with the scenographic arrangement of the whole auditorium, and derived a unique arrangement of seats and set-pieces for each production. He could do this easily, since his theater was nothing more than a cavernous, brick-lined, arched chamber which could seat only a few dozen spectators. At first his scenography reflects little more than successively more daring forays by the actors out into the audience: they act in the center aisle (*Cain*), then they perform in the center of the hall between two blocks of audience (*Siakuntala*); finally they perform amidst spectators who are placed on seats scattered randomly throughout the auditorium (*Forefathers*). Each successive production brought Grotowski's actors closer to the spectators, but only in terms of physical proximity.

Beginning apparently with his adaptation of Słowacki's *Kordian,* Grotowski recognized the eclecticism of his experiments, and he began to search for the essential qualities of theater, which he would expose through a rigorous *reductio* of everything which he found extraneous to the theater event. Certain aspects of the Theater of 13 Rows already lent themselves to the explorations which resulted in his concept of a "poor theater." For one thing, Grotowski had always worked with only a handful of actors, and yet he had staged adaptations of classic texts which originally called for elaborate changes of locale and dozens of performers to play their many characters. Grotowski had already devel-

oped a kind of "abbreviated production" which reduced hoary romantic verse dramas to their essential scenes peopled by key protagonists,
and he conflated supernumerary roles into anonymous choral parts
spoken by one or two actors. In the process, he rendered several
nineteenth-century closet dramas stageworthy, and with *Kordian* he
recognized that his pragmatically derived technical success contained
the germ of ideas that could be further developed. In *Kordian* we first
see the notion of confrontation at work, between work and interpretation, and between actors and audience. Słowacki's romantic hero wan-
ders through a Europe in revolution, climbs Mont Blanc and imagines
there that he must shed his blood for his occupied nation; one scene
finds him imprisoned in a mental hospital on orders of the Czar who
then occupied Poland—even a century ago, certain Russians considered
a man crazy, not just criminal, if he resisted their authority.

Grotowski's *Kordian* has been brought into the present in one radical
gesture: the entire production takes place in the mental hospital, and a
mad Kordian raves about bleeding for his country atop Mont Blanc
when in actuality he is being bled ("medicinally") on the top bed of a
double bunk; as if in anticipation of *Marat/Sade* and Solzhenitsyn,
Grotowski's mental-hospital bureaucracy has replaced the civil government as symbol of omnipresent authority, and the nineteenth-
century dramatic "couple" of rebel and regent becomes transformed
into the more modern "couple" of patient and psychiatrist. On the
scenographic level, Grotowski's arrangement of platforms, hospital
cots, and bunks results in a proximity of actors and audience which is
also a significant statement in terms of the ideas being explored by
Grotowski-Słowacki. The hospital beds fill the hall, they are the only
element of décor and also the only available seats for the spectators;
actors playing patients, dressed in the same street clothes as the spectators, sit among the spectators and are periodically pounced upon by
white-robed psychiatrists, so that spectators observe and become ab-
sorbed in an action which shifts from place to place in the hall. They are
never certain whether the person sitting beside them will be revealed as
a "patient" and begin to "act"—and they fear that they may be mistaken for the "actors" they so much resemble, and will be treated as
"patients," or forced to act in Grotowski's play. *Kordian* remains one
of the more striking instances in the Grotowski canon in which the
scenic arrangement and textual adaptation result in the casting of the
audience in a significant role in the play.

This central period in Grotowski's career resulted in his thus far most
widely known theoretical statements and productions. Essays written
between 1964 and 1968 appeared in the latter year under the title
Towards a Poor Theatre, first published as a special English-language

number of the Danish theater journal *Teatrets Teori og Teknikk*[50] that was edited by Grotowski's early student Eugenio Barba and then appeared in an identical edition in the United States the next year. *Towards a Poor Theatre* also contains interviews with Grotowski and accounts of the development of his method of actor's training, as recorded by several European theater workers, and Ludwig Flaszen's poetic descriptions, written under the direction of Grotowski, of three major productions from the repertoire of the Laboratory Theater, of which Flaszen serves as dramaturg. All this material had appeared in program notes and theater journals in several countries, including Poland, but Barba provided a valuable service by collecting and translating it in an anthology which has since appeared in many European languages.

Grotowski has recently stated that *Towards a Poor Theatre* and the productions described in it mark the end of one period of his work. This rich period brought him from obscurity even in Poland to international renown; it also brought him from Opole to Wrocław, a larger town yet still barely a culture center even in Poland; there Grotowski was given the directorship of the Instytut Badań Metody Aktorskiej (Institute of Actors' Research) in 1965. This organization is primarily a research center (of humanistic "science"); secondarily, it is an actors training school which uses Grotowski's core company of Polish actors as source material for the institute's researches, and as instructors for propagating the results of these researches among an international student company whose membership changes constantly (in contrast to the permanent Polish actors who have worked with Grotowski since the beginning of the sixties). As Grotowski sees it, during the "poor theater" period his primary function lay in furthering knowledge of the actor's art and its connection to the audience's own participation in theater; to achieve and demonstrate this interaction, he also staged model productions under the rubric of the Teatr Laboratorium, or Laboratory Theater. The productions which mark this phase of activity are Marlowe's *Doctor Faustus*, Wyspiański's *Akropolis*, Calderón's *The Constant Prince* in the Polish version of Słowacki, and most recently *Apocalypsis cum figuris*, which Grotowski considers a transitional piece between his "poor theater" work and his present activities. Flaszen describes *Faustus, Akropolis*, and *The Constant Prince* in *Towards a Poor Theatre*; the last two plays and *Apocalypsis cum figuris* have played at various theater festivals in Europe and also in the United States. In addition to a note on *Apocalypsis* in Grotowski's book, a full description by Ludwig Flaszen has appeared in English, in the form of a program note given to foreign visitors to the Wrocław auditorium (or at touring presentations abroad, as at the Munich Olympics!). This program note has also been printed in the American journal *The Drama Review*.[51]

All this creative activity, which roughly spans the sixties, is marked by Grotowski's reading of Artaud. Although he first read *The Theater and Its Double* in 1964, he was already working in a Polish theater milieu which was beginning to feel Artaud's influence in terms of scenic arrangement and treatment of the actor; discussion of Artaud in the Polish theater press (especially in *Dialog*) began about the time Grotowski became director of the Theater of 13 Rows. Grotowski's *reductio* towards a poor theater parallels to a surprising extent the less coherent process of elimination found in Artaud's theories, more so than Grotowski acknowledges in his essay on Artaud, "He Wasn't Entirely Himself."[52] In an important sense, they both begin and énd with a concept of empty space. But Grotowski has managed to preserve the sanctity of the space at the same time that he has found a way to bring it into the life and work of his theater, renewed on a daily basis, as the center of his encounter with audiences—or in his more recent terminology, his encounter with the quotidian, nontheatrical world. Instead of ending with the pristine and perhaps sterile space of potentiality arrived at in *The Theater and Its Double*—and to a certain extent, by the *reductio* of *Towards a Poor Theatre* and the ambiguous conclusion of *Apocalypsis cum figuris*—Grotowski has recently proclaimed a concept of *place;* to paraphrase some of his recent statements, it is an existential place in which we might live authentically.

No new production embodying this concept of place has appeared from Grotowski's company, and he has recently stated that *Apocalypsis cum figuris* is to be the last play by his company that will distinguish between actors and spectators. And Grotowski appears to have abandoned the formal essay as a means of conveying his theoretical ideas, for the moment at least. "The word" from Grotowski increasingly takes on the prophetic connotations of that phrase; when he speaks to gatherings of theater people, he delivers public lectures in the guise of answering (actually, rephrasing) questions from the floor. Some of these performances, like the six-hour session I attended in Los Angeles in March 1973, take on theatrical aspects of their own. That particular evening, half of the spectators walked out in frustration with his manipulation of the questioners and his efforts to "purify" their questions by rephrasing them. But the other half of the audience was won over, and by the end of the evening they began to think and speak in his new quasi-theoretical, quasi-mystical language, a language which resisted both causal logic and any kind of theatrical application to the extent that Grotowski never mentioned any of his famous productions and even resisted using the word "actor." I understand that the session continued beyond 2:30 A.M. in a neighboring restaurant, with about thirty listeners in attendance—which happens to be the ideal number of spectators at a Laboratory Theater performance, according to Grotowski. Needless to say, accounts of these public sessions vary widely, and they are not readily available in print in English. In my discussion, I have drawn upon reports from sessions in New York and Warsaw and upon my own observation of such sessions in Wrocław, Los Angeles, and Bloomington, Indiana. And descriptions of what Grotowski now calls his "special projects" have begun to appear. According to Richard Mennen, the Laboratory Theater company is now a coalition of related sublaboratories, each headed by an actor, the dramaturg Flaszen, or by Grotowski himself, devoted to projects with names like "Methods of the Event," "Meditations Aloud," and "Acting Therapy." The prospectus currently circulated by the Laboratory Theater describes additional sublaboratories such as the "Working Encounter Laboratory," the "Laboratory of Happening Methods," and the "Laboratory for Cooperation with Psychotherapy." In a lecture at Indiana University, Bloomington, on April 23, 1978, Grotowski invited interested persons to apply for membership in week-long "special projects" held in the Polish countryside during summers, and he circulated a questionnaire for all applicants to complete. The principal questions read: "1. How do you earn your living? 2. What is your creative work? 3. What needs could you hope to fulfill through participation in our experiences (work)? 4. Tell me something you think is essential for you to tell me."[53]

In spite of the random circumstances by which Grotowski has made his latest views public, a common theme emerges from all of them that allows us to map out the shape, if not the particular contours, of his emerging theory, and make conjectures about its applicability to theatrical experimentation in recent years. Still, the probability that no further production will emerge from Grotowski's own company nags all the Grotowski-watchers; this thought colors our readings of his earlier reductio and his recent disavowals of all theater but the place in which the "human act" occurs. It would be an ironic but not unfitting end to this discussion of modern acting theory to announce that its most recent major theoretician had abandoned the theater on theoretical grounds. To reduce this temptation toward an overly progressive and causal reading of modern performance theory, I conclude this study with a discussion of a play by Peter Handke, which begins with the Grotowskian reductio as a given, and proceeds to open up a new realm in which plays may be written—a place in which the theater event can take place and take its place.

One premise stands at the center of all Grotowski's theater work and thought: he defines the theater as "what takes place between spectator and actor."[54] He considers all the other elements which we normally associate with theater to be supplementary, and he suggests that although some of these elements may be necessary occasionally, ideally the theater should "give them back" to the disciplines from which it has eclectically borrowed them. Rejecting Wagner's belief in a synthesis of all the arts, Grotowski would return elaborate auditoriums with fixed seats and stages to the realm of architecture; he would give representative stage design and scene-painting back to the plastic arts (even a costume must not have any intrinsic beauty or suggest an autonomous meaning until the actor wears it and gives it a referent by manipulating it physically); Grotowski shuns sound effects produced electronically or by conventional musical instruments, and "sends this back" to the discipline of music, preferring to use his actors' bodies and vocal resonators to produce the sound score. Grotowski also avoids any competition with electronic media such as film or television, shuns elaborate lighting effects, projections, the use of film, anything which would "enrich" his theater mechanically or make it a "total theater." In his *reductio* toward the essence of the theater event, he even eliminates literature to a certain extent: theater can exist without texts, and perhaps the theater should abandon the notion of illuminating and illustrating the holistic, permanently relevant literary art object—the "play" or piece of "dramatic literature"—and return that notion to the field of literature, where it does belong.

Through this process of elimination Grotowski arrives at a concept of the "poor theater," which consists of the encounter between actor and audience. His metaphor of poverty suggests the monastic quality of life at the Laboratory Theater, a sense which emerges from each of the productions as well. Grotowski undoubtedly recognizes that complete poverty of production elements is a theoretical ideal which cannot be realized on the stage; in fact, photographs of several of his productions indicate the beauty and resonance which emerge from the stovepipes, rags, and simple platforms scattered about the Grotowski auditorium. But this does not contradict his theory of poverty, for higher meaning arises from Grotowski's banal objects only in their relation to the actors who use and arrange them during performance. Grotowski has not dismissed the technical sophistication of modern staging just to replace it with another set of autonomous objects which elicit an audience response before performance and actor manipulation have given them significance (the phenomenon we see at work when, for example, the audience applauds the set design when the curtains part). Grotowski would be shocked if anyone applauded his bare stage or heap of stovepipes, although the objects which reappear habitually in his productions have been exploited for just such an autonomous "significance" by Grotowski's less creative followers.

As we can see, problems understandably arise when we try to isolate the positive value of a term like "poor theater," for the fecundity of Grotowski's imagination lends a richness to the most "poverty-stricken" elements in his productions. In fact, Grotowski avoids talking about the positive aspect of poverty in his theater and emphasizes the sense in which poverty is the antithesis or negation of our rich or synthetic theater (rich in flaws, he claims). (In Polish, Grotowski does not employ the expected antonym of "rich" [*bogaty*] in the phrase "a poor theater," that is, *biedny* ["poor"]; instead he uses a word derived semantically from *bogaty*, *ubogi*, which literally means "impecunious," "meager," or "unrich.") At the end of his *reductio* of nonessential stage and literary artifacts, Grotowski remains curiously silent about what he will put in their place.

Similarly, he refuses to specify the goal which his actor reaches at the end of the *via negativa*, Grotowski's famous series of physical and psychological exercises which compels the actor to abandon pre-conceptions, clichéd habits, mimetic reproductions of banal realistic behavior, and all the "proper" techniques of breathing, speaking, and moving taught in conventional acting schools. Grotowski denounces all of these as defenses behind which the actor hides his true self. Every actor assembles a collection of such received gestures, or in Grotowski's own words, "a bag of tricks"; he constantly seeks to acquire new skills, asking "how to do" certain stunts on stage—physical or emotional turns. But Grotowski forces his actor to assume the opposite attitude: instead of asking "how to do" something, he *resigns from not doing it.*"[55]

Is Grotowski suggesting that, in some unspecified way, this eradication of blocks allows the "part" or role called for in a particular performance situation to "shine through" the actor who has opened himself up to it? In part, this is true. The idea particularly suits Grotowski's choice of themes and play texts. One of his constant themes is the idea that ordinary, petty men unconsciously enact the mythologies and archetypes which stand behind their tradition: in his adaptation of *Akropolis*, concentration camp victims act out parables and legends from the Old Testament and classical Greek civilization; in *Apocalypsis cum figuris*, the figural tradition of interpretation is applied to the drunken revels of some sadistic peasants, who force the village idiot to play the part of Christ to their mocking portrayals of Apostles, until they realize with horror that the Simpleton has apparently become the part they forced him to play. In Grotowski's theater, the complement of the un-witting biblical figuration is the scapegoat, the man who takes on the punishment or suffering for certain offenses for the sake of onlookers, "saving them" from having to perform certain acts or sufferings at the same time as he indicts their complicity. Thus, Grotowski's Faustus investigates forbidden and inevitably fatal knowledge for the spectators present at the banquet held during his last hour on earth; Grotowski's Constant Prince takes on the burden of constancy, of remaining faithful to a hopeless and wrong-headed ideal—he defines himself in terms of the monomania and purity of his self-conception at the same time as his physical body is being tormented by his torturers, all "flexible" men who will not have to suffer the consequences of constancy because he has done this for them. Although the actor's skills involved in creating the part of the Constant Prince have caused this to be Grotowski's best-known production, the suffering undergone by the victim in *Apocalypsis cum figuris* is more central to Judeo-Christian conceptions of the scapegoat than Calderón's obscure Portuguese prince in the hands of the Moors; in this later work, Grotowski's actor is required to take on the sufferings of Christ himself—or rather, these sufferings, and the responsibility for other men which they entail, *come to him* through the agency of mocking and torture initiated by other men, and compel him to accept them in spite of his initial resistance. In the conceptions of the Constant Prince and the Simpleton of *Apocalypsis cum figuris* (both played by Ryszard Cieślak), we can see the most complete realization of the *via negativa* as a theoretical end in itself, as well as its most masterful employment as an actor's technique.

I suggested earlier that we can understand the *via negativa* in part as Grotowski's belief that the role can shine through and illuminate the actor who has rid himself of physical and psychic blocks. This is an innovation in acting technique, although Grotowski has not succeeded in specifying just how this may be accomplished. In fact, Grotowski does not explain the *via negativa* beyond giving us convincing arguments for eliminating extraneous decorative and literary elements from production, and listing the elaborate psycho-physical exercises practiced in the Laboratory Theater. Beyond this point, Grotowski cannot help the actor build a characterization. We should not view this as a shortcoming in Grotowski's theory, however; as we shall see, Grotowski moves from a notion of the actor who plays a "part" (character creation) to a theory of the actor who takes on a *social* role in the theater context (as opposed to the context of a particular play).

Grotowski's reluctance to explain exactly how the *via negativa* works and why it succeeds with some actors and some audiences acknowledges the extent to which factors like chance, inspiration, and belief play a part in acting; as for the question of whether a particular acting technique actually convinces a given audience of its verisimilitude, Grotowski would probably argue that all audiences have to be educated in, and sensitized to, the mimetic value of representational techniques foreign to them. To this extent, the *via negativa* is another convention, like Stanislavski's affective memory or Brecht's *Verfremdungseffekt*, and it seems most convincing to an audience of initiates. The Laboratory Theater has certainly attracted that audience, but so has the Moscow Art Theater and the Berliner Ensemble—and Brecht and Stanislavski would have to agree with Grotowski that, just like the *via negativa*, the techniques of affective memory and *Verfremdungseffekt* ultimately depend upon faith and shared conventions in order to "work." But all three theoreticians move beyond an analysis of their techniques of character creation to speculations about the way these techniques ideally affect the actor who uses them and the audience which watches them being used. Before we discuss this affective aspect of the *via negativa*, though, we should continue our examination of its conventional aspect as a technique.

Grotowski dealt with this primarily during his preparation of the productions discussed in *Towards a Poor Theatre*, culminating with Ryszard Cieślak's portrayal of the Constant Prince. During this period, his actors experimented with a variety of meditative techniques, each of which seeks to rid the meditator of blocks, to educate him into a closer knowledge of repressed inner impulses and to extend his physical limitations. Grotowski cites judo rituals and Hatha yoga (a yoga which links breathing patterns and physical exercises with introspection), along with exercises used in actor training, such as Dullin's eurhythmics (body motions performed to rhythmical and musical accompaniment) and Delsarte's hieroglyphic system of fixed facial expressions and body positions, each of which is supposed to convey a particular emotion (Delsarte enjoyed much popularity during the era of nineteenth-century melodramatic acting). We might add to this list some techniques which Grotowski does not record, such as Ignatian meditation and Reichian psychoanalysis, as it is used in extroversive activities like the current psychodramas, encounter groups, and so on. These activities share two assumptions: the belief that our authentic natures lie hidden beneath social facades which in turn have imposed physically inhibiting patterns of motion and emotion-registering on our bodies; and the belief that when we eradicate these blocks, we not only release authentic feelings and movement-patterns, but we also allow forces outside ourselves (which our resistances had previously blocked out) to penetrate us and work through us. Grotowski calls this "psychic penetration."[56] As a synthesis of previously unconnected meditative techniques and psychological assumptions from Western and Oriental traditions, it is one of the richest of conglomerations, but it is still a combination. To the extent to which it shares the first assumption mentioned above, that the extreme excitation of emotion purifies us of the adverse effects of emotion, it can be placed in the tradition of cathartic theories which includes the Renaissance interpretation of Aristotle, Freudian psychoanalysis, and Stanislavskian acting. To the extent to which it shares the second assumption—that the newly purified man acts as a medium for the transmission of certain unspecified forces which exist outside him—it can be placed in the mystic tradition which includes archetypal analysis and belief in "eternal return" associated with the Cambridge anthropologists; Jungian predication of "racial memory"; and, at the core of Grotowski's European Catholicism, the figural interpretation of the Scriptures and of history. (His obsession with Catholicism is in no way negated by the fact that he admits to being an atheist.) In terms of acting technique, Grotowski's contribution lies in the way he links the two beliefs, catharsis and *figura*.

We might outline a scheme for this process as follows. His actor undergoes an intensely grueling psychophysical process to discover a hidden aspect of his personality which resembles the "role" (the part which he has been asked to play); this role—constancy, Faustian overreaching, etc.—is also a social force or value acknowledged by society (the audience), but one which society cannot often perform with any degree of authenticity. Playing the role as part, the actor exposes his own congruence with the character—masochistic sufferer, sadistic torturer—and excites the emotions associated with these patterns of behavior, so that the role as behavior pattern is expended by his physical and psychological apparatus simultaneously with his playing out of the role as part (catharsis). But he has done this in the presence of an audience, spectators who share complicity with the actor in two ways. They have been cast in a significant role in the play's system of meanings (patients in *Kordian,* guests at Faustus's final banquet, and so on) so that they are "part of the play" along with the actor. And they consent to watch an exhausting and potentially degrading psychophysical exposure which the actor consents to conduct *in their presence:* their presence thrusts roles (in the sense of social functions, not parts) onto the actor (he is their *figura*), who performs them for an audience which will not have to take them on itself (it has made him a scapegoat). But though the audience has avoided certain roles which its presence has nonetheless brought into being (in the sense that, having made the actor a scapegoat, the spectators have re-created the efficacy of the values and forces which they have forced him to take from them onto himself), nevertheless, the audience has fallen into another set of roles (in terms of theater performance, not of its "part" in the play): it has been the voyeuristic sadist to the actor's exhibitionistic masochist.

Reading *Towards a Poor Theatre*, one cannot avoid noticing Grotowski's rich language, drawn from the vocabularies of religious and postreligious thought (his "holy actor" achieves a "secular *sacrum*,"[57] and from the language of sexual domination and submission. (Grotowski talks of "the masochistic component in the actor" as a "negative variant of what is creative in the director in the form of a sadistic component,"[58] and it is easy to substitute "audience" for "director" in Grotowski's theory, for he thinks of the audience as a single body, one-half of the actor-audience pair which is essential to theater; the audience is the manipulating and provoking body to which the actor reacts in performance, just as he reacts to the director during rehearsal. Unlike Artaud, Grotowski does not mistake the *metteur-en-scène* for "the supreme actor" on his stage; in fact, during performances, he always sits inconspicuously among the spectators, observing but still guiding the actors by means of his presence.) My schematic discussion of the relationship between catharsis and *figura* in Grotowski's acting technique has acknowledged the traditional religious and erotic bases of his synthesis, at the same time that it has already begun to move from Grotowski's combination of received elements (catharsis, the scapegoat, *figura*) to his real innovation: the involvement of the audience not only in the circumstances of the play (which, after all, is an age-old technique) but also its complicity in the circumstances of performance. But before we go on to Grotowski's innovations, let us conclude our examination of his attitude toward the tradition from which he has emerged.

First, we should correct a common misunderstanding about the role of literature in Grotowski's theater. In spite of his radical rearrangement of the texts which he used in productions preceding *Apocalypsis cum figuris*, Grotowski's work has not been antiliterary. That misunderstanding has stemmed in part from critical conservatism, and in part from the phenomenon of Grotowski's esteem outside of Poland (which is probably greater than at home): audiences and critics who do not understand Polish rationalize the fact that his performances affect them—in spite of linguistic barriers—by believing that the word plays no vital role in his theater. We should listen to a Polish critic like Andrzej Wirth, who has called Grotowski's theater a "literature-oriented theatre," and who says that "the word of the poet remains holy for him. He treats the classic texts as reservoirs of mankind's experiences; as material in which archetypes of elementary human situations are recorded."[59] Grotowski's choice of repertoire indicates his admiration for traditional texts and the legends they contain. But beyond this obvious admiration lies the more profound belief that, in so contemporary a context as the theater, we cannot present a historical reconstruction of the original text. This would violate our respect for the fact that, in its own time, the author's written text was a contemporary art object. Through historical scholarship, we can learn something of the nature of the text's particular immediacy and its particular effect on its original audiences, but the same historicism demonstrates at once that the age and the audience which could *directly* receive the author's play (in the immediate way which he originally intended) has passed away forever. Because Grotowski deeply respects this shared transaction of affectivity between minds—those of creators, those of recipients of their creations—he attempts to bring about an equivalent effect in his contemporary context. And we should bear in mind that this contemporaneity itself has two aspects—it belongs to the late twentieth century (as opposed to the Romantic era or the Renaissance, the periods from which Grotowski chooses his play texts), and it belongs to the present instant of performance, which always happens "now" and which makes *every* former transaction between creation and recipient a historical act, a part of the work's history of interpretations.

Hence, Grotowski's concern with "the classics" as opposed to contemporary plays really demonstrates his belief that *every* written text, no matter how recent, already exists in and is limited by a historical context—it is already a classic. As Grotowski says of the literary art object, "The entire value of the text is already present once it has been written: this is literature, and we may read plays as part of 'literature.'"[60] In reading, we can try to receive this value by the historical act of mentally reconstructing the original circumstances of performance and the audience assumptions of the time, and by erecting a similar construct drawn from our own history, that is, a circumstance in which we could react to the text as did its original audience. In short, we have made an interpretation of the artwork in the process of authentically reading or receiving it. Grotowski respects both of these activities, the recapitulation of a historically fixed object (the text) which indicates the continuity of the human mind over centuries, and the contemporary transaction (the interpretive reading of the text) which is unrepeatable but the unrepeatability of which attests to the persistence of the historical object's affective quality. Since this affective quality stands at the center of his theater in his concept of the encounter between actor and audience, it follows that Grotowski believes that theater can only present an interpretation of the text, not "the thing itself" (in that objective sense in which a work is contained and preserved within the pages of a book) but a *reading* which is contemporary in its twentieth-century metaphors and in the sense that its performance-based affectivity always happens "now." The interpretation Grotowski presents often rearranges and cuts the play's lines, and sets it action in an anachronistic setting (such as in Wyspiański's *Akropolis*, which Grotowski transposes from Wawel Cathedral to Auschwitz, a more contemporary "cemetery for the tribes," to cite Wyspiański's obsessively repeated appellation for the Cathedral). Grotowski also casts his audiences in significant roles in each production—for example, in *Akropolis* the spectators are understood to play "the living" while the actors play "the dead." He does this to involve the audience in the interpretation of the play, for in the sense that it plays a theatrical "part," the audience fleshes out the interpretation by embodying a part of it, and the audience acknowledges the interpretation's affective presence by helping to create the interpretation. By drawing the audience into the activity of creating the interpretation, as opposed to just passively receiving it (hearing and watching), Grotowski has drawn it into another responsibility which it shares with the actors and director who originally structured the performance by distorting, cutting, and "violating" the literary text. The actors and director rearranged the text *because* they understood its meaning and affective quality in its historical context, and respected the wholeness of this assemblage of words, referents, and affective responses which comes down to us as "all the words of the text in order" and which may "be read": they violated these "ordered words'" to *make a reading* of them, we might even say that they violated the text in order to save it. By bringing the audience into the act of violation, instead of simply demonstrating the results of the violation (the interpretation) to it, Grotowski makes his audience responsible for knowledge of the assemblage of values present in the original text, as well as for the new set of values which results from the confrontation with or interpretation of that text.

This places a great responsibility upon the audience and greatly complicates the director's activity; he must "manage" not only the production as it evolves and partially yields an interpretation of the primary text, and not only the actors who help in part to further this process of evolving and to embody the results which evolve, but he must also "manage" the audience which, each evening, completes both the evolution and the embodiment of interpretation. (At the linguistic level, we might see this more easily through the French phrase for the English "to watch a play": *j'assiste à une pièce*, I help at making a play.)[61] Zbigniew Osiński has observed the importance of Grotowski's "directed" audience:

> One of the most essential and most meaningful assumptions in each spectacle lies in Grotowski's theatrical practice of simulta-

neously directing two companies—actors and audience—or directing them as one collectivity participating together in theatre space-time.[62]

But even though our close analysis of Grotowski's "casted audience" has yielded the impetus for his supposedly antiliterary violation of texts, and demonstrated Grotowski's profound respect for both literary texts *and* the interpretive act of reading, problems arise at once. How can the audience be held responsible for knowledge of a primary literary text which is not literally present, which is signified only by its palimpsest, the Grotowski version? Foreign audiences face the additional problem of not understanding the language of either the original text or Grotowski's palimpsest. Another problem: Grotowski's actors sometimes reduce words to pure sounds, distort them into songs, screams, groans, and speak a very rapid Polish which not every native speaker can follow precisely; furthermore, even Poles often receive the literary palimpsests (Grotowski's versions) at a degree of removal caused by the intrusion of translation. Grotowski's repertoire has mainly consisted of Polish translations of foreign plays (*Dr. Faustus, El Principe Constante* in the famous Słowacki translation) or of Polish classics which deal with the retelling of old legends (*Akropolis*), a retelling which automatically imposes a palimpsest upon the obliterated original. Since every audience must necessarily fail to know fully the original text as well as the director and actors know it, should we assume that Grotowski's oft-proclaimed setting up of a confrontation between original text and theatrical interpretation is a failure?

Before we come to this conclusion, we should be aware of a "meaning" inherent in this very failure. To the extent to which the audience does not succeed in arriving at the same re-creative knowledge of the original literary object as does Grotowski's actor, who has spent months of rehearsals analyzing it intellectually and emotionally, tearing it apart and reassembling it, this "unsuccessful" audience thus becomes aware of the *distance* between itself and the art object, the extent to which any contemporary interpretation/re-creation inevitably fails to capture some facet of the primary art experience. Each spectator becomes aware of loss over time, of the human world's continual dissolution, of the omnipresent void between his consciousness and those of others—poets who initiate aesthetic transactions by creating artworks, actors who further these transactions by embodying them. The hermeneutic tradition to which Grotowski is an heir has always taught us both our capacity for recapturing primal wisdoms and ancient meanings, and the *distance* between ourselves and "the word" which can never be fully mediated and which should remind us of existential limitations; given this understanding, interpretive palimpsests do not so much intrude between ourselves and "the word" as they pay homage to human persistence—in the face of failure—in approaching the word. We should also observe that when Grotowski demands an unrealizable responsibility for the literary artwork from his audience, he is exposing the necessity of reducing the distance between actors and audience in terms of their function in generating a performance. Clearly, the only audience member who could have the same emotional-intellectual knowledge of the original literary text that the actor has, and who would also completely understand the relationship between the original and the distortions performed (the Grotowski version), would be an audience member who had attended every rehearsal. Only Grotowski, the ideal audience member, can make this claim. When he limits his audience size to thirty spectators, he does this partially to acknowledge that only a very responsible, emotionally and intellectually knowledgeable, and necessarily small number of people may legitimately take part in such a project as his; he calls this group of initiates "an elite of the soul," as opposed to a monied or educated elite, the two usual audiences for theater. But as I just observed, only the director of such an ensemble can be fully aware of both text and interpretation, and the subtle relationship between them which is publicly manifested by the distorted and wrenching violations of the text which the actors speak and perform; following this logic, Grotowski could legitimately limit his "audience" to himself—that he limits it to thirty, points to his *reductio*'s belief that, essentially, it could be still smaller. (But again, Grotowski moves from the purely negative aspect of his *reductio*—eliminating the audience from a fully realized encounter with the literary art object—to the positive position of making an encounter with the actor who embodies the art object, an encounter which can come about because, in a certain sense, the art object has been eliminated.)

Another barrier stands between Grotowski's spectators and the art experience that they ought to be acknowledging, participating in, and helping to create: the "parts" they are supposed to play in particular productions. Need Grotowski's audiences be consciously aware of these "parts," such as "the living" in *Akropolis* or Faustus's banquet guests in *Dr. Faustus*? Many spectators claim that they have felt completely engaged in Grotowski's performances without ever having been aware of their dramatic "part" in it. Furthermore, Grotowski does not always specify the exact nature of the part: watching *The Constant Prince* from a steep angle of elevation from behind a baffle which comes to eye level, the single row of audience members may imagine that they sit either in a hospital operating amphitheater or overlooking a circus ring or a bull ring, each vantage point being a location which would cast the audience in a different "part." Donald Richie has commented on this apparent discrepancy:

> Of help to [the actors]...is the casting of the audience in the play. In *Cain* we are the descendants of Cain; in *The Ancestors* we are courtiers; in *Doctor Faustus* we are the guests; in *Akropolis* we are the living.
>
> All this is no help to us. And, indeed, we do not feel ourselves to be any of these things. But it is of enormous help to the actor. He needs a context badly and we are it.[63]

To the extent that the informed audience mentally "knows" the identity of its "part" but does not "feel" it, to use Richie's term, and to the extent that the actor assumes a certain "cast relationship" between himself and the audience but *of which the audience is unaware*, Grotowski has deliberately erected another barrier between his audience and its full apprehension of the artwork. Perhaps this conviction on his actor's part that we play a part of which we are either unaware or unconvinced accounts for the profound uneasiness felt by spectators at Laboratory Theater performances. They report that Grotowski's actors "look without seeing," that they seem to "look through us," that they seem "possessed of a special knowledge which we are denied." As I see it, this deliberate withholding from the audience of knowledge about its "part" and Grotowski's preventing the audience from experiencing conviction in the part in which it nonetheless has been cast represents one of his greatest provocations of his audience, an aggressive act committed by his actors which nevertheless attests to their profound love for those people who have gone to such an apparently frustrating effort to be, authentically, part of Grotowski's audience. His actors look at us as if they know something about us which we have not yet discovered about ourselves. What is this knowledge? Our secrets? Our sins? The certainty of our deaths? The verbal elements in the Grotowski repertoire of plays support each of these interpretations yet lend certainty to none of them.

Let us return to Donald Richie's statement which seemed to undercut the notion of the "casted audience"; perhaps a solution lies in the very dichotomy which Richie points out. He claims that the actor needs a context badly, and we audience members are that context. But before saying this, Richie points out that the audience does not need to share the context if this is seen as being based on the circumstances inherent in the play text, the character "parts" played by actor and audience. But what results if we locate this "context" in the circumstances inherent in the *act of performance*? This performance is the only entity actually present in the moment of "now," and it exists partially to acknowledge our distance from, and the absence of, the play text, literary artwork, or "the word" that we should like to reverse and recapitulate, but that fades from us as we seek to know it and make it ours by interpreting it (placing a palimpsest over it). The "we" who engage in this activity include both audience and actor. But beyond our failure to achieve a complete and immediate reception of the artwork (a failure, moreover, which is different for actor and audience, who have differing degrees of knowledge of and emotional engagement in the work—we do not all share even the same failure), there exists a transaction which *is* successful, which results in a success that makes our failure to receive the artwork authentically seem like a heuristic device which has served to bring us—actor and audience—into another ultimately more profound encounter than the unsuccessful aesthetic encounter.

This is the encounter I sense when Zbigniew Osiński states that Grotowski simultaneously directs actors and audience "as one collectivity participating together in theatre space-time." It is the kind of encounter which results in the audience's recognition of the actor behind the character he performs, of the man behind the part, of the nature of man which compels him to mask, play roles, and act at the same time that he most wants to break down defenses, narrow distances, and unmask. On the actor's part, it is the kind of encounter with spectators that allows him to recognize the people behind the "dramatic parts" in which they have been cast, and behind the "social roles" they play as onlookers—onlookers to a victimizing (the scapegoat function), onlookers to a display of masochistic exhibitionism (their complicitous function of sadistic voyeurism), even, finally, the role of onlooker-as-the-other, the spectator who gives the watched man existence by watching him. Grotowski's tortuous attempt to set up public encounters in which these artificial "parts" and "roles"—for they are one—may be taken on, used up, and, it is hoped, cast off results in his ultimate notion of catharsis. In its final cause, this catharsis brings about an encounter between people which lies beyond artifice, imitation, theater—ultimately, beyond art and aesthetics themselves—yet which we can reach by having gone through all these things. Although they are the logical conclusion of Grotowski's thought in *Towards a Poor Theatre*, these ultimate notions lie largely outside that work, and outside any concept of theater, no matter how "poor." In his recent uncollected statements, Grotowski has made an attempt to define this encounter which seems to have cathartic properties in itself. Perhaps it lies in the very nature of such a project that Grotowski's definitions seem incomplete, not open to rational apprehension, ultimately unverbalizable. When successful, this kind of encounter should demonstrate the limitations of artifice and words; the encounter itself attempts to transcend them. We probably cannot both *live* it and *name* it. Short of learning its true name, we might follow Grotowski and refer to this ultimate encounter simply as "the human act."

6. *Apocalypsis cum figuris* and the Return of the Theater

Grotowski published *Towards a Poor Theatre* in 1968, the same year in which his actors first performed *Apocalypsis cum figuris* before an audience. They had rehearsed *Apocalypsis* over four hundred times. Since 1968, no new Grotowski production has appeared, and Grotowski has not published any essays which rival those found in *Towards a Poor Theatre* in terms of rigor and organization of argument. But Grotowski has not remained completely silent. In his impromptu discussion sessions with audiences following performances of *Apocalypsis*, he speaks at length about the continual crisis involved in theater work, and his own crisis in particular. Although Grotowski speaks through indirection and metaphor, his public pronouncements reveal some information about his newest direction. I suspect that it will result in either a radical deviation from the theater we know today, or in his departure from theater altogether.

Grotowski has said that *Apocalypsis* marks the conclusion of a phase of theater work which evolved through the activity recorded in *Towards a Poor Theatre*, and perhaps a new beginning as well. This turning point is most apparent in his treatment of the literary text. Like the productions of the "poor theater" period, *Apocalypsis* is an intense distillation and blasphemous testing of revered myths and poetic passages. Like earlier productions, it plays for about an hour on a bare stage; its cast consists of six actors, who take on all the roles and also provide the extensive sound score of songs and screams, through which the play's words are refracted. But unlike earlier productions, the "script" of *Apocalypsis cum figuris* has no independent existence as literature. All the words which the actors speak are quotations drawn from classic sources—the Scriptures, Dostoyevsky's *Brothers Karamazov*, the prose of Simone Weil, and the verse of T. S. Eliot. But Grotowski's actors are not simply illustrating their favorite quotations. They developed the action, characterizations, and themes of their play through improvisation during years of rehearsals. Until relatively late in this process, they improvised their own words to accompany the visual-vocal partitur. (Notice that the actors and director created *Apocalypsis* through the same process of "actualizations" described by Aristotle, beginning with action, plot, characters, and idea, and adding specific words much later.) When the gestural score was "set," Grotowski and his actors substituted the classic quotations for their own phrases. In a program note to *Apocalypsis,* Grotowski explains, "The idea was that, wherever the spoken word was essential, it should appear in the form of quotations from sources which could be regarded as the work not of one writer but of the whole of mankind."[1]

Has Grotowski created his most universal work by freeing it from the bounds of literature entirely? He has certainly escaped from the confines of Polish romanticism, the important but obscure national literature which provided the springboard for most of his earlier productions. *Apocalypsis* also approaches universal significance by dealing explicitly with the myth of Christ and his figural reappearance. But beyond the appeal of this theme, the circumstances behind the creation and performance of *Apocalypsis* make it compelling to any sympathetic audience. For creation and performance occur simultaneously here, and, to a larger extent than with any of the other plays discussed in this study, the play is re-created with each new performance.

However, there is very little "free improvisation" during performances of *Apocalypsis.* Grotowski does not introduce chance into his finished work, for he believes that the place for exercises and fortuitous improvisations is in the rehearsal stage during which he "writes the production." He does not write the play's words, of course, and even with *Apocalypsis* he felt compelled to dip into world literature for his script. But just as in the cases of film directors who are called the *auteurs* of their cinematic works, Grotowski aspires toward an authorship of all the elements of his productions, including the management, "casting," and "directing" of their audiences, as we have seen. This *auteur* temperament prizes the total aesthetic control which the monastic performance conditions of the Laboratory Theater afford; random improvisation in performance and unpredictable audience participation stand at the opposite pole from such total control, and have more to do with group psychology and audience sociology than with aesthetics. Characteristically, Grotowski has avoided randomness in his most mature productions, concluding with *Apocalypsis.* (More recently, he has expressed dismay with all theater and a new interest in what he calls "paratheatrical phenomena,"[2] but although this development is anticipated by *Apocalypsis,* it lies outside the boundaries set by that production, and will not be discussed until later.) Before we discuss the aspects of *Apocalypsis* which his actors re-create with each new performance, though, we ought to examine the fixed partitur which provides the boundaries for their creation. For the sake of convenience, let us call *Apocalypsis* "a play," although the Polish loan-word *spektakl* ("spectacle") might be a better name for the piece. For if, as I suggested earlier, the play was created through a process of Aristotelian "actu-alizations" which begins with more intellectual elements such as ac-tion, theme, and character—what we might call "creation from the top down"—it is first perceived by the audience through the play's *spectacular* and visceral elements, "from the bottom up" (or phe-nomenologically, as I argued of Artaud's theater). What we see and feel in Grotowski's theater seems to be separated from what we know and hear in it. Consider for a moment what Grotowski's spectacle shows us visually. He confronts us with six tortured actors who perform a harried yet evocative mime of caresses, beatings, derisions, and ecstasies. Gradually, as we watch, the actors take on separate identities as characters, and their gestures begin to become "decodable" as bibli-cal figurations, although their blasphemous behavior does not compel us to see Christian mythology as the only system of referents. The actors break and share bread, but they also cast it at one another, and mastur-bate into it. A white cane carried by the village idiot suggests the staff of some good shepherd to us, but it also suggests blindness (although none of the characters is blind). In visual terms, the play falls into two parts: the first half is lighted by two white spotlights which stand on the stage floor and point upward; the second half of the play takes place in darkness which is punctuated by the flames of several altar candles, until one by one, these flicker out. During the second half, the character playing the village idiot is stretched out on the floor in a posture of crucifixion, but later he rises from this death to whip the others with a towel; still later, two secondary characters stand in buckets and splash water about their feet, while the tormented hero confronts his inter-locutor for their last argument, which concludes with the extinguishing of all the candles. When the lights come back up, all the actors are gone. This account leaves the reader unenlightened by the spectacular ele-ments, the "visuals" and the "vocals" which it perceives as no more than songs and screams if the Polish text is not translated. Visually, we do not even perceive the narrative outlines of a concrete story, which con-ventional pantomime and ballet would have afforded us.

Clearly, Grotowski's "spectacle" does not stand alone, or explain it-self, although the spectacular is the aspect of *Apocalypsis* which can most obviously be attributed to his "creation." But if we return to the play with some knowledge of the script's words, and also consider it in the light of his written intentions found in the program note, we begin to notice the coherence and wholeness of a work which is more than vocalized pantomime. What strikes the audience which apprehends *Apocalypsis* intellectually as well as by means of its spectacle is the deliberateness and unity with which the entire production is "written"—and the perverse contradiction between its verbal poetry and its gestural agony.

Let me describe this play's action a second time. It takes place in a bare, windowless room, on a level floor which has no stage or separation from the handful of onlookers (who sit one row deep around the four walls, upon the floor). Five men and one woman, wearing contemporary dress, lie on the floor in the empty space Grotowski has allotted them. One by one, they awaken from drunken stupor and all but one (the man with the white cane) begin to assign one another names—Simon Peter, Mary Magdalene, John, and Judas. Judas calls the last of them "Savior," but Simon Peter intervenes. Simon Peter quickly assumes the role of master of ceremonies, and decides that Lazarus would be a better identity for the fifth of their party. Their "Savior" might be played, Simon Peter suggests, by a pathetic man who is still lying on the edge of the playing space, the man whom the program note identifies as "the Simpleton." He wears nothing but a black raincoat; the others are dressed in stylish white clothes. At first he responds positively to Simon Peter's "casting," and seems to relish any role which will draw him into the acceptance of the group. His big eyes moon and roll; he grins and looks ingenuous; and Grotowski's sophisticated audience of intellectuals is suddenly surprised that the Laboratory Theater can be *funny*, for the Simpleton almost looks foolish. But there is an edge to his idiocy, and we remember that this same actor had once played the tortured Constant Prince. The Simpleton's eyes also register a consciousness of his mental deficiency, and a knowledge of the idiocy of his having been chosen to play Christ; the eyes anticipate the mockery which he will soon suffer.

At first the revelers pretend to accept the Simpleton. They draw him into their circle and Simon Peter addresses him as if the Simpleton were Christ: "You were born in Nazareth," "You died for them on the cross," "But they failed to recognize you." But he speaks each sentence as if it were a taunting insult, and others punctuate his statements with guffaws of derision. Simon Peter even briefly carries the Simpleton on his back, but the ride ends brutally when he suddenly mounts the Simpleton and whips him into a frenzy, riding him around the periphery of the playing space until the Simpleton rears and throws off his oppressor. He races around the group of tormentors and pounds the floor with rhythmic beats, transforming his protest into a kind of Dionysian dance. Then he falls to the floor. He has begun to believe in his role as Christ—and to resist it.

The play now begins to resemble a curious exorcism, for the Simpleton tries to cast off his role as Savior at the same time as the revelers goad him into accepting it. They refuse to acknowledge him unless he responds "in character" as Christ, but when he does this, they revile him for being Christ. The Simpleton himself is torn between the longing for acceptance by the group, self-preservation, and the temptation to take on so fine yet so devalued a role as that of the Savior; at the same time, however, he registers an idiot's fear that his desire to be Christ smacks of *hubris*.

We can observe this complex evocation and derision of the Christ *figura* in the episode of Lazarus. Until this point in the play, the actor who was called Lazarus has done nothing to justify the biblical associations with his name. In fact, Grotowski's program note informs us that, in Polish, Lazarus is a "term of abuse for a feckless wretch and so does not conjure up solely Gospel associations."[3] Suddenly, this fellow lies upon the floor and pulls his T-shirt over his face. The others begin a noisy wake for him, which encourages the Simpleton to join in the game and complete the identification of the biblical story: he calls out, "Lazarus, come forth." But Lazarus's reaction undercuts the parable's beatific implications. He gets up, swaggers resentfully toward his savior, and breaks open the loaf of bread which had been blessed—and also cradled and then stabbed by Mary, and masturbated into by John. Then he pelts the Simpleton with hunks of bread, all the while reciting from Scripture. But he does not speak the words of the biblical Lazarus; instead he cites Job's lamentations, cursing the day of his birth. Job's words concerning man's emergence from the womb parallel Lazarus's situation of emerging from the grave, but the words hold up both passages to scorn:

> There is a man-child conceived. Let that day be darkness; let not God regard it from above, neither let the light shine upon it; let the blackness of the day terrify it. Let the stars of the twilight thereof be dark; let it look for light, but have none; neither let it see the dawning of the day; because it shut not up the doors of my mother's womb, nor hid sorrow from mine eyes. Why died I not from the womb? Why did I not give up the ghost when I came out of the belly?[4]

Lazarus curses a savior who will not let him die. He defends man's right to the certainty of existential limits and the choice of reconciliation to one's own death without the need for a concept of "hereafter" or divine intervention. He flings back at the Savior the very symbol of the Savior's "meddling" in human affairs, the bread which represents Christ. Konstanty Puzyna compares the gray Polish bread to a decomposing corpse, and observes that Lazarus returns his own flesh for Christ's offer of his body:

> He is stoning him with bread, but with his own corpse as well, with a gray, shapeless, sticky pulp. His eyes light up as though his retaliation for an idiotic infraction of the human right to burial were a relief.[5]

But Lazarus has defended his right to death with the pessimistic words which Job spoke *during* his dark night of the soul, not *after* God had restored him. Lazarus's wish to taunt the Simpleton-Savior so overtakes him that he carries his legitimate defense of man's finitude to the extreme of exalting nihilism and praising death. And Lazarus senses this exaggeration, at the same time as he regrets the human self-sufficiency which compels him to turn down so generous an offer as Christ's body, Christ's gift of life for men and his restitution of the worth of life through the very act of dying as a man for the sake of other men. Christ and Lazarus seem to be competing for a monopoly on death: if the traditional Christ had died for men like Lazarus, the Grotowskian Lazarus wants to spite idiotic remnants of Christ's *figura*—at the same time as he registers the agony of being driven to arguing for death when confronted with the possibility that Christ may have returned, even in the guise of an imbecile.

These complicated dialectics lie under each of the sacral parodies in *Apocalypsis,* and they account for the mutual agony which both the revelers and the Simpleton feel during each enactment. The play does not portray a simple mockery of Christ, an action which would be both easy and pointless. Instead, *Apocalypsis* presents the agony felt by contemporary men when they find themselves having to resist the Christ-impulse when it possesses one of their number, as well as the torture felt by the victim visited by the role of Savior.

Although the sacrifice of the protagonist in *Apocalypsis* resembles the martyrdom of the Constant Prince, Grotowski's latest production offers a more sophisticated treatment of the theme. More emphasis falls on the group of tormentors here; they seem to equal the Simpleton in terms of stature as characters, and perhaps in terms of suffering. *Apocalypsis* is more an ensemble play than the solo tour de force of *The Constant Prince.* This shift in emphasis is important, for the characterizations of the ensemble members are also the roles which the audience members most often play: as audience, we do not see ourselves as the Simpleton, or as any kind of individual protagonist, but we can readily accept the choral, communal function of onlookers. And as I argued earlier, Grotowski's audience also acts as a kind of instigator to his actors' reactions, a voyeur to his actors' exhibitionism, and a sadist to his actors' masochism. All these social roles are concretized in *Apocalypsis* as character traits of the drunken revelers, who often "watch" while the Simpleton "acts out" his *figura*. The audience's similarity, in function and characterization, to the revelers explains why Grotowski departs from his usual practice of assigning a literary character "part" to the audience of *Apocalypsis*. For once, we are not "the living" or "Faustus's guests," we are simply "the audience." Grotowski can avoid the artificial mechanism of casting us because the action and theme of his play invest our simple identity as "audience" with the properties of a complex role-function. We do not simply "identify with" the characters in Grotowski's play who most resemble us: our act of watching the play calls into being relationships between men which the play also happens to discuss "thematically," discursively.

Grotowski also complicates the audience's relationship to his production within the play itself. Returning to my statement that the audience does not necessarily identify with the revelers simply because it most resembles their function, I would go further and suggest that the audience empathizes with the play's protagonist more than with its "chorus." But while the Simpleton captures our attention, he does not always allow us to see our own identities in his character. He is more uninhibited and also more complicated than most of us would want to be. Even his name suggests several contradictory systems of reference. As "the Simpleton," he suggests the holy fool who often appears as the personification of Christ in Slavic legend and in its literature—for example, the epileptic Prince Mishkin in Dostoyevsky's *The Idiot*. The Polish word *ciemny* can refer to a simpleton, but it literally means "dark"—like the dark black raincoat which the character wears, but also as in "the dark one" of Satan. Perhaps Grotowski is suggesting that a visitation by Christ's presence is akin to Satanic possession in a world which no longer needs a savior—or does he suggest that our fallen world would regard the return of Christ as a visit from the devil? *Ciemny* can also mean "unenlightened," "ignorant," even "blind" —again we must ask whether these qualities refer to the sighted man who carries a white cane, or to his tormentors (and the audience which abets them). The word's secondary meanings of "pessimistic," "obscure," and "suspicious" also fit both protagonist and chorus. The "choral" audience expects to feel suspicion and doubt about both the Simpleton's divine visitations and the worth of his mission—we spectators can rationalize this in ourselves as "healthy skepticism"—but we are startled when the Simpleton demonstrates the same doubts about the divine burden he bears. What kind of Christ is this who joins with his scoffers in questioning the value and even the existence of his mission? Gradually, we understand that the Simpleton belongs to both companies in the play and in the production, and that he has internalized the confrontation between them in his tormented person. In the play, he first belongs to the company of revelers (or exists outside it, wanting entrance); his paradox consists of the fact that he can gain admission only through another expulsion, being thrust out into the lonely company of the derided divine. In the production, he belongs to the company of actors, but the others desert him by going over to the side of the audience; his paradox consists of wanting to join the company of onlookers and instigators, but being left outside it, the lonely object of the other's gaze, the man who reacts to its provocation—the only "actor" left in the play. Or to reduce this to a formula, Grotowski equates the actor with the Savior and suggests that the audience's complicated attitude of admiration and rejection of the actor is like its attitude toward Christ.

This relationship prevails in each of the biblical episodes portrayed in *Apocalypsis*. The play does not present the life of Christ chronologically, but thrusts a seemingly random collage of biblical episodes at its audience. In each scene, Grotowski finds a graphic visual metaphor for biblical symbols which fixes it in an actor's wordless gesture—but which also reduces it to a literal, gross significance. I discussed the demythologizing of the Lazarus story, and other examples could be related. Grotowski conveys the symbolism contained in the sacrament of Communion by directing his actors to gnaw at one another's sides, and then to mime the swallowing of blood and to react as if it were liquor; as they do this, their bellies seem to swell like leeches. They reverse the direction of meaning in Christ's command that we think of the symbolic properties of his blood when we drink wine, and show us men slurping feigned blood as if it were wine. Christ's intercession for Mary Magdalene becomes an erotic scene between the Simpleton and the woman reveler: divine love is literalized as sex. This Christ scourges the temple (the theater?) by whipping the revelers with a towel; the various scriptural references to ritual washing (Christ's baptism, the washing of his feet, and finally, the washing of his corpse) become conflated in *Apocalypsis* to the scene of two peasant women noisily wading in buckets of water.

The biblical episodes are further complicated by the literary quotations which Grotowski has appended to the play's action as "dialogue." Through their juxtaposition, they ironically undercut the biblical parables. Lazarus's words come from Job, and plead for death instead of resurrection. Mary Magdalene's lines come from the Song of Solomon, but their eroticism no longer suggests divine love, only nymphomania. Concerning Judas's lines, Grotowski writes, "His speeches are almost entirely parables from the Gospels, but so scissored and interpreted as to give their moral a dubious ring and make him sound like an informer or agent provocateur."[6]

The other characters speak lines which come from modern literature. When the Simpleton scourges the temple, John suddenly stops him, fends off the towel which whips him, and holds the Simpleton's arm with love and regret. John is no longer playing a moneylender waiting to be driven out, but stands as a sorrowful, simple man who regrets that he cannot fully remember or respond to Christ's love. His words, taken from Simone Weil, indict the fury of the Simpleton, a curious Christ who has been caught in the act of beating his flock:

> Sometimes I can't keep from repeating, with fear and a remorseful conscience, a little of what you told me. But how can I convince myself that I remember: You won't tell me, you are not here. I well know that you don't love me. How could you have loved me? And yet, there is within me something, a small part of me which, in the depths of my soul, trembling with fear, cannot defend itself against the thought that maybe, in spite of everything you.... Oh, Jesus![7]

Simon Peter's treatment of the Simpleton is more severe. At the end of the play, after communion, crucifixion, and a rejected resurrection, they confront one another alone on the candlelit stage. The episode suggests Christ's temptation in the desert, but he is tempted by a man, not a devil, and the tempting arguments come from the Grand Inquisitor in Dostoyevsky's *Brothers Karamazov*. Simon Peter attacks a Christ who grants his followers freedom to decide personally between good and evil, who grants them as their model only his own image and mission. This Christ expects men to love him freely, yet he refuses to ease their problem of choice by handing down "the stern ancient law":

> But did you never imagine that [man] would eventually reject and challenge even your image and your truth, if he were weighted down with so fearful a burden as freedom of choice? In the end they will cry out that the truth is not in you, since they could not have been left in greater confusion and suffering than you have done by leaving them with so many cares and impossible problems.[8]

At this point in the play, the audience should feel some sympathy toward Simon Peter's diatribe, for its members have been placed in a similar position, confronted with a complex and ambiguous Christ whose return can be seen as both an offer of salvation and a disruption of social harmony, even a demonic possession. Certainly the Simpleton seems to have failed his mission by the end of the play; he does not defend himself through strong words but uses gestural language to protest his divinity and the sincerity of his self-sacrifice. In contrast to the actor's mimed protestations, his words express despair, old age, tiredness, and loss. Appropriately, the Simpleton's lines are mainly drawn from Eliot's verse:

> I no longer strive to strive towards such things
> (Why should the agèd eagle stretch its wings?)
>
> [History] . . . gives too late
> What's not believed in, or if still believed,
> In memory only, reconsidered passion. Gives too soon
> Into weak hands, what's thought can be dispensed with
> Till the refusal propagates a fear.[9]

These verses summarize *Apocalypsis cum figuris* in its grandeur and despair. The Simpleton stops striving to convince the revelers of his truth, but they do not succeed in convincing him that their nomination of him as Christ was merely a cruel game all along. The Simpleton grows into the part—or the identity—of Christ, of the agèd eagle, as the play progresses. He laments what he thinks to be his failure to affect the others, the world of men: he came too late, after they had stopped believing in him except in memory; or he came too soon, and being too weak a vessel for the Word, he gave men the impression that the Word could be rejected. Since it cannot, its refusal bred fear in men and caused them to turn on the frail bearer of the Word. But just as Eliot's verses express the idea of despair but possess a kind of stature and even grandeur in their form, the Simpleton's exalted physical appearance at the end of the play indicates the victory of Christ within him which his speeches do not betray. The Simpleton has been fully convinced that he is Christ, and that this identity has failed to affect the others. Full of regret, he withdraws from the men who rejected him:

> I have lost my passion: why should I need to keep it
> Since what is kept must be adulterated?
> I have lost my sight, smell, hearing, taste and touch:
> How should I use them for your closer contact?[10]

The lights flicker out as he recites a lamentation in Latin. The last voice we hear in the darkness belongs to Simon Peter, who apparently addresses the Simpleton-Christ to expel him: "Go and come no more."

Whom is Simon Peter turning out? The question suggests that the play is open to a number of interpretations, but establishing any one of them as the "final meaning" presents some problems. Grotowski poses the question himself in his program note, and suggests three contradictory solutions. The Simpleton may be "a bearer of higher values whose very presence has dislocated life's everyday routine," or "a troublesome drinking companion who, just by turning up, has soured a celebration, making it an agonized confrontation between [the celebrants] and their own anxieties," or he may be "a personification of flawed or false values."[11] But Grotowski offers no code which would allow us to isolate one of these readings.

The first problem to be faced by anyone wishing to interpret *Apocalypsis* is to determine which play he will examine as the central one. Paradoxically, there seem to be several layers of meaning here, or of potential meaning—does one govern all the others, and ironically undercut and hence "correct" all the layers which contradict it (and each other)? We have noticed that this is a play-within-a-play: at the center stands the life of Christ, and it is framed by the modern-day situation of the drunken revelers who enact it. Since their Christ is played by a man whom Grotowski calls "the Simpleton," a kind of village idiot, and since Grotowski refers extensively to peasant superstition and rural religion in his program note, we might expect that these revelers are "really" drunken peasants—who else, even in Catholic Poland, would undertake so cruel and so outmoded an entertainment as to play these biblical charades with an imbecile? However, before we carry this "peasant reading" to an extreme, we should observe that nothing in the production's style of representation urges us to look for verisimilitude: peasant behavior does not identify the revelers as rustics who could be "expected to believe in such superstitions," and the six actors wear rather urban and stylish clothes which do not tie them to any geographical region.

If we have difficulty choosing between the "peasant" frame-play or the "biblical" play-within-a-play, we also have difficulty deciding between the text and the gestures which so contradict them. Do the exalted literary passages elevate agonized pantomimed action which Grotowski's actors developed independently of a literary text? Or do the gross gestures debunk altogether certain hollowed poetry, and the notion of literature as an integral part of dramatic art? Grotowski has certainly reached the end of his *reductio* of literature here; it is hard to imagine a "poor theater" which could reduce the text even further and not cross the boundary between theater and pantomime.

Apocalypsis contains another semantic contradiction within the gestural language it employs. The sacramental parodies all depend upon a separation between sign and referent. Bread and wine refer to Christ's body and blood, but this divine cannibalism refers in turn to the spiritual sustenance that belief in Christ and acceptance of him as a model can offer to men. But Grotowski's visceral pantomimes of real cannibalism and blood-sucking prevent us from making the leap from the sign to its symbolism. He asks us to consider the gesture for *what it is,* and what it is can terrify us. In an essay called "Grotowski—Destroyer of Signs,"

Seweryna Wysłouch suggests that Grotowski's real shock-value does not lie in the eroticism and cruelty of his gestures per se, but in his elimination of the traditional referents for which signs have mediated in the past.

> Twenty centuries of our culture have shaped the whole richness of signs with the aid of which we indicate love or lust, beginning with the heart pierced with an arrow and ending with the subtle gestures of the romantic ballet. With Grotowski, however, eroticism and orgy are shown literally. The gesture doesn't refer to anything except itself, it means nothing beyond what it tangibly displays—and thus it loses the character of being a sign. This is what really shocks the viewer, who—through his whole life having to deal with signs—suddenly perceives that the age-old tradition has been brutally thrown out....[12]

In the verbal text, Grotowski's treatment of the individual poetic passages also sets up a distance between the literal meanings of words and the interpretations which their speakers make of them. Not only do his performers "act against the text," by ironically undercutting or over-inflating the sentiments found in the quoted passages; they sometimes distort words so much by groaning or screaming them that the words lose all semantic value. Wysłouch calls this "desemanticization" and discusses this in terms of the distinction between sign and referent:

> The text "tacked on to gestures" vanishes amidst the pressure of scenes and images—we may even say it vanishes at birth, speaking quietly and indistinctly, smothered by plastic gestures. The muffled word loses its range and sense. It stops referring to the essence hidden behind it, stops "meaning," because the tension between its sound (*signifiant*) and that which it designates in language (*signifié*) suffers a slackening. Only noises dart forth to the audience: cries, song, the blow of the body against the parquet floor, and vocal sounds stripped of meaning, the semantics of a living language.[13]

Such desemanticization would lead an interpreter to believe that Grotowski wants us to regard the gesture exclusively for *what it is*, not for what it refers to—Wysłouch makes this conclusion, and decides that Grotowski has destroyed the elaborate system of referents which signs have accrued over the centuries to confront us with primal appetites, sexual instincts, and "corrupt human nature."[14] Can we be so certain that the referents exist only as memories in Grotowski's theater, though, a pantheon of values and meanings to be debunked? We have already discussed the ways in which the Grotowskian artwork must be seen to contain elements which are not literally present or apparent in his plays—the "roles" to be played by the "casted audiences" in earlier productions, or, in *Apocalypsis*, the information found in the program note, which identifies the ambiguous Christ-figure as the Simpleton and sets up the contradictory meanings his name may take on in Polish. In his earlier productions of classic plays, Grotowski expected his interpreters to possess a knowledge of the original texts that served as springboards for, but which were not contained in, his distorted reading of the texts. With *Apocalypsis*, we are expected to know something about the original contexts of the quoted passages, to understand how they function ironically in the new context of this play, but also to be able to determine whether Grotowski somehow restores to them their original value and power in his independent creation.

This possibility of restoration has led several critics to believe that *Apocalypsis* does not eliminate the semantic nature of literature from the theater but somehow "redeems" it. Jan Błoński calls the work both a Passion play and a tragedy, a tragedy about the possibility of tragedy today and about the existence of values themselves. He goes on to claim that Grotowski is the true *auteur* of the play:

> we are justified in saying that he used the Bible, Dostoyevsky and Eliot to "write" *Apocalypsis cum figuris* himself. The words come from sources already known to us, but their composition (i.e., what determines their theatrical value) calls into being an original action, and an original meaning. In the final analysis then, "poor theatre" indirectly regains all that it previously rejected by a gesture of asceticism, including literature.[15]

Konstanty Puzyna has written two excellent essays about *Apocalypsis*. His careful nonevaluative description of the play in "A Myth Vivisected" is a model of documentation and an invaluable summary of the play's major actions.[16] *Apocalypsis*, he suggests, does not deal with the hackneyed statement that God is dead, but with the more provocative question of whether God—or the God-like—has died out among men. Puzyna dwells on the play's literary themes, particularly the biblical episodes, and provides the closest thing we have to a text for this scriptless play. After writing this essay, Puzyna returned to the play because he was dismayed that he had captured so little of the actors' gestural score in his description of the literary elements, and he was convinced that the gestural text provided a whole layer of meaning which qualified the literary quotations and the pantomimed myths and sacraments. Puzyna's second essay, "Addendum to *Apocalypsis*," is a curious achievement. The author describes many of the play's extraliterary gestures, demonstrates how they tie the play into a single unified work, and formulates three rules governing the gestural holism of the piece. First, the gestures are ambiguous, each possessing a multiplicity of contradictory referents; second, the gestures are simultaneous (or synchronic), which means that we cannot understand particular gestures one at a time as they occur, but must read later gestures in terms of related earlier ones, and, more difficult for the audience which watches the play chronologically and diachronically, we must read *earlier* gestures in terms of related *later* ones; third, the play obeys "an ambiguous law of universal analogy," a phrase which Puzyna does not explain, but which suggests that any metaphor can be made to refer to any referent or any further metaphor.[17] Puzyna concludes by likening the play to Joyce's *Ulysses*! Setting out to isolate what he calls the exclusively "actorly" aspects of the piece, he finally suggests that the actors' score can be best understood in the way we understand a symbolist poem. We must sympathize with the critic, for it is difficult to talk about a nonliterary theater spectacle without erecting a substitute literary text in its place, and description of even a small number of the "actorly" elements in a production takes up considerable space in print. These elements are also the most difficult to convey to readers who have not seen the particular production, and descriptions of acting convey only the bald outline of the artwork which an audience to that acting received. Puzyna is essentially correct in his comparison of *Apocalypsis* to symbolist literature, but he does not provide the explanation which allows us to choose between the sacred and profane layers of the play and select one of these as the foundation.

Perhaps we should step outside the confines of the play itself and consider whether a governing frame of reference might exist in the circumstances of its performance. At the beginning of this discussion, I argued that creation and performance exist simultaneously in *Apocalypsis*, not through audience participation or actor improvisation during performance, but because the audience merges with the function of the drunken revelers: they conspire to incite and then to reject the Simpleton, whose fate the play equates with that of both the actor and of Christ. This is not a conscious conspiracy, of course; the audience never departs from its passive, watchful position seated around the playing space, and neither the Simpleton nor the revelers make any direct addresses to their onlookers.

Still, a number of elements in the production draw our attention away from the play as a representation of a past event (drunken mockery or biblical Passion) peopled by localized characters (peasants, or Christ and Apostles); these elements call our attention to the present moment and location in which performance occurs. For example, Grotowski's program note informs us:

> When the audience enters the hall before the performance begins they come in contact with actors who belong here and now, not to

some other age, or some other time and place. They have not stepped out of a different period from ours or out of a different story. It is here that they are stretched out.[18]

In what sense do we share "the same story" with the actors? Grotowski does not call them *characters* at this point in his program note, which would have suggested certain contemporary peasants or revelers who still manage to become interested in the possibility of Christ's return. If we shared that "same story," we would presumably be expected to criticize or sympathize with folkways, but the revelers' religious orgy would be something we *learned about* in Grotowski's theater, as portrayed or narrated by his actors playing character parts, not something which happens because we consent to be an audience in the presence of his actors performing. And clearly, his actors are stretched out in front of us *here*, since neither the bare playing space nor any gestural or verbal elements suggest that the stage represents any other place. As for the actors being here *now*, their clothes are contemporary, and we know that their performing space (in Wrocław at least) is also the general exercise hall and rehearsal room where they lead whatever part of their existences they spend in the identity of actors. Considering the monastic and psychically demanding regimen of the Laboratory Theater, which is a kind of testing-ground of values and life roles for its members, these actors have as much right to be here *now*, as *actors* (not particular characters), as we have. We are virtually intruding upon their territory—except for the fact that they need an audience to complete their identity as actors, so we belong here in some essential way, too.

So far, we share "the same story," if we enter Grotowski's auditorium with some foreknowledge of his expectations about the function of actors and audience in his ideal theater. The program note gives another indication of this when it warns us against reading the word "apocalypse" in the title in terms of the Book of Revelation, and the second coming of Christ found there: whatever happens in Grotowski's theater will not illustrate a biblical apocalypse, but it does share the colloquial connotations of the word "apocalyptic," he tells us. That term has been overworked lately, but if it has an authentic meaning for us, it should be tied to the meaning which it possesses in slang speech: the curiously diminutive sense in which the world always seems to be on the brink of dissolution, so that we may have an apocalyptic experience in each evening's news headlines (or with the purchase of each new rock album). Yet we pursue each catastrophe anxiously, believing against the lesson of experience that this particular new one, *here and now*, will change our world unalterably, will be the true apocalypse.

Each evening of performance must seem like that to a playwright, director, actor, or spectator who believes in the affective potentiality of theater. Together, they conspire to bring about the change which they believe theater can effect—the playwright constructing his play in such a way that the audience finds itself in a certain stance or posture toward the artwork and more susceptible to the message it delivers via this stance; the director devising styles of acting which hold up behavior models for the audience or remold the actor's psycho-physical apparatus itself; the actor undergoing this strenuous regimen so that he will be remade as a person and will also temporarily embody an artwork which otherwise exists independently of his organism; and the audience returning night after night to receive and partially create all this activity, to change something or to be changed by the theater event, *do* something or at least be *done* to. The Greek root for "drama" initially means "to do." The theater event provides an apocalypse every evening, but also an apocalyptic sense of futility when no tangible change results, when each party to the theater event realizes that he may have created or received something in terms of aesthetics, but that the prevailing order, separation between men, and need for revelation and apocalypse still exist. The affectivity of theater and the value of its catharsis do not seem to be transportable outside the realm of the art experience, much as contemporary theater theory would like to have it be otherwise. Brecht assigned change and affect to the Marxist future, Artaud located them in an ideal and unenterable "space of potentiality"—neither could achieve them here and now, and both feared that this meant that they could never be achieved in real terms, outside of ideal systems.

Grotowski wants the affectivity to occur here and now, too, and his dismay at the possibility of this failing to happen has driven him into a posture of worshiping the apocalypse, to the point where his latest production takes this for its theme. First, in his *reductio*, he eliminated all the production elements which might stand in the way of this essential change in the nature of theater's human participants; he even eliminated literature. For a time, he used myths and archetypes as the subject matter of his theater, believing that the violation of these myths could somehow restore their power to affect us: this culminates in the blasphemous Christian figurations of *Apocalypsis*. But already in that play, and even in *Towards a Poor Theatre*, Grotowski was beginning to suspect that beneath the "timeless" myths lies another, more essential entity, whose presence in this theater has more power to affect, to shock, and to move than any objects or beliefs borrowed from the realms of aesthetics, religion, or cultural history. He refers to the existential reality of the people who take part in his theater, his actors and audience. Consider this passage from *Towards a Poor Theatre*:

> Even with the loss of a "common sky" of belief and the loss of impregnable boundaries, the perceptivity of the human organism remains. Only myth—incarnate in the fact of the actor, in his living organism—can function as a taboo. The violation of the living organism, the exposure carried to outrageous excess, returns us to a concrete mythical situation, an experience of common human truth.[19]

I find this "fact of the actor" embodied in the themes and in the performance of *Apocalypsis*. The common sky of belief does not exist for the drunken revelers in the play, even the Simpleton would like to shake it off, and his ambiguous demonic and imbecilic qualities suggest that belief may be a curse or an illusion. In performance, in spite of the historical interest of the rich biblical allusions, the sifting-over of various figurations does not draw us to Grotowski's theater, or hold his actors there. It is certainly not the element which stimulates affectivity in his art. But we *are* drawn by the willingness of his actors to give themselves up to us, to expose their most private fantasies and psychological substrata in beautiful, technically perfect contexts of art experiences which use the actors' living bodies and existential identities as component parts. This aesthetic "violation of the living organism" is entered into willingly by all parties in the hope that it will change all of us, redeem us in a way Christ or the Christ-like man once might have done. *Apocalypsis* deals with a return of Christ because the function of Grotowski's actor is to take on the corporeal and philosophical functions of Christ for modern theater audiences, and to the extent that his monastic theater is a way of life and part of the "real world," the actor takes on a savior's function for all the world. This is an extremely risky and egotistical position to be in, and Grotowski's audience shares the risk by attributing such messianic capacities (even in the abstract) to theater art in general.

Eventually, the moment of collapse intrudes, at the end of the *reductio*. Or perhaps a sense of omnipresent collapse has permeated the whole process, so that apocalypse seemed immanent throughout. Both senses of an ending inform *Apocalypsis*—the sense that at the end of this particular performance a change in the essential relationship between actors and audience will have occurred, or, at the end of this particular production, the *reductio* of theater will either eliminate it or transform it into something essentially new; and the more continuous catastrophic sense that plays and performance situations are doomed to repeat their pleas for an apocalyptic ending which never materializes.

Now the rejection of the Simpleton in the play's plot and the pathos of the actors who must force themselves to reject him take on another significance. As actors, they have finally become conscious of the fact that theater consists in essence of their ineffectual martyrdom, that their confrontation with the audience had not dealt primarily with literary creations, the portrayal of characters, or even the alienation from and *reductio*-style violation of all these foreign myths. Conscious of the way in which acting results in a violation of their living organism, they have conspired to renounce and expel this function from the theater, even if it results in the apocalyptic destruction of the theater altogether. Their Christ-like martyrdom has become a demonic burden to them, one which the evolution of affectivity in art since Stanislavski has developed into expressly the social function which they must discharge, but a martyrdom which, as people who have learned from art and been changed by participation in its discipline, they would like to exorcise. And so, "here and now," "once and for all," they have gathered in the theater to expel the need to be its scapegoats. They awaken the Christ-function in one of their number—ironically, the man who had been their most accomplished actor—simply by setting up a theatrical situation, by acting and by looking on. But ironically, when they side with the audience as onlookers, they have legitimized the theater once again, gone over to the enemy who exists to attend their perpetual martyrdom. Hence their agony and their paradox. They have forced themselves to make the supreme gesture of sacrificing one of their number to exorcise the role of actor-as-demonic-Christ, and they have given up the identity which they once held as actors—but *they are not even successful in the effort*. To make the Simpleton into an authentic scapegoat-actor for them, they have been forced to assume the complementary role of audience-victimizers.

The Simpleton's behavior also astonishes them: at first, he is reluctant to take on the Christ-function, since, as a veteran of Grotowski's *reductio*, he desires to side with the others and expel the burden of the actor. But once he is goaded into the martyr's role, he must play it doubly well in order to discharge it, and when he does this, its old narcotic appeal takes hold of him. Now he wants to be the Christ-actor for all the others, the revelers and the audience which they have gone to join. They protest in the words of Dostoyevsky that they have no further allegiance to that role:

> We are not with you but with another; that is our secret.
> We have not been with you but with another for a long time.[20]

And they cite Simone Weil to argue that the notion of theater as a location in which such painful communion must take place is no habitation for them:

> You came into my room and said: "Poor is he who understands nothing and who knows nothing. Come with me and I will teach

you things you never dreamed of." You told me to leave and go with you to the attic, where from the open window one could see the entire city, a sort of wooden scaffolding and a river on which boats were being unloaded. We were alone. From a cupboard you took bread which we shared. The bread truly had the taste of bread. Never again did I perceive such a taste. You promised to teach me but you taught me nothing. One day you told me: "and now go." I understand you came to me by mistake. My place is not in that attic. Anywhere else: in the prison cell, a railroad waiting room, anywhere, but not in that attic.[21]

The attic mentioned by Weil as the room which Christ's interlocuter disclaims as his own bears a striking resemblance to the auditorium of the Laboratory Theater in Wrocław, which is also housed in an attic, under the high, slanting ceiling of the top story of a building in the city square. The function of Christ-like martyrdom had touched all the participants in the Laboratory Theater—actors and audience, both of whom thought they could see a world from its elevation, but both of whom now sense that the experience has taught them nothing, that the role came to them by mistake, that it will expel their individual identities ("and now go") if they do not expel its potency first, and depart from the attic which is not their authentic location.

Simon Peter ends this ritual of disillusionment by paraphrasing Simone Weil's "and now go." In the final darkness, he tells us to "Go and come no more."[22] Has he finally cast out the actor-function by expelling the Simpleton? Or is he addressing the audience, whose complicity in the secular *sacrum* undertaken at the Laboratory Theater had made that tempting martyrdom possible? Whichever apocalypse he wishes to achieve, it will not be a conclusive one, yet; although *Apocalypsis cum figuris* may be the last play which Grotowski prepares, he has not yet been able to take Simon Peter at his literal word and terminate the activity of performance. But his public pronouncements indicate that he would like to accomplish this, perhaps through a qualitative alteration of our understanding of the theater event, perhaps through a continuation of his *reductio* until he reaches its termination. He recently said in an interview, "It seems to me that the prevailing or professional theatre must proceed along the road it goes—up to its extinction."[23] Although his extreme form of theater could hardly be called "prevailing," Grotowski himself possesses a strong tendency toward artistic self-annihilation.

On the other hand, he also feels that there might be another, more profound encounter between humans than any act undertaken by means of theatrical artifice. He refers to this rather mystically as "the human act," and claims that although it may lie beyond theater, theater may be a means of approaching it. Or better still, theater might be a place in which the human act occurs, even though this act need not be associated exclusively with theater. Some of Grotowski's recent statements on the theater as an existential *place* resemble Artaud's earlier notion of theater as an empty space, waiting to be filled with human content:

> Q.: What, for you, is the Laboratory Theater?
> A.: At the beginning it was a theater. After that a laboratory. And now it is a place, where I hope to be true to myself . . . . it is a place where an act, a testimony, is given by actual people, and which will be concrete and corporeal. . . . It isn't essentially what we call a laboratory, it isn't even essentially what will be generally called a theater. Ultimately it is this *place*. If theater had not existed, some other pretext would have been found.
> . . . theater doesn't interest me now, only what I can cause *by means of theater*.
> I cannot say "I love the theater," as many do. I don't love the theater. It is just a domain, just a place, just an occasion whereby we encounter other people and through which we perform an act of love.
> Abandon theater as a goal. Treat it as a place, a territory. Can something important happen in this place? Yes, a human being who discovers himself, who goes beyond this semi- or half-existence. Is it theater? It transgresses what in the past we've called theater. It's like going toward an authentic adventure, because it touches our concrete, carnal, real life.[24]

Grotowski's new project seems to address a comment made by Richard Gilman, who was speaking however about the actor-training and sense of the actor's mission which prevailed at the Laboratory Theater during the "poor theater" period. Gilman first speaks of the Grotowskian actors' resolution "to relearn their lives, to submit to a process of education for authenticity, for a break into a new and postnatural being," and then he concludes that Grotowski "has prepared his actors not so they will be more 'life-like,' but so that they will be ready for new life . . . ."[25]

The benign and somewhat sentimental tone of Grotowski's most recent pronouncements seems to indicate that whatever dark night of the soul he experienced during his creation of *Apocalypsis cum figuris*, that ordeal has passed and the process has led him closer to the "authentic adventure" he seeks. In spite of that play's pessimism about the possibility of material affectivity in the theater and genuine change through participation in it, Grotowski and his actors seem to have experienced some kind of catharsis. And *Apocalypsis cum figuris*, that somber masterpiece of performance theater, continues in Grotowski's repertoire. It is his only current production, the last hallmark of the "poor theater" period, but possibly a seedbed for whatever new direction awaits him as well. Recently, Grotowski has expressed interest in reintroducing the concept of *święto* to his theater. This Polish word literally means "holiday,"[26] but its secondary definitions which Grotowski enthusiastically cites suggest several of the ends which his cathartic secular *sacrum* sought to accomplish. *Święto* has connotations of "festival," but also "the holy," "the sacred," implications of "plenitude," the qualities of "the joyous" and of "the free," Grotowski told a student audience in Los Angeles. When one of the students asked him what new production the Laboratory Theater was preparing at the moment, Grotowski replied, "Now we're in holiday: our relationship among one another is explored without reference to texts or legends." And he has recently reported that the company's continuing work of *Apocalypsis* moves that play ever closer toward the state of holiday, even though this stage has not been attained as yet.[27] Our culture's most deathless myth about the birth of theater out of communal ritual returns in Grotowski's notion of theater as a liberating and authenticating holiday, or at least a place in which such a holiday might occur. But whether Grotowski's *święto* will result in a rebirth of his theater is a question which cannot be answered here.

Afterword: *Offending the Audience* and Embracing It

The language of gestures and the desemanticization of verbal elements in *Apocalypsis cum figuris* push that work to the limits of verbal art in theater. *Apocalypsis* may also be an end-point or at least a turning point for its creator, but the play does not exhaust the possibilities of performance theater. Peter Handke's dramas present an alternative to the destruction of the word wrought by Grotowski: they are full of words, and his earliest plays contain nothing but words.

Handke calls these short pieces "Sprechstücke." They consist of blocks of text, paragraphs containing simple, declarative sentences; all the sentences in a particular block often conform to the same grammatical model, so that hearing them reminds one of pattern-drills in a language laboratory. The plays contain no characters, plots, stories, fictional times or places; Handke does not even assign the individual sentences to particular actors, but leaves this up to his directors. Each play is a litany of verbal elements on a particular theme indicated by its title— *Crying for Help, Prophecy, Self-Accusation*. They are addressed by speakers directly to the audience, and Handke specifies that these announcers are speakers, not actors playing particular roles or even stepping out of characters to comment upon them. If they have stepped out of character, Handke's speakers have stepped out of the function of being actors to comment on the circumstances of theater itself. This is particularly true of the first *Sprechstück* Handke wrote, in 1965, *Offending the Audience (Publikumsbeschimpfung)*.

The piece is scored for four speakers. They address the audience directly throughout, sometimes to describe the play which they are "performing":

> This is no play. We don't step out of the play to address you. We have no need of illusions to disillusion you. We show you nothing. We are playing no destinies. We are playing no dreams. This is not a factual report. This is no documentary play. This is no slice of life. We don't tell you a story. We don't perform any actions. We don't simulate any actions. We don't represent anything. We don't put anything on for you. We only speak.[1]

and sometimes to describe the audience out front:

You are not listening to us. You heed us. You are no longer eaves-
dropping from behind a wall. We are speaking directly to you.
Our dialogue no longer moves at a right angle to your glance. Your
glance no longer pierces our dialogue. Our words and your glances
no longer form an angle. You are not disregarded. You are not
treated as mere hecklers. You need not form an opinion from a
bird's or a frog's perspective of anything that happens here.[2]

Most of the sentences contain negations: the audience is told what it is
not seeing and what it is *not* experiencing more often than what it is in
fact taking part in. After about an hour of this dissection of the theater
event, the speakers suddenly inform the audience that they will be
offended before the piece ends, and begin to hurl hundreds of insults
across the footlights:

...you would-be revolutionaries, you reactionaries, you draft-
card burners, you ivory-tower artists, you defeatists, you massive
retaliators, you white-rabbit pacifists, you nihilists, you individ-
ualists, you Communists, you vigilantes, you socialists, you minute men....[3]

But the insults contradict each other, as the descriptive sentences about
theater performance did earlier in the play. No particular audience
member need feel insulted by such an undifferentiated barrage of language: the common avant-garde tactic of *épater le bourgeois* is not being
employed by Handke so much as it is being *played with*. Does the piece
amount to no more than a clever "acoustic pattern," as the speakers
themselves say of the insults they hurl? And if it does aspire to significance, can we call this a play at all, and not a discursive essay?

Handke defends his pieces as theater, claiming that they employ only
the speech forms that are uttered orally in real life, and therefore require
an auditor. He says in a note to the play, "The speak-ins employ natural
examples of swearing, of self-indictment, of confession, of testimony,
of interrogation, of justification, of evasion, of prophecy, of calls for
help. Therefore they need a vis-à-vis, at least *one* person who listens;
otherwise, they would not be natural but extorted by the author."[4]
Handke's sentences are not arranged as dialogue, they cannot find their
listener in another character—the individual speakers portray no
particular characters; also, the speakers cannot be said to speak
"monologues" and therefore to be listening to themselves. The sentences require an audience to justify their existence as oral speech. But
the sentences, although they are often exhortative and phrased in the
imperative voice, do not resemble colloquial speech. They are formal,
dry, legalistic—Handke trained as a law student before studying literature. Their abstract quality addresses the audience as a corporate body

waiting to be instructed intellectually rather than moved to pity or fear. The didactic tone of the *Sprechstücke* shows their resemblance to Brecht's *Lehrstücke*. But Handke's lectures contain no explicit "teaching," instead they exploit the posture of public instruction to play with the notion of didacticism itself.

Handke's translator, Michael Roloff, renders "Sprechstück" as "speak-in," a term which reminds us of the "sit-ins" and "teach-ins" of the sixties, political gestures, virtually guerilla theater, in which the gesture and form of the forbidden political act became more important than the content of the act itself. (It was more important to visibly occupy a segregated restaurant seat than to eat the meal which one might be served there—the sit-ins assumed a certain amount of accord between the antagonists involved, for the "actors" were "influencing public opinion" more than they were "fighting for their lives," and they played their gestures directly to the audience of restaurant patrons, law officials, and television viewers.) Likewise, a theatrical speak-in primarily seeks to militantly occupy and protest against the theater understood as the "establishment's property," but in Handke's case, the theater's *mimetic* tradition is being protested more than the politics of its audience. Only secondarily does a speak-in contain a particular lesson about the lives of its auditors, and speak-ins refuse to portray these lives. Handke writes in his note to the play that they are "spectacles without pictures, inasmuch as they give no picture of the world. They point to the world not by way of pictures but by way of words; the words of the speak-ins don't point at the world as something lying outside the words but to the world in the words themselves. The words that make up the speak-ins give no picture of the world but a concept of it."[5]

As Handke's work evolves, this separation between the world of things and the world of words obsesses the playwright more and more. His later plays are tragedies of language, acts of "speech torture," as he says of his masterpiece, *Kaspar*. (One of the dozens of insults hurled at the end of *Offending the Audience* is "you *pain* in the mouth.") Words give us a false sense of control over the reality of objects, the unrepeatability of experiences, and the intangibility of emotions, and they allow us the illusion of complete communication or "oneness" with other people. Yet language is a fragile illusion, and employing it to escape from one's existential isolation and the omnipresence of the abyss is like "skating over thin ice," the metaphor behind another full-length play, *The Ride Across Lake Constance*. At any moment we can "fall through" language into despair. Returning to Handke's *Sprechstücke*, we can sense his Wittgensteinian doubt of language even in these early plays: *Offending the Audience*, its speakers tell us, will be a "comedy of words," not a "comedy of insidious objects."[6] As his note to the *Sprechstücke* insists, a literary artwork made up of words must deal with the problem of words, this is their essential subject matter, and they are "word-plays" as much as speak-ins. Martin Esslin suggests this literal translation for *Sprechstücke*: "word-plays"captures the sense in which these plays use words as their subject matter as well as their vehicle of expression.[7] Words also demand a listener, since they have no existence independent of communication; hence, word-plays are theatrical, for the theater concretizes the communication transaction of linguistic expression. The term "word-play" also captures the *playful* quality of these pieces, which charm us because of their manipulation of the formal qualities of speech, sentence patterns, acoustic patterns, and so on. (Handke's neologism *Sprechstück* may also make a passing reference to Schoenberg's *Sprechstimme*, "spoken voice" singing which assigns the separated quality of spoken words to the words sung in his vocal music; Handke, on the other hand, borrows the abstract acoustic qualities of music for his spoken lines.)

The obsession with words and the formal-acoustical qualities of language which mark Handke's later plays show his connection to the fellow Viennese Ludwig Wittgenstein. By announcing that speaking and words are the essential subject matter of verbal art, Handke performs a hyperbolic *reductio* similar to that of the *Tractatus Logico-Philosophicus,* in which Wittgenstein concludes that what cannot be spoken about must be consigned to silence. Handke shares Wittgenstein's radical distrust of the metaphysical statements which words permit us to delude ourselves by, and he sides with the later Wittengenstein of the *Philosophical Investigations* in his belief that banal statements from everyday speech provide quite enough problems for linguistic analysis; even in his verse, Handke resists and attacks the impulse to write in heightened, "poetic" language. But his personal *reductio* has not thrust him across the watershed from speech to silence, mainly because he believes that what we *can* speak about is speech itself. Also, it must be admitted that even Handke finds it impossible to eliminate all "pictures of the world" and extra-linguistic themes and referents from his drama: as is usually the case, Wittgenstein's severe *reductio* stands as an ideal for Handke, not a model for imitation.

Still, as a work of minimal theater, *Offending the Audience* dispenses with almost everything which earlier drama found necessary. It has no action, plot, characters, metaphysical speculation, or individuating diction; Handke permits his piece to retain the *melos* of acoustic patterns, but forbids any *opsis*, or visual spectacle. He does not approve of tricking up his *Sprechstücke* with film projections or choreography. The play does retain a bit of illusionistic spectacle, but this takes place "before" the play begins. Handke instructs the theater management to handle the ticket-taking and ushering in an extremely ceremonial manner; the ushers will turn away any patrons who come improperly dressed, the stagehands will make noises backstage before the curtains part to give the illusion of scenery being set up, and the house lights must be dimmed even more slowly and dramatically than usual. Then, the audience will be properly startled to see no conventional play upon the stage when the curtains part. This little joke of Handke's is a feeble alienation effect which succeeds in calling the audience's attention to its identity as audience, but smacks too much of a time-bound *épater le bourgeois* attitude to harmonize with the more abstract and universal statements spoken in the play's text.

The anatomy of performance Handke makes in *Offending the Audience* emphasizes the radical contemporaneity of any theater event, the fact that it is not so much *about* a modern-day situation as it *is* a situation itself, today. What happens on stage takes place in the present:

> This is no drama. No action that has occurred elsewhere is re-enacted here. Only a now and a now and a now exist here. This is no make-believe which re-enacts an action that really happened once upon a time. Time plays no role here. We are not acting out a plot. Therefore we are not playing time. Time is for real here, it expires from one word to the next.[8]

The present tense and presence of theater extend to the audience and provide it with a link to the speakers, those "actors" who both transmit and embody the artwork.

> By always speaking directly to you and by speaking to you of time, of now and of now and of now, we observe the unity of time, place, and action. But we observe this unity not only here on stage. Since the stage is no world unto itself, we also observe the unity down where you are. We and you form a unity because we speak directly to you without interruption. Therefore, under certain conditions, we, instead of saying you, could say we.[9]

This radical unity of time, place, and action even allows the speakers to conclude, "Therefore this piece is classical."[10] Handke's citation of the neoclassical unities refunctions them to suggest an ideal accord between actor and audience members—the actors call them "we" instead of "you."

If the audience is one with the actors, it also takes part in the artwork, it does not simply receive it passively. The artwork which is contained in any theater event changes with each performance: some of the difference stems from changes in the actor's behavior, intonation, emotional state, and so on, but an equal part of the theater event's uniqueness stems from the differing composition of its audience, the personal contributions made by each audience member as an individual. This encounter between unique and changing individuals, Grotowski's essence of the theater, also stands at the center of Handke's concept of theater event. In *Offending the Audience*, the speakers dwell on the un-repeatable quality of theater in an effort to make the audience aware of its creative share in performance:

> Time is not repeatable even if we repeat our words, even if we mention again that our time is your time, that it expires from one word to the next, while we, we and you, are breathing, while our hair is growing, while we sweat, while we smell, while we hear. We cannot repeat anything, time is expiring. It is unrepeatable. Each moment is historical. Each of your moments is a historical moment. We cannot say our words twice. This is no make-believe. We cannot do the same thing once again. We cannot repeat the same gestures. We cannot speak the same way. Time expires on our lips. Time is unrepeatable.[11]

As the play progresses, the speakers shift their emphasis from state-ments about what the play "is not" to statements about the condition and participation of the audience. There are long passages about the way in which diverse citizens become an intentional though uncon-scious collectivity, become an audience. Spectators had walked from *different* directions *toward* one goal (the theater), they had dressed accordingly, looked at themselves in mirrors, checked their makeup, awaited the curtain anxiously—this abstract language might be de-scribing an actor's preperformance preparations as much as a spec-tator's, and Handke is trying to diminish the essential distance be-tween them in terms of theatrical function. Both parties observe the other, and somehow give the other authenticity. His actors watch his audience, and comment upon the fact that the lighted auditorium which Handke requests in performance allows them to do this more easily (whereas the darkened hall of proscenium staging allows only a one-way view from anonymous spectator to spotlighted actor).

The lighted auditorium also forces the audience to be more aware of itself. This self-awareness is not the aggressive kind in which the spec-tator is isolated to be scrutinized (as is the case of the spotlighted actor of proscenium staging). In fact, that claustrophobic isolation plagues the audience in the conventional theater only when there is no "play" visible to avert the audience's introspective gaze—before the curtains part.

> You watch. You stare. By watching, you become rigid. The seating arrangement favors this development. You are something that watches. You need room for your eyes. If the curtain comes to-gether, you gradually become claustrophobic. You have no van-tage point. You feel encircled. You feel inhibited. The parting of

> the curtain merely relieves your claustrophobia. Thus it relieves you. You can watch. Your view is unobstructed. You become uninhibited. You can partake. You are not in dead center as when the curtain is closed. You are no longer someone. You are something. You are no longer alone with yourselves. You are no longer left to your own devices. Now you are with it. You are an audience. That is a relief. You can partake.[12]

This claustrophobia which an audience experiences sitting before closed curtains corresponds to the actor's stage fright which he feels anticipating the isolation and scrutiny of performance; we might call it "audience fright." When the curtains part, the audience no longer has to be "someone," it can be "something," and loses awareness of itself. Handke wants to move his audience into a mutual and egalitarian position in relation to his actors, not isolate either group in hostile territory. The act of making the audience aware of itself should have educational and therapeutic qualities, not contain the humiliation of unmasking. Handke has said of *Offending the Audience*,

> The play has not been written so that the usual audience should make way for a different audience, but that the usual audience should become a different audience. The play can serve to make the spectator pleasantly or unpleasantly aware of his presence, to make him aware of himself. It can make him aware that he is there, that he is present, that he exists.... It can make him attentive, keen of hearing, clearsighted, and not only as a playgoer.[13]

In the text of his play, Handke is not always so philosophical about this gift of awareness which his actors arouse in the audience. At times the speakers describe the intimate bodily functions of the spectators: as they become aware of the fact that they are sitting in a theater, they also become aware of the flow of their saliva, the beating of their hearts, the desire to scratch themselves, the sweat under their armpits. This anatomization ends ironically: "You become aware of the air you are inhaling and exhaling through your mouth and nose. You become aware of our words entering your ears. You acquire presence of mind."[14] Next, the actors dare the spectators not to perform the automatic body functions of which they have suddenly become aware: "Try not to blink your eyelids. Try not to hear anything. Try not to breathe. Why, you are breathing. Why, you are salivating. Why, you are listening. Why, how terribly self-conscious you are."[15] This is easy humor achieved by the clever juxtaposition of statements which belong to different semantic categories but which may be expressed in identical syntactic patterns, the kind of word-play Handke delights in. But the point behind the anatomy lesson is to hold up the reality of the spectator's physical body sitting in a theater seat as an example of the reality, specificity, and importance of his existential presence in the theater event. Handke does not allow his spectators to acknowledge that they are "here" only in the abstract, in the sense that intellectually they "know" that some notion of audience presence plays a role in Handke's theory of theater. He wants a more bodily and individual awareness, he wants each spectator to acknowledge that he *personally* makes a difference to whatever transpires. When he feels that his spectators are sufficiently engaged in an active way, Handke reveals to them the coup which they have unconsciously performed. Directly following the investigation of the spectators' bodily functions, Handke reveals to them that *they* are the real protagonists of any theater event.

> You are now aware of your presence. You know that it is *your* time that you are spending here. You are the topic. You tie the knot. You untie the knot. You are the center. You are the occasion. You are the reasons why. You provide the initial impulse. You provide us with words here. You are the playmakers and the counterplotters. You are the youthful comedians. You are the youthful lovers, you are the ingenues, you are the sentimentalists. You are the stars, you are the character actors, you are the bon vivants and the heroes. You are the heroes and the villains of this piece.[16]

As the speakers had intimated earlier in the play, "You are an event. You are *the* event."[17]

These compliments resemble the accolades which drama critics reserve for characters and actors, and they reappear at the end of the play when Handke's actors hurl the more than one hundred and fifty separate insults at the audience. But before the actors begin their insults, they explain the function of insulting the audience. In terms of Handke's dramaturgy, the insults do provide a climax to his otherwise formless *Sprechstück*, but hurling a string of insults would seem to be a callous way to treat the people who have just been acclaimed as the real heroes of the play. Handke's speakers mention some other explanations. Offending the audience is one way of speaking to it, they say, and the communication transaction which forms the basis for a Handkean speak-in is concretized most explicitly in the vocative and imperative forms of address. (In other words, two parties and their mutual interaction are required for an insult to "work"—the insult demands and acknowledges the presence of the other, and even if it offends him, it grants him the minimal beneficence of acknowledging him.) Handke's speakers go on to admit that their insults will address no one in particular, and will contradict each other, so that no one need feel personally offended. They add that the audience has been warned in advance about the insults, anyway, so it need not be offended by this "acoustic pattern." Then they undercut all these apologies with the accurate perception that "Since you are probably thoroughly offended already, we will waste no more time before thoroughly offending you, you chuckleheads."[18]

Most audiences are offended already by this piece of antitheater. Its lack of plot, imitation, and dialogue offends the audience's expectation of what a proper play should be. And the speakers' close verbal scrutiny of the audience throughout the play has reversed the master-servant relationship which usually prevails between patron and performer, and thrust the audience into a hostile spotlight. Robbing a spectator of his anonymity probably offends him more than insulting him with invective. But Handke's speakers have not wrenched the audience out of its protected territory and identity simply to abandon it: they reveal a new and heroic identity for the audience to assume, that of protagonist in the theater event, not just passive recipient. The old identity of the theater-goers as *audience* is offended and insulted in Handke's play, to the extent to which this implies passivity, snobbery, and respect for the artificiality of mimetic art. However, Handke's speakers compensate the theater-goers by granting them a new identity: the speakers take them over to their side, and make them actors who will experience the presence and authenticating quality of performance. As the insults roll out in comic profusion, we hear compliments in between, the praises which drama critics sing of good actors:

> You let the impossible become possible. You were the heroes of this piece. You were sparing with your gestures. Your parts were well rounded. Your scenes were unforgettable. You did not play, you *were* the part. You were a happening. You were the find of the evening. You lived your roles. You had a lion's share of the success. You saved the piece. You were a sight. You were a sight to be seen, you ass-kissers.

> You were one of a kind. You had one of your better days tonight. You played ensemble. You were imitations of life, you drips, you diddlers, you atheists, you double-dealers, you switch-hitters, you dirty Jews.

> You were the right ones. You were breathtaking. You did not disappoint our wildest hopes. You were born actors. Play-acting was in your blood, you butchers, you buggers, you bullshitters, you bullies, you rabbits, you fuck-offs, you farts.[19]

Although the compliments diminish in proportion to the number of insults as the litany progresses, the nomination of the audience as actors spares the play-goers the burden of receiving any particular insult which may happen to sting them. They begin to join in the play of this word-play, revel in the Rabelaisian hyperbole of it all, indict all the human foibles and uncomplimentary identities which they may possess as audience members but of which in the theater they have been relieved. Handke's scattershot technique extends to indict the very notion of mortality itself, the greatest insult to the human spirit. His penultimate paragraph is a devastating evocation of disease and the causes of death, but it is also a virtuoso piece, an acoustic pattern which bravely opposes corporeal decay with whatever permanence abides in verbal creation and the experience of art.

> O you cancer victims, O you hemorrhoid sufferers, O you multiple sclerotics, O you syphilitics, O you cardiac conditions, O you paraplegics, O you catatonics, O you schizoids, O you paranoids, O you hypochondriacs, O you carriers of causes of death, O you suicide candidates, O you potential peacetime casualties, O you potential war dead, O you potential accident victims, O you potential increase in the mortality rate, O you potential dead.[20]

The acting play-goers have even found a way momentarily to assert themselves in the face of death.

Handke ends with a long coda in which both the insults and the rave reviews return. One of the more clever ones is "You milestones in the history of the theater. You historic moments."[21] Perhaps Handke has an eye on history himself, for *Offending the Audience* itself has proved to be something of a milestone in the history of recent theater. But the final evocations which signal his total acceptance of the audience as fellow-participant have nothing to do with theater, role-playing, role-switching, or even with performance. The play ends in an encounter beyond the theatrical level, perhaps in a Grotowskian "human act."

> You architects of the future. You builders of a better world. You mafiosos. You wiseacres. You smarty-pants. You who embrace life. You who detest life. You who have no feeling about life. You ladies and gents you, you celebrities of public and cultural life you, you who are present you, you brothers and sisters you, you comrades you, you worthy listeners you, you fellow humans you.

> You were welcome here. We thank you. Good night.[22]

And then Handke instructs his stage manager to pipe the taped sound of roaring applause into the auditorium, and to continue applauding the play-goers until they leave the theater, just as they would have applauded the actor of a conventional play until he left the stage.

Whatever catharsis is contained in *Offending the Audience* is a catharsis achieved by actors and audience, to the extent that they are able to exchange these roles and social functions, and, ultimately, to abandon them. This catharsis involves a purgation of whatever is inhibiting about belonging to the ranks of either the actors or the audience, and, at the same time, it makes the participants aware of whatever is liberating and authenticating about theater. It confronts our most basic notions of what dramatic literature and theatrical art consist of, insults whatever is ossified and stale about them, and prepares us for a new life of play-going and plays, acting and acts. In her essay on Artaud, Susan Sontag makes a statement which might be applied to Handke: "Insulting art (like insulting the audience) is an attempt to head off the corruption of art, the banalization of suffering."[23] "Suffering" is perhaps too strong a word in the context of *Offending the Audience*, which after all is a comedy. A comedy of words, Handke tells us; his later plays are as obsessed with words but more aware of the suffering they cause. Handke's early comedy displays as much passion, though of another kind. It would be shortsighted to call his writing cold or emotionless simply because it resorts to the style of legal argument and philosophical reduction rather than to the language of sentimental naturalism. Any writer like Handke who is possessed enough to drive language to this extreme, and forge from it a new theatrical diction, displays a special kind of passion. As Richard Gilman says of him, "even when the philosophical style is entirely dry, systematic, and abstract, there may be a drama of the self on display more compelling than most outright fiction."[24] Still, the state into which Handke's catharsis of actor and audience propels them lies beyond words, in spite of the playwright's mastery of language. As with Grotowski's extreme example of purity and holiness in acting, Handke's dramaturgy in *Offending the Audience* pushes dramatic literature to an extreme beyond which it may not be able to proceed and retain its identity.

However, Handke's first play did not prove to be his last, and the lessons which it taught him about the paradox of language and the paradox of performance continue to inform his playwriting. The affectivity of performance theater like Handke's and Grotowski's may not change the world or save the theater, as Brecht would have demanded of it. But it is an education in authenticity for its participants, a preliving of future roles and parts which we may choose to play, a prologue to experience. Handke calls his speak-ins "autonomous prologues to the old plays,"[25] and they have also proved to be prologues to his more mature playwriting. But *Offending the Audience* is another kind of prologue as well. In the words of its speakers:

> This piece is a prologue. It is not the prologue to another piece but the prologue to what you did, what you are doing, and what you will do. You are the topic. This piece is the prologue to the topic. It is the prologue to your practices and customs. It is the prologue to

your actions. It is the prologue to your inactivity. It is the prologue to your lying down, to your sitting, to your standing, to your walking. It is the prologue to your future visits to the theatre. It is also the prologue to all other prologues. This piece is world theatre.[26]

Notes

INTRODUCTION

1. *Aristotle's Poetics, a Translation and Commentary for Students of Literature,* trans. Leon Golden, commentary by O. B. Hardison, Jr. (Englewood Cliffs, New Jersey: Prentice-Hall, 1968). I cite all translations of Aristotle from this edition. Golden explains his interpretation of *katharsis* as "clarification" in "Catharsis," *Transactions of the American Philological Association* 93 (1962).

2. Golden and Hardison, *Poetics,* p. 117. I am indebted to Hardison for the discussion which follows, most of which summarizes his own arguments.

3. G. F. Else believes that the clarification of incidents also connects catharsis to *hamartia:* it clarifies the protagonist's tragic "mistake" (not "flaw"). See Else, *Aristotle's Poetics: The Argument* (Cambridge, Mass.: Harvard University Press, 1957).

4. Golden and Hardison, *Poetics,* p. 117.

CHAPTER ONE

1. Strindberg approaches this position most specifically in his Preface to *Miss Julie* (1890), where he says that the actor becomes "part and parcel of the situation and is imbued with the mood of it," and in his "Notes to the Members of the Intimate Theatre" (1907), where he suggests that the actor goes into a trance, "actually becoming the person he is supposed to represent." The quotations come respectively from *Seven Plays,* trans. Arvid Paulson (New York: Bantam Books, 1970), p. 65, and *The Chamber Plays,* trans. Evert Sprinchorn (New York: Dutton, 1962), p. 210.

2. Constantin Stanislavski, *Building a Character,* trans. Elizabeth Reynolds Hapgood (New York: Theatre Arts Books, 1949), p. 279.

3. Constantin Stanislavski, *My Life in Art,* trans. J. J. Robbins (Boston: Little, Brown, 1935), p. 351.

4. *My Life in Art,* p. 461.

5. Constantin Stanislavski, "The Art of the Actor and the Art of the Director," in *Stanislavski's Legacy,* ed. and trans. Elizabeth Reynolds Hapgood (New York: Theatre Arts Books, 1958), pp. 168–82.

6. Constantin Stanislavski, *An Actor Prepares,* trans. Elizabeth Reynolds Hapgood (New York: Theatre Arts Books, 1936), p. 14. Burnet M. Hobgood has suggested more accurate translations for many of Stanislavski's special terms in "Central Conceptions in Stanislavski's System," *Educational Theatre Journal* 25, no. 2 (May 1973): 147–59. The phrase which Hapgood translated as "living the role" should be translated as "experiencing the role," according to Hobgood,

and the full Russian title of *An Actor Prepares* is *The Actor's Work on Himself in the Creative Process of Experiencing*. Stanislavski's concept of "experiencing" a role rather than "living" it emphasizes the actor's consciousness of his own identity throughout performances (something which Stanislavski repeatedly stressed): the actor knows that he is not really Uncle Vanya, so he can perform activities like following blocking, picking up cues, etc., things which would be outside the consciousness of the character he plays. Still the effect is the same as it would have been could he literally "live" the role: he gives up his own personality traits to the demands of the character, and the audience reads his acting as if he "were" the character. Hobgood concurs: "When an actor experiences a role, Stanislavski believed, the fully realized personality of the character so dominates the occasion that the actor's own personality virtually disappears" (p. 150).

7. *An Actor Prepares*, p. 112.

8. *Building a Character*, p. 108.

9. *An Actor Prepares*, p. 49.

10. Ibid., p. 188.

11. Ibid., p. 243.

12. *Building a Character*, p. 27.

13. *An Actor Prepares*, p. 233.

14. Ibid., pp. 158–59.

15. *Stanislavski's Legacy*, p. 175.

16. *Building a Character*, pp. 134–35.

17. *My Life in Art*, p. 361.

18. *An Actor Prepares*, p. 295.

19. Ibid., p. 164.

20. *Stanislavski's Legacy*, p. 129.

21. Ibid., p. 76.

22. Marcel Merleau-Ponty, *Eloge de la philosophie et autres essais* (NRF, "Collection 'Idées,'" 1960), p. 96. Cited and translated by Philip E. Lewis, "Merleau-Ponty and the Phenomenology of Language," in *Structuralism*, ed. Jacques Ehrmann (1966; reprint ed., Garden City, N.Y.: Doubleday, 1970), p. 29.

23. Lewis, "Merleau-Ponty," p. 19. The quotation he translates is from Merleau-Ponty, *La Phénoménologie de la perception* (Paris: Gallimard, 1945), p. 214.

24. Merleau-Ponty, *Eloge de la philosophie*, p. 99. Quoted and translated by Lewis, "Merleau-Ponty," p. 29.

25. Alain Robbe-Grillet, *For a New Novel*, trans. Richard Howard (New York: Grove Press, 1965), p. 111.

26. *Building a Character*, p. 279.

27. *My Life in Art*, p. 85. Quoted from Shtchepkin's letter to Shumsky.

28. Ibid., p. 88; *An Actor Prepares*, p. 14.

29. *An Actor Prepares*, p. 157.

30. Ibid., p. 162.

31. Ibid., p. 163.

32. Sigmund Freud, "Psychopathic Characters on the Stage," trans. Nora

Beeson in *The Psychoanalytic Quarterly* 11 (1952): 459–65; reprinted in *Theatre in the Twentieth Century*, ed. Robert W. Corrigan (New York: Grove Press, 1963), p. 207.

33. Ibid., p. 208.

34. Ibid., p. 209.

35. Ibid., p. 211.

36. Ibid., p. 211.

37. John J. Sullivan, "Stanislavski and Freud," in *Stanislavski and America*, ed. Erika Munk (New York: Hill and Wang, 1966), p. 107.

38. Ibid., p. 107.

39. Richard Schechner, "Exit Thirties, Enter Sixties," *in Public Domain; Essays on the Theatre* (New York: Bobbs-Merrill, 1969), p. 8.

40. Ibid., p. 8.

41. Bertolt Brecht, "Notes on Stanislavski," in *Stanislavski and America*, p. 132. The quotations from Brecht used in this chapter were translated by Carl R. Muller from Brecht's *Schriften zum Theater*, vol. 8 (Frankfort: Suhrkamp Verlag, 1963–64), pp. 187–219; the materials date from 1952–53.

42. *An Actor Prepares*, p. 267.

43. *Building a Character*, p. 22.

44. *An Actor Prepares*, p. 294.

45. *Building a Character*, p. 244. Tortsov retains the sense of reality to allow one of his skeptical students to object at his point that "no such theatre exists in the world" (p. 244).

46. Ibid., p. 282.

47. *My Life in Art*, p. 537.

48. Renato Poggioli, *The Theory of the Avant-Garde*, trans. Gerald Fitzgerald (Cambridge: Harvard University Press, 1968), pp. 20–21.

49. Constantin Stanislavski, *Creating a Role*, trans. Elizabeth Reynolds Hapgood (New York: Theatre Arts Books, 1961), p. 213.

50. *Building a Character*, p. 236.

51. Vladimir Prokofyev, "Stanislavski Preserved," in Munk, *Stanislavski and America*, p. 69. In *Creating a Role*, Stanislavski claims that tangible results come from his system of physical actions with almost mechanical inevitability: the system "automatically analyzes a play," "automatically induces organic nature to put its important inner creative forces to work to prompt us to physical action," and "automatically evokes from inside us live human material with which to work" (p. 349).

52. Richard Schechner, "Exit Thirties, Enter Sixties," p. 7.

53. Vsevolod Emilevich Meyerhold, *Meyerhold on Theatre*, trans. and ed. Edward Braun (New York: Hill and Wang, 1969), p. 177. (Meyerhold is paraphrasing the rebellious playwright Konstantin from *The Seagull*, Act One, a part he played in Stanislavski's premiere production.)

54. Meyerhold, *Meyerhold on Theatre*, p. 199.

55. Jerzy Grotowski, *Towards a Poor Theatre*, trans. T. K. Wiewiorowski (Holstebro, Denmark: Odin Teatrets Forlag, 1968), p. 16. An identical edition was published by Bobbs-Merrill of New York in 1969.

56. Brecht, "Notes on Stanislavski," p. 129.

CHAPTER TWO

1. *Stanislavski's Legacy*, p. 110.

2. Ibid., p. 123.

3. Ibid., p. 110.

4. *My Life in Art*, pp. 373–74.

5. Maurice Valency, *The Breaking String: The Plays of Anton Chekhov* (New York: Oxford University Press, 1966), p. 209.

6. *Stanislavski's Legacy*, p. 81.

7. Ibid., p. 82.

8. *Building a Character*, p. 205.

9. Valency, *The Breaking String*, p. 45.

10. Robert W. Corrigan, "Stanislavski and the Playwright," in *Theatre in the Twentieth Century* (New York: Grove Press, 1963), p. 190.

11. John Gassner, *Directions in Modern Theatre and Drama* (New York: Holt, Rinehart and Winston, 1965), p. 152.

12. Paul Gray, "From Russia to America: A Critical Chronology," in Munk, *Stanislavski and America*, p. 143.

13. Robert Brustein, *The Theatre of Revolt, An Approach to Modern Drama* (Boston: Little, Brown, 1962), p. 152.

14. Richard Schechner, "Approaches," in *Public Domain*, pp. 90–91.

15. Anton Chekhov, *The Three Sisters*, 1900. I quote from the translation of Ronald Hingley, which appears in *The Oxford Chekhov*, vol. 3 (London: Oxford University Press, 1964), but I prefer to adopt the character names preserved in Randall Jarrell's translation (London: Macmillan, 1969). Hingley translates common Russian names like "Andrei" into English equivalents, and this strikes me as unnecessary and too "British." Occasionally I cite Jarrell's translation, and refer to it by name when I do. This quotation, however, is from Hingley, p. 76.

16. Hingley, *The Three Sisters*, p. 76.

17. Ibid., p. 139.

18. Jarrell, *The Three Sisters*, p. 20.

19. Hingley, *The Three Sisters*, p. 135.

20. Ibid., p. 99.

21. Ibid., p. 100.

22. Ibid., p. 138.

23. Ibid., p. 73.

24. Ibid., p. 139.

25. Jarrell, *The Three Sisters*, p. 96.

26. Hingley, *The Three Sisters*, p. 23.

27. Jarrell, *The Three Sisters*, p. 97.

28. Hingley, *The Three Sisters*, p. 133.

29. Ibid., Appendix, p. 316. Quoted and translated from the actor V. V. Luzhsky's recollections as included in *Chekhov i teatr: pisma, felyetony, sovremenniki o Chekhove-dramaturge*, ed. E. D. Surkov (Moscow, 1961).

30. *My Life in Art*, pp. 347–48.

31. M. N. Stroyeva, *The Three Sisters* at MAT," trans. Elizabeth Hapgood Reynolds, in Munk, *Stanislavski and America*, p. 56. Stroyeva was the Russian

editor of volume 1 of *Stanislavski's Theatre Legacy* (Moscow: State Publishing House, 1955), which recounts the first five years of the Moscow Art Theater, and from which Hapgood takes her translation.

32. Valency, *The Breaking String*, p. 221.

33. Francis Fergusson, *The Idea of a Theatre: The Art of Drama in Changing Perspective* (Princeton University Press, 1949; reprint ed., Garden City, N.Y.: Doubleday Anchor Book), p. 191.

34. *The Three Sisters*, p. 75.

35. Ibid., p. 122.

36. Ibid., p. 100.

37. Jarrell, *The Three Sisters*, Notes, p. 148. Jarrell's notion of a character's collected speeches as an "aria" comes directly from Stanislavski's notion of an actor's "score" for his characterization. See, for example, *Creating a Role*, p. 80, where the actor is instructed "to compose a score of lively physical and psychological objectives" and "to shape his whole score into one all-embracing supreme objective"; when the two activities are performed simultaneously they constitute the process of living the role. Jarrell's adaptation of the concept of "score" demonstrates how Stanislavski's interpretation of Chekhov influences our reading of the playwright to this day; it is not surprising that Jarrell prepared his translation for a 1963 production of *The Three Sisters* by the Actors' Studio, the home of "method acting."

38. Hingley, *The Three Sisters*, p. 75.

39. Ibid., p. 86.

40. Jarrell, *The Three Sisters*, pp. 66–67.

41. Hingley, *The Three Sisters*, p. 95.

42. Ibid., p. 133.

43. Ibid., p. 133.

44. Jarrell, *The Three Sisters*, Notes, p. 140.

45. Hingley, *The Three Sisters*, p. 93.

46. Brustein, *The Theatre of Revolt*, p. 163.

47. Schechner, *Public Domain*.

48. Jarrell, *The Three Sisters*, Notes, p. 110.

49. Ibid., p. 120.

50. Ibid., p. 137.

51. Hingley, *The Three Sisters*, Appendix, p. 311.

52. *My Life in Art*, p. 410.

53. *Stanislavski's Legacy*, p. 111.

54. *My Life in Art*, p. 361.

55. Valency, *The Breaking String*, p. 247.

CHAPTER THREE

1. Bertolt Brecht, *Brecht on Theatre: The Development of an Aesthetic*, trans. John Willett (New York: Hill and Wang, 1964), p. 87. Unless otherwise noted, all translations of Brecht's theoretical writings come from this edition, abbreviated as *Brecht on Theatre*.

2. Ibid., p. 57.

3. Ibid., pp. 50, 57, 91.

4. The only other time Aristotle employs the word catharsis in the *Poetics* occurs in section 17; here Aristotle is discussing Euripides' plotting of *Iphigenia in Tauris,* and catharsis has the limited meaning of the purification ritual which Orestes underwent as part of his expiation for his mother's murder.

5. *Brecht on Theatre,* p. 282.

6. Ibid., p. 181. Unless otherwise noted, citations of Brecht's theoretical writings in German are taken from *Schriften zum Theater* (Frankfort on the Main: Suhrkamp Verlag, 1957).

7. John Willett, *The Theatre of Bertolt Brecht: A Study from Eight Aspects* (New York: New Directions, 1959), p. 110.

8. Maria Ley-Piscator, *The Piscator Experiment* (Carbondale: Southern Illinois University Press, 1968), p. 182.

9. *Brecht on Theatre,* p. 152.

10. Ibid., p. 92.

11. Walter H. Sokel, "Brecht's Split Characters and His Sense of the Tragic," in *Brecht: A Collection of Critical Essays,* ed. Peter Demetz (Englewood Cliffs, N.J.: Prentice-Hall, 1962), pp. 127–37.

12. *Brecht on Theatre,* p. 193 ("Organum," paragraph 74).

13. *The Theatre of Bertolt Brecht,* p. 193.

14. Martin Esslin, *Brecht: The Man and His Work* (1960; reprint ed., Garden City, N.Y.: Anchor Books, 1961), pp. 141–42.

15. *Brecht on Theatre,* pp. 15–16.

16. Ibid., p. 227.

17. Ibid., p. 58.

18. Edward M. Berckman, "The Function of Hope in Brecht's Pre-revolutionary Theatre," in *Brecht Heute/Brecht Today,* 1 (Frankfort on the Main: Athenäum Verlag, 1971), pp. 25–26.

19. *Brecht on Theatre,* pp. 92–93.

20. Ibid., pp. 277–78.

21. Ibid., p. 27.

22. Walter H. Sokel, "Brecht's Concept of Character," *Comparative Drama* 3 (Autumn 1971): 181.

23. *Brecht on Theatre,* p. 14.

24. Ibid., p. 183 ("Short Organum," paragraph 12).

25. Ibid., p. 193.

26. Ibid., p. 186 ("Short Organum," paragraph 24).

27. Ibid., p. 205 ("Short Organum," paragraph 77).

28. Ibid., p. 277.

29. "Brecht's Concept of Character," p. 186.

30. All subsequent readers of Brecht are indebted to his first major critic, Walter Benjamin. Lecturing about epic theater in the late 1930s, Benjamin isolated the centrality of its dialectical nature years before Brecht considered changing the name of his theatrical form from "epic" to "dialectical" theater. Benjamin also observed that the Brechtian actor is the essential conveyor of the dialectical attitude, and that the performance situation, not the literary text, is

the decisive locus of meaning and of didactic "teaching" for Brecht. Consider, for example, these statements from "What is Epic Theatre?":

" . . . the actor . . . in epic theatre . . . finds himself beside the philosopher. His gesture demonstrates the social significance and applicability of dialectics. It tests the conditions on men."

"For [the epic theater's] performance, the text is no longer a basis of that performance, but a grid on which, in the form of new formulations, the gains of that performance are marked."

" . . . the educative effect of epic theatre is immediately translated into recognitions—though the specific recognitions of actors and audience may well be different from one another." Benjamin's lecture is reprinted in *Understanding Brecht*, trans. Anna Bostock (London: NLB, 1973), pp. 12 and 25.

CHAPTER FOUR

1. Darko Suvin, "The Mirror and the Dynamo," *The Drama Review* 12, no. 1, reprinted in *Brecht*, ed. Erika Munk (New York: Bantam Books, 1972), pp. 95–96.

2. Julian H. Wulbern, *Brecht and Ionesco: Commitment in Context* (Urbana: University of Illinois Press, 1971), p. 140. Wulbern's example of an Ionesco play which suffers from engagement is *Rhinoceros*, while *Exit the King* illustrates concerns beyond commitment.

3. A translation by Eric Bentley of Alfred Kurella's essay "What Was He Killed For?" appears in Bentley's edition of *Lehrstücke, The Jewish Wife and Other Short Plays by Bertolt Brecht* (New York: Grove Press, 1965), pp. 163–72. The essay first appeared in *Literatur der Welt Revolution*, no. 4 (Moscow, 1931).

4. Ernst Schumacher, *Die dramatischen Versuche Bertolt Brechts 1918–1933* (East Berlin, 1955), p. 365, trans. Martin Esslin, in *Brecht: The Man and His Work*, p. 156.

5. "Anmerkung zu den Lehrstücke," *Stücke* (Frankfort on the Main: Suhrkamp-Verlag), 5:276; trans. Martin Esslin, *Brecht*, p. 157.

6. Reiner Steinweg, *Das Lehrstück, Brechts Theorie einer politischästhetischen Erziehung* (Stuttgart: J. B. Metzlersche Verlagsbuchhandlung, 1972), p. 87. Steinweg traces the probable origin of the *Lehrstück* to drama-therapy rehabilitation exercises conducted by the Russian director Asja Lacis with juvenile delinquents after the Revolution; she worked with Brecht as assistant director for *Eduard II* in 1924. See Steinweg, pp. 148–49.

7. Esslin, *Brecht*, p. 157.

8. Willett, *The Theatre of Bertolt Brecht*, p. 118.

9. Ibid., p. 134.

10. *Europe* (Paris) (January–February, 1957), p. 173, trans. Martin Esslin, in *Brecht*, p. 157.

11. Reiner Steinweg, *Das Lehrstück*, p. 62.

12. Lionel Abel, *Metatheatre: A New View of Dramatic Form* (New York: Hill and Wang, 1963), p. 91.

13. Robert Brustein, *The Theatre of Revolt: An Approach to Modern Drama* (Boston: Little, Brown, 1962), pp. 250–51.

14. Peter Demetz, Introduction, in *Brecht: A Collection of Critical Essays*, p. 10.

15. Cited by Frederic Ewen in *Bertolt Brecht: His Life, His Art and His Times* (New York: Citadel Press, 1969), p. 253.

16. Willy Haas, *Bert Brecht*, trans. Max Knight and Joseph Fabry (New York: Frederick Ungar, 1970), p. 71.

17. Esslin, *Brecht*, p. 156.

18. Hannah Arendt, "The Poet Bertolt Brecht," trans. J. F. Sammons, in *Die Neue Rundschau* 61 (1950), pp. 53–67, reprinted in Demetz, *Brecht: A Collection of Critical Essays*, p. 44. In this vein, Willy Haas found the play to also be "a prologue to the tragic events of 1940 and 1941," namely, the Stalin-Hitler pact! See Haas, *Brecht*, p. 81.

19. Kurella, "What Was He Killed For?" in Bentley, *Jewish Wife*, p. 166.

20. Schumacher, *Die dramatischen Versuche Bertolt Brechts 1918–1933*, pp. 365, trans. Esslin, in *Brecht*, p. 156.

21. Ronald Gray, *Bertolt Brecht* (New York: Grove Press, 1961), p. 52.

22. Bertolt Brecht, *Versuche 11–12: Der Jasager und Der Neinsager; Die Massnahme* (Berlin: Gustav Kiepenhauer Verlag, 1931), following p. 358.

23. *The Jewish Wife*, p. 98. Unless otherwise noted, all quotations in English come from this edition. Occasionally, I have translated excerpts from the edition of 1931 (*Versuche 11–12*) that do not appear in Bentley's translation of the 1930 version.

24. Ibid., p. 79.

25. Ibid., pp. 81–82.

26. *Versuche 11–12*, p. 357 (my translation). Reiner Steinweg has edited a critical edition of *The Measures Taken* which includes five different versions of the play. Brecht's changes tend to add epic narration (the "he said") and to add emotional depth to the Agitators in their difficult decision to eliminate the Young Comrade. In a polemical "Afterword for Drama- and Agitprop-Groups," Steinweg recommends that each group reassemble the text according to the political circumstances surrounding the group's production of *The Measures Taken*. See *Die Massnahme, Kritische Ausgabe mit einer Spielanleitung* (Frankfort on the Main: Suhrkamp Verlag, 1972), p. 478.

27. *Jewish Wife*, p. 107.

28. *Versuche 11–12* , p. 365. My translation.

29. Andrzej Wirth has detected a "syllogistic principle" in Brecht's songs in *The Measures Taken*, whereby "two statements fill the role of quasi-premises from which follows the third statement . . . obviously, it is not a sequence in the logical sense, but an order of images imposed by the poet. . . . The syllogistic principle, employed in lyric verse, imposes onto poetry the rigor of utter terseness and economy of means, and gives to this verse a special 'matter-of-fact' quality which is very modern and intellectual" (*Siedem Prób* [Warsaw: Czytelnik, 1962], p. 17, my translation). These metaphoric syllogisms mask the antitheses of a dialectical pattern upon which Brecht builds his verse.

30. *Versuche 11–12*, p. 334. Bentley's translation in *Jewish Wife*, p. 83.

31. *Jewish Wife*, p. 83.

32. Ibid., p. 101. Bentley emphasizes the preposition "with"; Brecht does not.

33. Contrast the prominence of the pronoun "I" in this scene with the ab-

sence of the expected pronoun in the speech "Who fights for communism..." recited by the Control Chorus in scene 2, *Versuche 11–12*, p. 334. In this formal litany, the Chorus avoids using the subject "he" in a series of parallel "sentences" which describe the qualities of the fight for communism. Grammatically, each of these sentence fragments is understood to be preceded by "er muss" ("he must"): "die Wahrheit sagen und die Wahrheit nicht sagen; Dienste erweisen und Dienste verweigern; Versprechen halten und Versprechen nicht halten...," ("speak the truth and not speak the truth; perform services and not perform services; keep promises and not keep promises"—my translation). Brecht inserts the pronoun when he concludes his list with the one quality which is constant and not subject to pragmatic manipulation: "Wer für den Kommunismus kämpft, hat von allen Tugenden nur eine: dass er für den Kommunismus kämpft" ("Who fights for Communism has only one of all the virtues: that he fights for Communism"—Bentley, *Jewish Wife*, p. 82). The fighter for communism gains even this pronominal identity only when his one virtue is mentioned, the quality which links him with his submission to the struggle for communism.

34. In Brecht's later revisions, he added another chorus at the very end of the play, which reemphasizes the necessity of changing the world, the various dangers that besiege both the "one" and the "all" ("Begreifen des Einzelnen und Begreifen des Ganzen"), and the Control Chorus concludes with the admonition that only having learned from reality can we change reality: "Nur belehrt von der Wirklichkeit, können wir/Die Wirklichkeit ändern (see Steinweg's critical edition of the play, Suhrkamp Verlag, 1972, pp. 96, 101, 134).

35. *Jewish Wife*, p. 101.

36. Sokel, "Brecht's Split Characters," p. 133. Another approach to the question of this play's "tragic" nature is to argue that the Young Comrade is well-intended yet in error, and that when he realizes his errors the tragic clash of two opposing positive values is alleviated; the play becomes an "optimistic tragedy." Walter Weideli proposes that the play's conflict be seen in terms of an antagonism between "traditional morality" and the "morality of combat," resolved in the view that "subjective kindness will no longer suffice: henceforth, it must be effective" (*The Art of Bertolt Brecht*, trans. Daniel Russell [New York University Press, 1963], p. 49). Wolfgang Schivelbusch distinguishes between "premature humanity" and "communist humanity," and argues that in the Young Comrade's belated realization of his mistaken behavior, we find a continuation of the tradition of optimistic tragedy ("Optimistic Tragedies: The Plays of Heiner Müller," *New German Critique* 2 [Spring 1974], 104–13).

37. Ewen, *Bertolt Brecht, His Life, His Art, and His Times*, p. 255.

38. Ibid., p. 255.

39. Reinhold Grimm, "Ideologische Trägodie und Trägodie der Ideologie,'" in *Interpretationen 2: Deutsche Dramen von Gryphius bis Brecht* (Frankfort on the Main: Fischer Bücherei, 1956), p. 316, trans. Wulbern, in *Brecht and Ionesco*, p. 114.

40. Ibid.

41. *Jewish Wife*, pp. 96–97.

42. *Versuche 11–12*, p. 348.

43. Sokel, "Brecht's Split Characters," p. 135.

44. Ibid., p. 136. Charles R. Lyons expands on this tragic reading in *Bertolt Brecht, The Despair and the Polemic* (Carbondale: Southern Illinois University Press, 1968), distinguishing an antithesis between the Young Comrade's "vital human will" and the "strong willed consent" of the Agitators; he finds it a "tragic paradox" that willed submission is presented as the only possible control of instinctive energy, but that such submission results in "the destruction of the individual identity, the merging of the individual will with the collective" (p. 77). I argue that individual identity in this play originally emerges from the collective.

45. Sokel, "Brecht's Split Characters," p. 136.

46. *Brecht on Theatre*, p. 204 ("Short Organum," paragraph 74).

CHAPTER FIVE

1. Michael Kirby, "Introduction," *The Drama Review*, 17, no. 52 (Fall 1971): 4.

2. Peter Brook, *The Empty Space* (New York: Atheneum, 1968), p. 9.

3. Richard Schechner, "Actuals," *The Theatre Quarterly* 1, no. 2 (Spring 1971).

4. Richard Schechner, *Environmental Theatre* (New York: Hawthorn Books, 1973).

5. Julian Beck, *The Life of the Theatre; the Relation of the Artist to the Struggle of the People* (San Francisco: City Lights, 1972).

6. Joseph Chaikin, *The Presence of the Actor* (New York: Atheneum, 1972).

7. See John Lahr's *Up Against the Fourth Wall* (New York: Grove Press, 1970).

8. Martin Esslin, *The Theatre of the Absurd* (Garden City, N.Y.: Doubleday, 1961).

9. Raymonde Temkine, *Grotowski*, trans. Alex Szogyi (New York: Avon Books, 1972), p. 144.

10. Brook, *The Empty Space*, p. 54.

11. Antonin Artaud, *Nerve Scales*, in *Collected Works*, vol. I, trans. Victor Corti (London: Calder and Boyars, 1968), p. 72.

12. Antonin Artaud, *Artaud Anthology*, trans. David Rattray (San Francisco: City Lights Books, 1965), p. 222.

13. See A. Alvarez, *The Savage God, A Study of Suicide* (New York: Random House, 1972); Naomi Greene, *Antonin Artaud, Poet without Words* (New York: Simon and Schuster, 1971), p. 120; and Paul Arnold, "The Artaud Experiment," *The Drama Review* 8, no. 2 (Winter 1963): 21. Martin Esslin argues that we should view Artaud as an "existential hero" in his study *Antonin Artaud* (New York: Penguin Books, 1977), p. 6: "What he did, what happened to him, what he suffered, what he *was*, is infinitely more important than anything he said or wrote."

14. Letter to Paulhan, January 25, 1936, cited by Eric Sellin in *The Dramatic Concepts of Antonin Artaud* (Chicago: University of Chicago Press, 1968), p. 93.

15. Susan Sontag, "Approaching Artaud," *The New Yorker* (May 19, 1973), p. 48. This essay was reprinted as the introduction to Sontag's *Selected Writings/Antonin Artaud* (New York: Farrar, Straus and Giroux, 1976).

16. Grotowski, *Towards a Poor Theatre*, p. 119. Hereafter cited as "Grotowski."

17. When he ranks the six elements necessary for tragedy in descending order below action (plot, character, thought, diction, melody, spectacle) Aristotle does not prescribe the actual order in which a poet must perform certain creative acts. Rather he is speaking about how a unified work comes into being from the point of view of ideal perception of the work. Several critics have extrapolated an ideal order of composition from Aristotle's ordering of parts; for example, Francis Fergusson calls this a "hierarchy of actualizations" in *The Idea of a Theatre*, pp. 48–50.

18. Antonin Artaud, *The Theater and Its Double*, trans. Mary Caroline Richards (New York: Grove Press, 1958), p. 37. Hereafter cited as "Artaud."

19. Artaud, p. 69.

20. Romain Weingarten, "Re-read Artaud," trans. Ruby Cohn, *The Drama Review* 8, no. 2 (Winter 1963): 76.

21. Artaud, pp. 37 and 78.

22. Ibid., p. 78.

23. Bettina Knapp, *Antonin Artaud, Man of Vision* (New York: David Lewis, 1969), p. 38.

24. Artaud, p. 94; the phrase is italicized in the original.

25. Ibid., p. 38.

26. Ibid., p. 72.

27. Ibid., p. 75.

28. Artaud, *Collected Works*, vol. 2, trans. Victor Corti (London: Calder and Boyars, 1968), p. 18.

29. Artaud, p. 98.

30. Ibid., p. 133.

31. Ibid., p. 138; p. 133.

32. Ibid., pp. 134–35. Artaud variously begins the word "double" with an upper- or lowercase letter.

33. Ibid., p. 126.

34. Ibid., p. 116.

35. Ibid., p. 8.

36. Ibid., p. 12.

37. Ibid., p. 13.

38. Grotowski, p. 125.

39. Artaud, p. 79.

40. Ibid., p. 52.

41. Ibid., p. 27.

42. Ibid., p. 31.

43. Ibid., p. 81.

44. Ibid., p. 79.

45. Ibid., p. 80.

46. Ibid., p. 82.

47. Ibid., p. 82.

48. For example, in photographs of that production the great actor Roger Blin, an extra in *The Cenci*, looks ill at ease and conscious of his overplaying (see, for example, Alain Virmaux, *Antonin Artaud et le théâtre* [Paris: Seghers, 1970], following p. 224).

49. Grotowski, pp. 133–73.

50. *Teatrets Teori og Teknikk* 7 (Holstebro, Denmark: 1968).

51. *The Drama Review* 14, no. 1 (Fall 1969).

52. Grotowski, p. 117–25.

53. Jerzy Grotowski, "Holiday," *The Drama Review* 17, no. 2 (Summer 1973); *The Village Voice* (December 31, 1970), p. 34; "Teatr a ritual" ["Theatre—and Ritual?"], *Dialog* 8 (August 1969); "Co Bylo" ["What Used to Be"], *Dialog* 10 (October 1972); "Jak żyć by można" ["How One Might Live"], *Odra* 4 (April 1972); "Takim, jakim sie jest, cały ["Such as One Is—Whole"], *Odra* 5 (May 1972); "Święto" ["Holiday"], *Odra* 6 (June 1972). See also Richard Mennen, "Jerzy Grotowski's Paratheatrical Projects," *The Drama Review* 17, no. 4 (December 1975): 58–69, and Tadeusz Buski, "Grotowski's Exit from the Theatre," *Le Théâtre en Pologne/The Theatre in Poland* 17, no. 7 (July 1975): 15–16.

54. Grotowski, p. 32.

55. Ibid., p. 17.

56. Ibid., pp. 37–38.

57. Ibid., p. 49.

58. Ibid., p. 48.

59. Andrzej Wirth, "Brecht and Grotowski," in *Brecht Heute/Brecht Today*, p. 191.

60. Grotowski, p. 55.

61. Peter Brook refers to this notion in *The Empty Space*, p. 140.

62. Zbigniew Osiński, "Apoteoza i szynderstwo" ["Apocalypse and Derision"], *Miesięcznik Literacki* 12 (1969): 60; my translation.

63. Donald Richie et al., "On Grotowski—a Series of Critiques," *The Drama Review* 14, no. 2 (Winter 1970): 210.

CHAPTER SIX

1. This twelve-page brochure, published in English, provides the most thorough record of *Apocalypsis cum figuris* to emerge from the Laboratory Theater. Presumably, it is a joint effort by Grotowski and his dramaturg Ludwig Flaszen, although neither author nor translator is credited, nor are the pages numbered. The program, to which I shall subsequently refer as "Notes to *Apocalypsis*," contains a brief description of the production, the plot, and characters, and some interpretation. Following this, the characters' speeches are quoted extensively, although none of the citations (or translations) from Scriptures, Dostoyevsky, Weil, and Eliot are specifically identified. Even in his program note, Grotowski playfully usurps the quotations, as if to make them "the work . . . of the whole of mankind."

2. *Le Théâtre en Pologne/The Theatre in Poland* 16, no. 1 (January 1974): 30.

3. "Notes to *Apocalypsis*."

4. Ibid.

5. Konstanty Puzyna, "A Myth Vivisected: Grotowski's Apocalypse," *The Drama Review* 15, no. 1 (Fall 1971): 41.

6. "Notes to *Apocalypsis*."

7. Ibid. (This passage is from the preface to *La Connaissance surnaturelle*.)

8. "Notes to *Apocalypsis*."

9. "Notes to *Apocalypsis.*" (These passages are from "Ash Wednesday" and "Gerontion.")

10. "Notes to *Apocalypsis.*" (This passage is from "Ash Wednesday.")

11. "Notes to *Apocalypsis.*"

12. Seweryna Wysłouch, "Grotowski—Niszcyciel Znaków" ["Grotowski—Destroyer of Signs"], *Dialog* 8 (August 1971): 129; my translation.

13. Ibid., p. 127.

14. Ibid., p. 130.

15. Jan Błoński, "Grotowski and His Laboratory Theatre," *Dialog* (special English-language issue, 1970): 150.

16. Konstanty Puzyna, "A Myth Vivisected: Grotowski's Apocalypse," *The Drama Review* 15, no. 1 (Fall 1971).

17. Konstanty Puzyna, "Addendum to *Apocalypsis,*" in *Burzliwa Pogoda* (Warsaw: Panstwowy Instytut Wydawniczy, 1971), p. 97; my translation.

18. "Notes to *Apocalypsis.*"

19. *Towards a Poor Theatre,* p. 23.

20. "Notes to *Apocalypsis.*" Simon Peter speaking as the Grand Inquisitor.

21. Ibid. John reciting Simone Weil.

22. This was the play's final line when it first opened; the phrase is also the last words of Dostoyevsky's Grand Inquisitor. More recently, Grotowski has allowed his actor to simply utter "Idź sobie"—"Get out."

23. *Le Théâtre en Pologne/The Theater in Poland* 16, no. 1 (January 1974): 30.

24. *"Co Było"* ["What Used to Be"], *Dialog* 10 (October 1972): 117; *"Święto"* ["Holiday"], *Odra* 6 (June 1972): 48; "Jak żyć by mozna" ["How One Might Live"], *Odra* 4 (April 1972): 33; *The Village Voice* (December 31, 1970), p. 51. Translations from the Polish are my own.

25. Richard Gilman, "The Theatre of Poverty," in *Common and Uncommon Masks, Writings on Theatre, 1961–1970* (New York: Vintage Books, 1972), pp. 303 and 306.

26. Some of Grotowski's interviews have been transcribed under the title of "Holiday." See *The Drama Review* 17, no. 2 (Summer 1973).

27. *Le Théâtre en Pologne/The Theatre in Poland* 16, no. 1 (January 1974): 30.

AFTERWORD

1. Peter Handke, *Offending the Audience,* in *Kaspar and Other Plays,* trans. Michael Roloff (New York: Farrar, Straus and Giroux, 1969), p. 9. Hereafter cited as "Handke."

2. Handke, p. 8.

3. Ibid., p. 31.

4. Ibid., p. ix.

5. Ibid.

6. Ibid., p. 11.

7. Martin Esslin, *The Peopled Wound* (New York: Doubleday, 1970), p. 231.

8. Handke, p. 15.

9. Ibid., p. 20.

10. Ibid.

11. Ibid., p. 16.

12. Ibid., p. 17.

13. Cited by Nicholas Hern, *Peter Handke, Theatre and Anti-Theatre* (London: Oswald Wolff, 1972), p. 43.

14. Handke, p. 21.

15. Ibid.

16. Ibid.

17. Ibid., p. 12.

18. Ibid., p. 29.

19. Ibid., pp. 29–31.

20. Ibid., p. 31.

21. Ibid., p. 32.

22. Ibid.

23. Susan Sontag, "Approaching Artaud," *The New Yorker* (May 29, 1973), p. 41.

24. Richard Gilman, "Peter Handke," *American Review* 17 (May 1973): 206.

25. Handke, p. ix.

26. Ibid., p. 28.

Index